Wm Washington

William Washington engraved by J.B. Forest (1836)
Courtesy of South Caroliniana Library

William Washington

Cavalryman of the Revolution

Stephen E. Haller

SE Haller

Williamsburg, Virginia
May 21, 2003

Heritage Books, Inc.

Published 2001 by

HERITAGE BOOKS, INC.
1540E Pointer Ridge Place, Bowie, Maryland 20716
1-800-398-7709
www.heritagebooks.com

ISBN 0-7884-1803-3

A Complete Catalog Listing Hundreds of Titles
On History, Genealogy, and Americana
Available Free Upon Request

*This book is dedicated
to the memory of American men and women
who have served their country*

contents

illustrations

preface

William Washington was one of a small, loyal cadre of key field officers who served with distinction in the Continental Army for almost the entire duration of the War of the American Revolution. His independent operations and dramatic accomplishments as a cavalry commander in the South were comparable to the exploits of many of his better-known fellow officers. Unlike William Davie, Henry "Light Horse Harry" Lee, Francis "Swamp Fox" Marion, Daniel Morgan and Thomas "Gamecock" Sumter—not to mention their famous British adversary, "Bloody" Banastre Tarleton—there has not been an extensive, published biography of William Washington. During the campaign in the Carolinas, General Nathanael Greene once referred to "Light Horse Harry" Lee as his "eye," but he called Colonel Washington his "arm."

Washington's six years in the war provide a first-hand view of the problems faced by the Americans in maintaining not only an army, but also particularly a cavalry corps. His story also offers new insights on the traditional views of senior American generals George Washington and Horatio Gates regarding the cavalry's role in the war. He constantly faced shortages in men, horses and supplies. Twice, because of these problems and battlefield reverses, he had to rebuild his cavalry command under very difficult conditions. In 1776 Washington distinguished himself at the Battle of Trenton as an infantry captain who, along with Lieutenant James Monroe (later the fifth President of the United States), led a decisive charge against a Hessian artillery battery. He transferred to the cavalry and served as a major and lieutenant colonel in the 4th and 3rd

Continental Light Dragoons in the Middle States (1777-1779). He is best remembered as a cavalry commander in the South under Generals Benjamin Lincoln, Daniel Morgan and Nathanael Greene in 1780-1781. His story provides a more thorough explanation of the American cavalry's actions during the British siege of Charleston in 1780 and many of the small-unit engagements typical of the war in the South. Washington went on to fight in all of the major battles in Greene's campaign to drive the British out of the Carolinas in 1781.

Washington was a gallant battlefield commander who personally led his men, and he was wounded on at least two occasions. His courage and good tactical sense glittered when he independently attacked Rugeley's Farm and Hammond Stores and made several decisive charges during the pitched battles of Cowpens and Guilford Court House. The Battle of Cowpens has often been compared to Hannibal's classic victory over the Romans at Cannae, and Washington's cavalry was surely as vital to Morgan as Hasdrubal's was to Hannibal. Washington's impetuous drive to bring an action to decisive conclusion also got him into trouble at the battles of Hobkirk's Hill and Eutaw Springs (where he was unhorsed, wounded and captured). Yet it is the mercurial aspect of his military career that makes this story an all the more believable, fascinating example of a soldier and cavalryman in the Continental Army.

Washington left only a handful of letters, unlike his more famous cousin George Washington. Most of these papers are preserved in the Nathanael Greene Papers at the William L. Clements Library and the Library of Congress and the George Washington papers also in the Library of Congress. A substantial number of primary sources and outstanding secondary sources regarding his peers and the War of the Revolution now make it possible to reconstruct the significant details of his military career. Although little is known about his youth in Virginia before 1776 other than an impression of those who helped form his character, several sources allow more than a glimpse of his life as a South Carolina planter, legislator and avid racehorse fan after the war ended. Many records of Stafford County, Virginia and St. Paul's Parish,

South Carolina were lost to fires during the Civil War. The story of rice heiress Jane Elliott's gift of a battle flag to Washington in 1780 and their marriage in 1782 offers a picture of a wartime romance and transition to peacetime. His deepest motives and personality are not easily revealed, but his battlefield dash and personal bravery appear balanced by modesty and selflessness on many occasions throughout his life. When approached to consider running for governor of his adopted state, he declined because he did not like to make public speeches and was not a native of South Carolina. Washington was foremost a soldier of the American Revolution, and consequently, this biography is primarily devoted to his war years.

acknowledgments

The assistance of a legion of librarians and archivists in locating sources for this biography began in the 1970s at Miami University in Oxford, Ohio when William Washington was the subject of my master's thesis. Most important then were Mary Persyn (now Director, Valparaiso Law School Library, Indiana) and C. Martin Miller, Jr. (now Head of Special Collections at Miami University's King Library). My advisor, History Professor Jeffrey Kimball, guided me through drafts and approval of the finished thesis with assistance from now retired department chairman Richard Jellison. When I resumed researching and writing in the late 1980s and early 1990s, the interlibrary loan assistance of Nancy Horlacher and Carole Medlar at the Dayton-Montgomery County Public Library in Ohio was vital. When I moved to Williamsburg, Virginia in 1996, Margaret Cook and others assisted me at Swem Library at the College of William & Mary where I spent many Saturday mornings. My colleagues at Colonial Williamsburg also offered guidance and advice (Joe Rountree, Gail Greve, John Turner, Marianne Martin and Suzanne Coffman—whose father, Henry F. Coffman, read the entire manuscript for fun and welcome criticism!). Also very helpful were: Lawrence Temple Washington of Alexandria, Virginia (4th generation nephew of William Washington), Jerrilynn Eby and George Gordon, historians of Stafford County, Virginia, Beth Bilderback at the South Caroliniana Library (University of South Carolina), James P. Lynch and the Rev. Christopher M. Agnew of St. Paul's Episcopal Church in King George County, Virginia and John A. Guy, III of the Washington Light Infantry in Charleston, South Carolina. Massey's Camera Shop in Williamsburg, Virginia was essential in creating several illustrations, and fellow Washington fan Sam Fore alerted me to the published diary of Baylor Hill. My family encouraged me the most by putting up with battlefield tours, library visits and contention for book shelf space, home computer time, etc. My wife Susan accommodated this extra personage on vacations and read the manuscript. My daughter Barbara, an architect in Columbia, South Carolina, grew up hearing about William Washington from her father since the 1970s. My son Elliott, now a teenager, happily tramped around places like Cowpens and Guilford Court House with me while we were on "vacations." Last, but by no means least, was the cheerful support and welcome improvements offered by Heritage Books editor Roxanne Carlson. Although I have received generous assistance with this work, I accept responsibility for any error or omission.

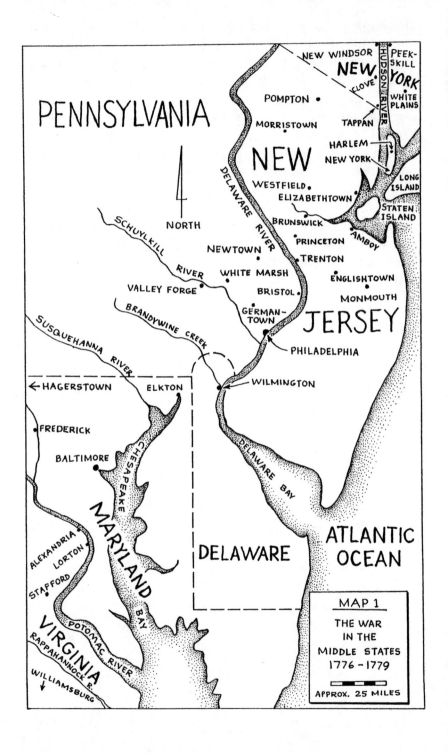

PENNSYLVANIA

NORTH

SCHUYLKILL RIVER

SUSQUEHANNA RIVER

← HAGERSTOWN

• FREDERICK

BALTIMORE •

VALLEY FORGE •

BRANDYWINE CREEK

ELKTON •

CHESAPEAKE BAY

MARYLAND

ALEXANDRIA
LORTON
STAFFORD •

VIRGINIA
RAPPAHANNOCK R.

POTOMAC RIVER

WILLIAMSBURG ↓

NEW WINDSOR

POMPTON •

MORRISTOWN •

DELAWARE RIVER

NEWTOWN •

WHITE MARSH •

BRISTOL •

GERMAN-TOWN •

WILMINGTON

WESTFIELD •
ELIZABETHTOWN •

BRUNSWICK •

PRINCETON •

TRENTON •

TAPPAN •

NEW
YORK

CLOVE

HUDSON RIVER

PEEK-SKILL

WHITE PLAINS

HARLEM
NEW YORK

LONG ISLAND

STATEN ISLAND

AMBOY

ENGLISHTOWN •

MONMOUTH •

NEW

JERSEY

PHILADELPHIA

DELAWARE BAY

DELAWARE

ATLANTIC OCEAN

MAP 1

THE WAR
IN THE
MIDDLE STATES
1776 - 1779

APPROX. 25 MILES

chapter I

THE MAKING OF A SOLDIER: 1752-1776

William Washington was born on February 28, 1752 in Overwharton Parish, Stafford County, Virginia at "Windsor Forest," his parents' home on the banks of Long Branch of Aquia Creek. This famous cavalry commander and hero of the Revolutionary War was the second-born son of Virginia planter Bailey Washington (1731-1807) and Catherine Storke (1722-1804). The daughter of Stafford County Sheriff William Storke, Catherine became Mrs. Washington when she married Bailey on January 12, 1749 in St. Paul's Parish of Stafford County. Bailey was the son of Henry and Mary Washington. Henry's father, John Washington, was the brother of Lawrence Washington—George Washington's grandfather. Their father, John Washington, had emigrated from England to Virginia in the late seventeenth century. William and George—his senior by 20 years—were thus second cousins, once removed.[1]

Little detail is known about William's life before the Revolution, except that he grew up with three brothers and two sisters on his family's 1200-acre Virginia plantation, which is now within the boundaries of the United States Marine Corps Base at Quantico. Bailey had received "all...lands at Acquia" in 1748 through his father's will, and his brother John inherited Henry's "home plantation." Agriculture in that part of Virginia was then centered mostly on tobacco, corn and other grains, apple orchards and raising livestock. Large cedar trees flanked the road leading to "Windsor Forest," which then included at least one permanent dwelling and eleven other buildings. With large chimneys on its east and west ends, this large frame house had a brick-walled cellar—an extravagance at a time when basements were dug out by hand. The other buildings included a tenant house and slave cabins. William's older brother, Henry, was born in 1749. After marrying Mildred Pratt in 1779, he would eventually choose the frontier life and move west to the Mississippi River region. William's two younger brothers, Bailey, Jr. and John, were born in 1753 and 1756 respectively. Bailey, Jr.—who married Euphan Wallace (step-daughter of Thompson Mason, George Mason's younger brother)—would later receive a 500-acre portion of Windsor Forest from his father in 1784. The young sisters, Elizabeth and Mary Butler, completed the family in 1758 and 1760. Elizabeth married William Storke, and Mary wed a local "medical doctor" (and Stafford County Clerk of Courts), Valentine Peyton. Bailey's ownership of Windsor Forest, as recorded in 1751, also included the notation that an undetermined number of African American slaves were living and working on this plantation.[2]

The elder Bailey was a man of sufficient local standing and reputation to be selected to serve as a Stafford County Justice of the Peace (1766-1773) and apparently was also a vestryman for Overwharton and St. Paul's Parishes of the Anglican Church. When a dispute arose regarding Stafford County's election of a member of the House of Burgesses in 1766, Bailey was one of six men designated to witness the taking of depositions in the county. He was quite active in church affairs in the early 1770's, a time of growing public dissent and dissatisfaction with paying tithes to support a church that was decreasing in attendance. Bailey joined with several other Overwharton Parish representatives to protest the irregular actions—"sundry and illegal and unwarrantable Proceedings of the Vestry...praying that the said Vestry may be dissolved." The Committee for Religion, although finding the grievances "reasonable," opined that the petitioners who sent the representatives should defray the expenses. The House in 1772 stirred up more resentment by assessing tithes to pay for the expenses incurred to settle the disputes. The rancor typical of the 1770's between the colonists and Royal Governor Lord Dunmore and his representatives continued. Bailey and ten other "Gentlemen (who refuse to act)" as Justices of the Peace forced the Council of Colonial Virginia to seek new local officials in late 1772 as long-established relationships disintegrated on the eve of the American Revolution. The Council issued Bailey a new justice's commission in the spring of 1773, however. In advance of the Convention of 1774, both Bailey and the St. Paul's Parish rector, Reverend William Stuart (who at the time was also young William's tutor) signed Stafford County's "sentiments of the freeholders and inhabitants" protesting British taxation "while parliament continues her attempts to enslave us." This strongly worded resolution also called for several forms of economic and political resistance. Years later, during the most desperate months of the War of the Revolution in Virginia in 1780-1781, William's father would also be elected Stafford County's representative to the Virginia House of Delegates and again serve as Justice of the Peace.[3]

Young William, now in his early twenties, had been studying for some time in preparation for the ministry when the Revolutionary War broke out. The Washington family initially attended services at St. Paul's Church (built c. 1750 and still active in what is now King George County) and later apparently attended the very nearby Aquia Church (built c. 1752-1757 and still active, located north of Stafford Courthouse and south of Quantico). The Reverend Doctor William Stuart, the popular rector of St. Paul's Parish noted for his eloquence from the pulpit, directed William's education. Bailey, and perhaps William, probably selected Stuart for this course of study for several reasons. He appears to have been educated at the College of William and Mary (although not a graduate) and later studied theology in England, where he was ordained by the Bishop of London and licensed for Virginia in 1746. He also performed the parents' marriage rites in 1749 and baptized young William in 1752.   Under Stuart, William acquired a special proficiency in Greek and the Classics, in addition to his theology studies.   A South Carolina contemporary later commented on William's education: "As a classical scholar, his merit placed him among the first on the list.   But that modesty, which is always the concomitant of worth, rather concealed, than displayed his talents—He was learned without ostentation." Washington's primary text would have been the Church of England's 1769 or 1771 edition of *The Book of Common Prayer, And Administration of Sacraments, And other Rites and Ceremonies of the Church.* It was common practice in Virginia at the time for local ministers to also provide a general education for the sons of landowners. Stuart may well have influenced William's character in other ways.   The Reverend's granddaughter fondly recalled that the clergyman's "pure, moral and religious character, high toned integrity, liberal education, and courteous genial deportment commanded the sincere regard and reverential respect of that gay, frolic loving but generous, noble hearted people." In the 1770's, this situation surely created some interesting dialogue (or debate), given his father's previously mentioned role in local church tensions. As a youth, William was athletic, good-humored, adept at fishing, swimming and hunting, and above all a superbly skilled horseman. In the social and economic environment of Virginia planter society, he would have been both expected and informally trained to assume a number of leadership responsibilities.   Ruddy-faced, auburn-haired William was also a very large young man for his time. One of his fellow officers, Henry "Light Horse Harry" Lee described him as "possessed [of] a stout frame, being six feet high, broad, strong and corpulent." As to Washington's interests and education, Princeton-educated Lee somewhat patronizingly observed that "his occupations and his amusements applied to the body, rather than the mind; to the cultivation of which he did not bestow much time or application, nor was his education of the sort to excite such habits, being only calculated to fit a man for the common business of life. In temper he was good-humored; in disposition amiable; in heart upright, generous, and friendly; in manners lively, innocent, and agreeable." His likable personality combined with his physical size to make him stand out among his peers. That William was pursuing the ministry, when he was second in line to inherit his father's estate (or a part thereof), may be an early indication of how he acquired his strong, life-long personal characteristics of humility, honesty, compassion, and benevolence. At his funeral, the eulogist and one of his contemporaries could "not fail to remark, the tone of character which he received from the impressions of his youthful studies. —During this course, his mind imbibed those strong and permanent impressions of moral and divine truth, and that firm religious conviction, which became stronger with his years, and ripened into maturity by reflection. These impressions, implanted in his mind that fine morality and rigid virtue, which through life shone so resplendent in all his actions."[4] William Washington's strong sense of right and wrong and his sense of duty led the young man to take up the earliest call of his fellow Virginians in the impending struggle with England.

When Virginia began raising troops to resist Great Britain, William gave up his studies and life as a planter's son to join the Patriot cause. In March 1775 Patrick Henry gave his "Liberty or Death" speech to the Virginia Convention meeting in Richmond, where they could avoid the reach of Lord Dunmore, Virginia's Royal Governor. Dunmore reacted to the signs of rebellion by removing the powder from the Public Magazine in Williamsburg on April 21 to keep it from falling into local hands. This aroused the Patriots even more, and one group of Patriots rallied in Fredericksburg near George Weedon's tavern and sent letters to surrounding counties for troops to march on the capital if necessary to support Patrick Henry's march from Richmond. Then the news arrived from Massachusetts detailing the April 19 Battles of Lexington and Concord. William Washington was among the first group of Virginia's youth to answer the call to arms, and he and his fellow "minute-men" from Stafford County formed a company in the early summer of 1775. Although Lord Dunmore managed to avoid armed conflict over the powder incident by arranging to reimburse the locals for the cost of the seized powder, this did not halt the Virginians' preparations for war. The Virginia Convention in Richmond created three infantry regiments, commanded by Patrick Henry, William Woodford and Hugh Mercer. At a September 12 meeting at Spotsylvania Courthouse of a "select committee" for four counties, William Washington and Townshend Dade were elected captains for Stafford County's companies of Colonel Hugh Mercer's "minute-men." Dunmore had fled to a ship in June, and by fall, he had "emancipated" Virginia's slaves who would desert their colonial masters and fight for the British. He then began conducting raids in the Tidewater area. By November, the Virginia Committee of Safety authorized up to £86 to Washington and two other officers to acquire muskets and rifles for their men. Woodford's regiment participated in the December 9, 1775 Battle of Great Bridge, where Lord Dunmore's troops were defeated. Dunmore retaliated by burning the port of Norfolk on January 1, 1776, further inciting Virginians to rid their land of the British and their Tory sympathizers. On January 13, 1776, the third regiment was completed, and its field officers were Colonel Hugh Mercer, Lieutenant Colonel George Weedon and Major Thomas Marshall. On February 3, the Virginia Committee of Safety authorized a cash advance of £72 to William Washington to begin recruiting men for his company, "taking care that they be at least five feet four inches high, healthy, strong made & well limbed, not deaf or Subject to fits...not to inlist any Servants, except Apprentices bound in this colony, nor without the Consent of their Masters in writing." Officers were further instructed to have any willing recruits sworn in within twenty-four hours and "pay them twenty shillings bountey money, taking a Receipt from each." On February 13, Congress designated Mercer's regiment the 3rd Virginia Continental Infantry Regiment. William was commissioned a captain in command of one of the regiment's ten companies (i.e., the 5th) on February 25, 1776 – three days before his twenty-fourth birthday.[5]

St. Paul's Episcopal Church in King George County
Courtesy of St. Paul's Episcopal Church

Aquia Church in Stafford County
Courtesy of Aquia Episcopal Church

Williamsburg became the Patriots' military headquarters in January, and William marched his company there with the rest of the regiment in early March. The officers used this time to begin transforming these untried troops into a cohesive force through daily discipline and drill in a training camp behind the College of William & Mary. From March 13 to March 20, William received funds to purchase "ruggs" and "Hunting Shirts" for his men. Mercer then marched the regiment 150 miles north to Alexandria to collect arms and equipment, and for a short time to guard the southeast shore of the Potomac River. While marching back to Williamsburg on April 2 on rain-soaked roads, Mercer decided to halt the regiment in Fredericksburg. The unit, whose men were dressed somewhat uniformly in fringed hunting shirts of similar cut and color, remained in the town for two weeks and continued to drill and parade. On April 6, the Committee of Safety determined that by lot, "the rank and preceedence as to the said Capt. Washingtons Company is...to be first [within the 3rd Regiment]." By mid-April, Mercer ordered Lieutenant Colonel Weedon to march the regiment back to Alexandria, where it remained for the next four weeks. While there, William used his time and over £180 to recruit additional men, repair arms and equipment and acquire more hunting shirts, bedding, rugs and blankets. By mid-May, William's regiment had made the return march of 150 miles to Williamsburg and they arrived in time for a grand review and other festivities held to mark the Virginia Convention's May 14 vote "to declare the United Colonies free and independent States." Many of the men of the regiment, tired and bored with the tedium of camp life and marching, were anxious to join the main army in the north where they could fight the main British army. Once again Mercer marched north in early June, this time 130 miles to the area near Lorton. Here the men continued their training and "for the protection of the inhabitants there" guarded against possible British landings along the Potomac River by Lord Dunmore's small but still dangerously mobile naval forces.[6]

While near Lorton, the Committee of Safety "Ordered that the Keeper of the Public Magazine do deliver...fifty eight Guns

<u>and Sixty-six bayonets</u> for the use of Captain Washington's Company...and return Seventeen Guns...unfit for use." As would be the case throughout the war, timely pay for the troops was not forthcoming. On June 11, Captain Washington received £205 "for the pay of his company to the 28th of February, & four hunting Shirts." On June 18, the Committee allowed him an additional £64 to purchase provisions. While in the vicinity, Washington also purchased a tent and rented barracks for his men in Alexandria. In late June the 3rd Virginia marched the 130 miles back to Williamsburg to become more fully equipped and undergo more intense and disciplined tactical drill. While marching through the Caroline District, Washington had to purchase forage for horses and rent a wagon to carry extra guns acquired for the regiment. Shortly after the regiment returned to Williamsburg, Congress promoted Colonel Mercer to brigadier general and ordered him north to join General Washington's army in New York. Weedon, now in command, led the regiment east to Matthews County to participate in the July 8 Battle of Gwynn's Island, where Lord Dunmore's raiders were finally driven off by artillery fire. The 3rd Virginia itself could not cross to the island due to a lack of sufficient boats. Upon returning to Williamsburg, the troops idled again through July, and they had to be warned to cease their gaming and gambling in Williamsburg. However, they paraded and fired salvos when word was received of the Declaration of Independence and the historic document was read to the troops near the Capitol. At the end of July, Weedon marched his regiment north again— this time to Westmoreland County opposite St. Mary's, Maryland, where Lord Dunmore was lurking after evacuating Gwynn's Island. When Dunmore left the Chesapeake entirely by August 7, Weedon marched the regiment back to Williamsburg to await further orders.[7] William Washington was becoming quite familiar with the marching and counter-marching that would characterize the war for the next five years.

Virginia Soldiers in Hunting Shirts
Colonial Williamsburg Foundation

New York and Trenton

Meanwhile, the large British army commanded by General William Howe that had landed on Staten Island in June now focused the war on New York and New Jersey for remainder of 1776. On July 22, Congress ordered the 3rd Virginia to march to New Jersey and join General Mercer's brigade. General Washington desperately needed additional troops to contend with the numerically superior British in New York. The 3rd and 9th Virginia Regiments were the first large, regular Southern regiments to march north.[8] The 3rd Virginia departed Williamsburg and halted at Fredericksburg for the men to exchange their weapons for newer ones at Hunter's Manufactory on the Rappahannock River. Here in Stafford County, William could have easily paid a farewell visit to his family as his regiment prepared for its long march to join the main army in New York. On August 13, Congress promoted Weedon to colonel of the regiment, and the Virginians resumed their 400-mile march north over back roads, enduring the hot and humid summer weather typical of the region.[9]

On August 27, General Washington's army suffered a severe defeat at the Battle of Long Island. Two days later he evacuated the army to New York Island and was again out-maneuvered, losing the city of New York to the British on September 15. However, Lord Howe's leisurely pursuit of the rebels enabled the Americans to rally and prepare defenses at the northern end of the island on the Harlem Heights. Weedon continued to hurry his regiment along, and he had to take a direct route through Maryland and New Jersey to avoid Philadelphia and its smallpox epidemic. Although the 3rd Virginia missed the Battle of Long Island, the men marched into the American camp on September 12 and 13 "in good spirits." The Virginians did not reach the forward lines until shortly before what would be known as the Battle of Harlem Heights. At this time, William's company had become badly depleted, suffering from sickness and desertion common throughout the army. The regiment had 408 men of its original 603 fit for duty, and young Washington reported only forty-three men present and fit for duty out of an original sixty-seven![10]

The terrain at the Battle of Harlem Heights consisted of interspersed woods and farms, which then separated the two armies south of the Heights.[11]   The opposing light infantry skirmishers opened the battle with several exchanges of musketry, and Colonel Thomas Knowlton's New England Rangers fought a running engagement with the British Light Infantry.   Initially the American light troops retreated, but General Washington saw an opportunity to entrap the confidently pursuing British, who had become separated from their main lines.   He quickly ordered forward some New England and Maryland troops—and the 3rd Virginia.   The three rifle companies of the 3rd Virginia, commanded by Major Andrew Leitch, immediately reinforced Knowlton's Rangers and began to envelop the British right flank and threaten their rear.   The remaining seven musket companies of the 3rd Virginia formed part of a frontal demonstration designed to engage the British and Hessians while Knowlton and Leitch completed their encircling movement.   The Virginians had been awake and under arms throughout the previous night and were no doubt weary from their month-long march, but the regiment advanced eagerly and smartly into its first fight.   *The Virginia Gazette* reported that "They all behaved with great bravery."   William's section of the regiment successfully defended a small pass while Knowlton and Leitch attacked the British right flank.[12]

The surprised British retreated after minor losses, and the Americans pursued them for a few hundred yards.   Both sides were gradually reinforced and the battle continued, ultimately involving 5,000 men from each army.   The Americans began to gain the upper hand for a change, and their performance against the British and Hessian regulars proved to be a welcome morale boost for the rebel army.   Washington, satisfied that his troops had partially redeemed their reputation from the Long Island and New York defeats, was the first to break off the action.   The general officially recognized the 3rd Virginia's active part in the battle, which provided both the regiment's and William Washington's baptism of fire. The regiment remained under arms, however, throughout the night of the 16th in anticipation of another British advance, which never materialized.[13]

William may well have been wounded at the Battle of Harlem Heights, and not, as some historians have claimed, in the previous Battle of Long Island. The 3rd Virginia was not in the American order of battle until September 10, *after* the August Battle of Long Island.[14] Although apprehensive from lack of both sleep and combat experience, he would have been eager to personally lead his men in their first fight, as he would always demonstrate throughout his battlefield career. One eyewitness described "a young officer on the right [of the regiment who] fired too early," drawing severe return fire from the British during the battle. The right wing of the regiment probably consisted of the 4th company and Washington's 5th company, the first three companies being the detached riflemen. Weedon reported losses of four killed, one ensign wounded and twelve others wounded or missing in action. Three men were reported wounded in the part of the regiment where William was probably posted, and his company return for September 21 listed one man wounded.[15] William would prove himself to be both brave and often impetuous in battle, and if he was in fact wounded in the New York campaign, it was at Harlem Heights!

The two armies remained opposite each other with very little activity for the closing days of September and the first part of October as the increasing autumn chill rolled in. General Washington treated the 3rd Virginia as somewhat of an independent command, declining to brigade it with other regiments. The commanding general's special attention was probably due to his need for a large unit of dependable regulars to be at his direct command rather than any favoritism toward his fellow Virginians.[16] The Americans continued, however, to suffer miserably from desertion and disease, to which the Virginians were not immune. On September 21, the 3rd Virginia reported only 383 men present and fit for duty of the unit's original 602 men. William's company maintained the regimental average: thirty-three men present and fit for duty of an original sixty-seven. The mundane and discouraging situation typical of camp life at this time was frustrating for most men, including William Washington. The men spent most of their time foraging for food, firewood and cover due to the constant shortage of supplies in this increasingly disorganized army. Young Washington was a man of action, and his boredom and discontent had to have been intensified by both his own company's and the entire army's inability to retain even half of their original numerical strength. Moreover, the Virginians had to perform their fair share of fatigue duty, the drudgery of which held no attraction for the action-oriented William Washington.[17] Thus, the condition of his company was somewhat typical of the distress of the army at this time. Indeed, the three Virginia regiments then in New York could muster only 1,011 men present and fit for duty of their original 1,663—a proportion slightly better than most other units in the army. Colonel Weedon once approached General Washington as to the possibility of recruiting replacements for the 3rd Virginia from other states' regiments whose terms of service were about to expire. This scheme apparently failed, because the October returns still listed only half of the regiment's men present and fit for duty.[18]

With the British Royal Navy operating unhindered on the Hudson River in early October, General Washington decided to withdraw his army from its vulnerable position at Harlem Heights and station it at White Plains. On the 17th, he attached the 3rd Virginia to Lord Stirling's brigade, which on the following day marched to White Plains as the army's advanced guard. On the 22nd, Colonel Haslet was detached with his Delaware regiment, picked men of the 1st and 3rd Virginia Regiments, and some Marylanders to cut off a 500-man Tory force at Mamaroneck near New Rochelle. Major Robert Rogers of French and Indian War fame commanded the Tory unit, the Queen's American Rangers. Lieutenant James Monroe (later the fifth President of the United States) and some of his riflemen from the 3rd Virginia took part in this operation, and Washington may have also been with this force when it surprised the Tories in a night attack. The Americans inflicted twenty casualties and captured another thirty-six men along with the unit's colors. The rebels suffered about a dozen casualties, and the victory helped to raise the fighting spirit of the American army. If William was not actually present, he certainly would have learned of the details. It is also not clear if the Virginia brigade fought a week later in the October 28 Battle of White Plains. Most of the fighting took place on the American right flank, where a force comprised of Delaware, Maryland, and New York regiments contested a combined British and Hessian advance for some time before the Americans pulled back in good order. An observer of this action, William had the opportunity to witness the impressive performance of the 16th British Light Dragoons when they charged and routed a number of American militia units. This enterprising officer would not forget such a tactical demonstration of the effectiveness of a charge by disciplined cavalry![19]

By early November, Washington had led his army to Peekskill on the east bank of the Hudson, where he prepared to cross the river in order to maneuver between the British and the Continental Congress' capital at Philadelphia. Stirling's brigade served as the advanced guards for this foray as well, which unfortunately turned into the famous retreat through the Jerseys.

Stirling found he had only 1,689 men present and fit for duty of his original 2,863 when he prepared to cross the Hudson in early November. The 3rd Virginia had 290 men present and fit, to which William's company contributed thirty-two. The majority of those men reported missing were either sick or deserters, rather than combat casualties. At this time, Weedon placed both the undermanned 4th and 5th companies under William's command—a total of fifty-seven men. By November 11, Stirling had crossed the Hudson and marched for Brunswick, New Jersey.[20]

Arriving at that town on the 13th, Stirling prepared to contest any potential British landings on the Amboy shore, a move that would threaten Philadelphia and General

Washington's line of retreat.   In the meantime, the British struck another blow to Washington's ability to remain in New York when on November 16 they captured Forts Washington and Lee, which were opposite each other on the Hudson River. Stirling remained in his position until the 18th, when he moved to Newark to cover the rear of the rest the ragged remnants of the American army as it retreated through New Jersey to Trenton on the Delaware River. Stirling's brigade—considered to be the elite of the army at this time—became Washington's rear guard and it slowly withdrew to Princeton on December 6, leaving only destroyed bridges and blocked roads in the path of the pursuing British. When this dispirited army crossed into Pennsylvania on December 7 and the last boats pulled to the western shore of the Delaware, the men found little food and shelter and stood nearly naked from lack of winter shoes, uniforms, blankets and tents. Moreover, the Virginians were still wearing their hunting frocks issued in the summer and the Stafford County men were not used to the harsh northern winter climate.   To make matters worse for General Washington's military prospects, most of his men's enlistments were to expire on December 31.[21]

Young William was learning a valuable tactical lesson of how to fight this war—that the Americans would have to often execute fighting withdrawals in order to survive to fight the British again. For the past three months, William Washington had participated in long marches, dreary encampments and retreats, with the action at Harlem Heights providing his regiment the only real combat with their enemy. Although the entire American army was safely on the Pennsylvania side of the Delaware River by December 17, General Washington described the desperate condition of his army and the cause of independence itself with a reference to the 3rd Virginia: "Weedon's, which was the strongest, not having more than one hundred and forty men fit for duty, the rest being in the hospitals."[22]

These discouraging, cold and hungry days of December of 1776 were what Thomas Payne described as the "times that try men's souls," when the nearly defeated Americans faced a much larger army of professional British and Hessian soldiers encamped across the Delaware River in New Jersey. In less than three months, this well-equipped and numerically superior army of professional soldiers had defeated the optimistic Americans in New York and chased them for more than 100 miles out of New York, across New Jersey and now into Pennsylvania. General Howe, however, failed to press his advantage and ordered his army into winter quarters, as was customary of 18th-century European armies. Howe's error prepared the stage for the Americans to launch a counter-stroke and achieve victories at Trenton and Princeton.[23]

On December 22, Stirling's brigade had only 505 men present and fit for duty, 134 of whom were from the 3rd Virginia. William Washington was by now well respected as an enterprising and capable junior officer. Prior to the famous crossing, William, James Monroe and several other officers were quartered for a time at William Neely's farmhouse. This Solebury farm was also being used as a hospital, and the owner later recalled William Washington as "a fine-looking man." Captain Washington was entrusted to lead a scouting party of fifty picked infantrymen on the enemy-occupied New Jersey side of the Delaware. He and his second in command, Lieutenant James Monroe, led reconnaissance and harassment missions in preparation for General Washington's planned— and desperate—surprise attack on the 1,300-man Hessian garrison at Trenton. Monroe described William as "an officer whose good conduct had already been noticed." On one occasion on December 25, another scouting party separate from Washington and Monroe (from the 5th Virginia) prematurely skirmished with a Hessian picket very near Trenton. This action temporarily alerted the sleepy garrison while the main American army was crossing the icy Delaware. Fortunately for the Americans, the Hessians discounted the incident as a harmless skirmish and Monroe recalled how William "executed his orders faithfully [and] took possession of the point to which he was ordered."[24]

William's detachment rejoined the main army once it finished crossing the Delaware, and he and Lieutenant Monroe

Trenton, 26 December 1776
U.S. Army Center of Military History

commanded the advanced guard of the left wing of the army, commanded by Generals Greene and Washington, as it approached Trenton in the early morning darkness of December 26. During this difficult night march when secrecy was paramount, William's party prevented anyone from preceding the army to warn the unsuspecting Hessians.[25] The surprise was complete, and the Americans severely defeated the Hessians, who suffered heavy losses in casualties and prisoners in a sharp pre-dawn fight later considered to have been one of the war's decisive battles.

William Washington was particularly active in the decisive early minutes of the battle. When the Hessians attempted to set up an artillery battery, William and Lieutenant Monroe led their companies in a bold, successful bayonet charge to capture the enemy guns before they could fire. Had these guns come into action firing grapeshot down King Street, Greene's column might have been stopped cold while the Hessian infantry formed up. The Hessian gunners, like most 18th-century professionals, fiercely defended their guns and wounded both American officers in the ensuing melee. Although the Americans prevailed, both Washington and Monroe soon had to be carried from the field. They were also ironically two of the small number of American casualties in the battle. William's fellow officers praised his gallantry and decisive action to prevent the Hessian artillery from forming during this critical stage of one of the decisive battles of the war. Monroe recalled how his commander "moved forward with the vanguard in front, attacked the enemy's picket, shot down the commanding officer, and drove it before him...rushed forward, attacked, and put the troops around the cannon to flight, and took possession of them."[26]

Immediately after the battle, General Washington gave the 3rd Virginia the honor of escorting several hundred Hessian prisoners to Philadelphia. Thus, the regiment did not partici-pate in the subsequent and equally impressive victory at Princeton on January 3, 1777. Sadly for the Americans and the men of the 3rd Virginia in particular, their original commander, General Mercer, was killed in the battle. William, recovering from the painful hand wounds he received at Trenton, was temporarily relieved of combat duty and accompanied his unit and the Hessian prisoners to Philadelphia.[27]

Although the winter campaign ended favorably for the Americans, General Washington experienced extreme difficulty in holding his little army together at their winter quarters in Morristown, New Jersey. The British and their Hessian mercenaries were still powerful, and they remained in New York and eastern New Jersey in force. Meanwhile, the 3rd Virginia was reorganized in January 1777 and, like many regiments, had to be recruited anew while remnants stayed in Philadelphia and Newtown. William probably remained in Philadelphia, recuperating from his wounds. Among other things, the New Jersey retreat had clearly demonstrated to George Washington and his generals the need for an effective American cavalry force. William Washington, a superb horseman whose recognized gallantry sometimes bordered on impetuosity, was naturally attracted to this new and promising branch of the army! His performance at Trenton surely distinguished him as a valuable officer, and whom one historian has included in the handful of officers in 1776 who "when the chips were down, were capable of delivering the best any general could demand."[28]

William Washington, in less than four months of active campaigning with the Continental Army, had proven himself on several occasions—to the point of being wounded while leading his men. He had become an officer who could be trusted with independent command and a battlefield leader capable of initiative and personal bravery at decisive moments. His grueling service in the New Jersey campaigns of 1776 gave him valuable exposure to the hit-and-run tactics necessary for the small American forces to eventually wear down the powerful British army. It was also clear that this war would be long and demand much of the band of dedicated officers who remained with George Washington's army. William's reassignment to the Continental Cavalry in 1777 would also provide him with experience on which he would later have to rely during his more notable exploits on horseback.

NOTES: CHAPTER I

[1] Douglas Southall Freeman, *George Washington: A Biography, Vol. I: Young Washington*, 225; George Washington Greene, *The Life of Nathanael Greene, Major General in the Revolution*, III, 115; George Harrison Sanford King (comp.), *The Register of Overwharton Parish, Stafford County, Virginia, 1723-1758*, 124; George Harrison Sanford King (comp.), *The Register of St. Paul's Parish, 1715-1798—Stafford County, Virginia, 1715-1776*, 148-149; *The National Cyclopaedia of American Biography; Being the History of the United States*, II, 492-493; Henry Lee, *Memoirs of the War in the Southern Department of the United States*, I, 398-399; Ella Basset Washington, "William Washington, Lieut.-Colonel Third Light Dragoons, Continental Army," *The Magazine of American History*, IX, 94; "William Washington of Stafford County, Virginia," *The William and Mary Quarterly*, 1st Ser., XV, 132-133; James Grant Wilson and John Fiske (eds.), *Appleton's Cyclopaedia of American Biography*, VI, 384. The most extensive Washington genealogy revealing William and George to be second cousins appears in Worthington Chauncey Ford (ed.), *The Writings of George Washington*, XIV, 317-430 passim and in Cowpens Centennial Committee, *Proceedings at the Unveiling of the Battle Monument in Spartanburg, S.C., in Commemoration of the Centennial of the Battle of Cowpens*, 129. George referred to William as his "kinsman." See George Washington to Edward Rutledge, June 16, 1791, in John C. Fitzpatrick (ed.), *The Writings of George Washington from the Original Manuscript Sources, 1745-1799*,   XXXI, 196. William Washington's name has occasionally been erroneously printed with a middle name "Augustine" or initial "A" in secondary sources. This has been confused with the name of George Washington's nephew, William Augustine Washington. All primary sources list Bailey's son as "William Washington."

[2] "Heads of Families—Virginia, 1785," in U.S. Bureau of the Census, *Heads of Families at the First Census of the United States Taken in the Year 1790 and Records of State Enumerations: 1782 to 1785*, 107; Jerrilynn Eby, *They Called Stafford Home: The Development of Stafford County, Virginia, from 1600 until 1865*, 143; Robert F. and Isobel B. Woodson (comp.), *Virginia Tithables From Burned Record Counties*, 113; King (comp.), *Overwharton Parish*, 123-124, 141 and 196; King (comp.), *St. Paul's Parish*, ix and 149-150; "Descendants of Two John Washingtons," *Virginia Historical Magazine*, XXII (1914), 329-330; Virginia State

Library, *Embrey's Index of Records: Stafford County Virginia Index of Grantees, 1664-1914*, Vol. 6, 2019; *Wills of Stafford County, Virginia, Book S,* 127; Therese A. Fisher (comp.), *Marriage Records of the City of Fredericksburg, and of Orange, Spotsylvania, and Stafford Counties, Virginia: 1722-1850,* 166.

[3] John Pendleton Kennedy (ed.), *Journals of the House of Burgesses of Virginia, 1766-1769,* Vol. 11, 20; John Pendleton Kennedy (ed.), *Journals of the House of Burgesses of Virginia, 1770-1772,* Vol. 12, 78; November 6, 1772 and March 11, 1773, in Benjamin J. Hillman (ed.), *Executive Journals of the Council of Colonial Virginia, Vol. VI: June 20, 1754 - May 3, 1775,* 512 and 520; Vinnetta W. Ranke (comp.), *Justices of the Peace of Colonial Virginia,* 17, 21, 22, 26, 32, 37, and 58; William J. Van Schreeven (comp.) and Robert L. Scribner (ed.), *Revolutionary Virginia: The Road to Independence, Volume I: Forming Thunderclouds and the First Convention, 1763-1774,* 159-162; Cynthia Miller Leonard (comp.), *The General Assembly of Virginia, July 30, 1619 - January 11, 1978: A Bicentennial Register of Members,* 139; Earl G. Swem and John W. Williams, *A Register of the General Assembly of Virginia,* 442.

[4] Cowpens Committee, Proceedings, 116; *NCAB,* II, 492; Felix B. Warley, "An Oration, Delivered in Saint Michael's Church, in the City of Charleston, the 19th June, 1810, on the Death of the Late Gen. William Washington", 7, 8 and 19; King (comp.), *St. Paul's Parish,* xxii-xxiii; Washington, "William Washington," 94 and 105; "William Washington," *William and Mary Quarterly,* 133; Wilson and Fiske (eds.), *Appleton's,* VI, 384; Lee, *Memoirs,* I, 402; *Proceedings at the Inauguration of the Monument Erected by the Washington Light Infantry to the Memory of Col. William Washington at Magnolia Cemetery, May 5, 1858,* 16; Guy Fred Wells, *Parish Education in Colonial Virginia* (New York: Columbia University, 1923), 22-23.

[5] *The Virginia Gazette,* September 22, 1775, 1; *The Virginia Gazette,* January 13, 1776, 3; Francis B. Heitman, *Historical Register of Officers of the Continental Army during the War of the Revolution, April, 1775 to December, 1783,* 574; Lee, *Memoirs* I, 399; Jacket No. 65, Revolutionary War Rolls, Record Group 97, National Archives; Journal of the Committee of Safety of Virginia, March 13 and April 6, 1776, in *Calendar of Virginia State Papers and Other Manuscripts,* VIII, 120 and 154-155; Robert L. Scribner and Brent Tarter (comps.), *Revolutionary Virginia: The Road to Independence, Volume IV: The Committee of Safety and*

the Balance of Forces, 1775, 405; Robert L. Scribner and Brent Tarter (comps.), *Revolutionary Virginia: The Road to Independence, Volume VI: The Time of Decision, 1776*, 15 and 49; Harry M. Ward, *Duty, Honor or Country: General George Weedon and the American Revolution*, 43-47.

[6] W. P. Cresson, *James Monroe*, 14-17; Richard Hanser, *The Glorious Hour of Lt. Monroe*, 45-48; George Mason to George Washington, April 2, 1776, in Jared Sparks (ed.), *Correspondence of the American Revolution; Being Letters of Eminent Men to George Washington*, I, 182; Scribner (comp.), *Time of Decision*, 205, 230, 339-341, 450 and 479-480; Journal of Committee of Safety, June 3 and 11, 1776, in *Virginia State Papers*, VIII, 185 and 198; Ward, *George Weedon*, 48-52.

[7] Journal of Committee of Safety, June 18 and 19 and July 4 and 5, 1776, in *Virginia State Papers*, VIII, 209, 212, 237 and 239; John T. Goolrick, *The Life of General Hugh Mercer*, 45-47; Hanser, *Lt. Monroe*, 49; *The Virginia Gazette*, July 20, 1776, 3; Ward, *George Weedon*, 54-55; Robert L. Scribner, and Brent Tarter (comps.), *Revolutionary Virginia: The Road to Independence, Volume VIII: Independence and the Fifth Convention, 1776*, 427, 437, 545, 703-704; 716.

[8] President of Congress to the Governor of Virginia, July 22, 1776, in Peter Force (ed.), *American Archives*, 5th Series, I, 494; Thomas Jefferson to Frances Eppes, July 23, 1776, in Edmund C. Burnett (ed.), *Letters of Members of the Continental Congress*, II, 22.

[9] *The Virginia Gazette*, August 9, 1776, 3; From the Journals of Council, August 10, 1776, in H. R. McIlwaine (ed.), *Official Letters of the Governors of the State of Virginia, Vol. I: The Letters of Patrick Henry*, 30; Force (ed.), *American Archives*, 5th Series, I, 1606; Cresson, *Monroe*, 19-20.

[10] Douglas Southall Freeman, *George Washington: A Biography, Vol. IV: Leader of the Revolution*, 189-190; Jacket No. 65, Revolutionary War Rolls, RG 97, National Archives; Hanser, *Lt. Monroe*, 59; Ward, *George Weedon*, 56-58. General information on the campaigns in New York and New Jersey is from John R. Sellers, *The Virginia Continental Line*, 6-7 and Christopher Ward, *The War of the Revolution*, I, 202-318.

[11] Information on the Battle of Harlem Heights is from Henry P. Johnston, *The Battle of Harlem Heights*; Sellers, *Virginia Line*, 8 and Ward, *War of the Revolution*, I, 231-252.

[12] Colonel David Griffith to Major Powel, September 18, 1776, and Captain Gustavus Brown Wallace to his brother, September 18, 1776, in Johnston, *Harlem Heights*, 119-120 and 171; George Weedon to John Page, September 20, 1776, in Richard B. Morris and Henry S. Commager (eds.), *The Spirit of Seventy-Six*, 470-471; Hanser, *Lt. Monroe*, 70-75; *The Virginia Gazette*, October 4, 1776, Supplement, 1.

[13] George Washington to President of Congress, September 18, 1776 and General Orders, Harlem Heights, September 16, 1776, in Fitzpatrick (ed.), *Writings of Washington*, VI, 68 and 56.

[14] The earliest reference to William Washington's alleged wounding at Long Island is in Benson J. Lossing, *Pictorial Fieldbook of the Revolution*, II, 435n. This error was perpetuated in Heitman, *Historical Register*, 574; *NCAB*, II, 492; "William Washington," *William and Mary Quarterly*, 133; and Wilson and Fiske (eds.), *Appleton's*, VI, 384. These claims may have been based on Lee, *Memoirs*, I, 399, but Lee clearly says that William fought at "York Island" (i.e., New York Island where Harlem Heights is), *not* Long Island. James Monroe also remembered Harlem Heights; see Stuart Gerry Brown (ed.), *The Autobiography of James Monroe*, 15 and 23. For a correct chronology, see also President of Congress to George Weedon, August 28 and 30, 1776, in Burnett (ed.), *Letters of Continental Congress*, II, 62 and 64; Returns, in Force (ed.), *American Archives*, 5th Series, II, 327-330; and George Washington to Hugh Mercer, September 11, 1776, in Fitzpatrick (ed.), *Writings of Washington*, VI, 43-44.

[15] Captain John Chilton to "My Dear Friends," October 4, 1776, in George P. Scheer and Hugh F. Rankin, *Rebels and Redcoats*, 185; Captain Wallace to his brother, September 18, 1776, in Johnston, *Harlem Heights*, 120; Jacket No. 65, Revolutionary War Rolls, RG 97, National Archives; Ward, *George Weedon*, 60-61.

[16] Return of Washington's Army at Kingsbridge, September 21, 1776, in Force (ed.), *American Archives*, 5th Series, II, 451-452; General Orders, Harlem Heights, September 26, 1776, in Fitzpatrick (ed.), *Writings of Washington*, VI, 119-120.

[17] Return of Washington's Army at Kingsbridge, September 21, 1776, in Force (ed.), *American Archives*, 5th Series, II, 451-452; Jacket No. 65, Revolutionary War Rolls, RG 97, National Archives; General Orders, Harlem Heights, September 30, 1776, in Fitzpatrick (ed.), *Writings of Washington*, VI, 134; Ward, *George Weedon*, 62-63; Sellers, *Virginia Line*, 9.

[18] Return of Washington's Army at Harlem Heights, September 30, 1776, and George Washington to President of Congress, October 2, 1776, in Force (ed.), *American Archives*, 5th Series, II, 607-608 and 841; Jacket No. 65, Revolutionary War Rolls, RG 97, National Archives; Sellers, *Virginia Line*, 10.

[19] General Orders, Harlem Heights, October 17, 1776, in Fitzpatrick (ed.), *Writings of Washington*, VI, 216; Ward, *War of the Revolution*, I, 258 and 262-266; *The Virginia Gazette*, November 15, 1776, 3. Monroe recalled being at White Plains; see Brown (ed.), *Monroe*, 15; Cresson, *Monroe*, 21; Hanson, *Lt. Monroe*, 86.

[20] Information on the retreat through New Jersey is from Ward, *War of the Revolution*, I, 275-290. Return of Washington's Army, November 3, 1776, and Return of the 3rd Virginia Regiment, November 5, 1776, in Force (ed.), *American Archives*, 5th Series, III, 499-500 and 515-516; George Washington to President of Congress, November 11, 1776, in Jared Sparks (ed.), *The Writings of Washington*, IV, 172; Ward, *George Weedon*, 68.

[21] Extract from a Letter from Fort Lee, November 13, 1776, in William S. Stryker (ed.), *Archives of the State of New Jersey*, Second Series: *Extracts from American Newspapers, 1776-1782*, I, 232; Hanser, *Lt. Monroe*, 93-104; Sellers, *Virginia Line*, 12; William S. Stryker, *The Battles of Trenton and Princeton*, 10 and 17.

[22] George Washington to Lund Washington, December 17, 1776, in Fitzpatrick (ed.), *Writings of Washington*, IV, 346-347; Ward, *George Weedon*, 70-72.

[23] Information on the campaign and battles of Trenton and Princeton is from Richard M. Ketchum, *The Winter Soldiers*; Samuel Steele Smith, *The Battle of Trenton*; Stryker, *Trenton and Princeton*; Ward, *War of the*

Revolution, I, 285-324; and W. J. Wood, *Battles of the Revolutionary War, 1775-1781*, 55-74.

[24] Return of the Army on the Delaware, December 22, 1776, in Force (ed.), *American Archives*, 5th Series, III, 1401-1402; William Gordon, *The History of the Rise, Progress, and Establishment of the Independence of the United States of America*, II, 395; W. W. H. Davis, "Washington on the West Bank of the Delaware, 1776," *Pennsylvania Magazine of History and Biography*, IV (1880), 141; Brown (ed.), *Monroe*, 25; Hanser, *Lt. Monroe*, 110, 118, 123-125 and 143-144; Sellers, *Virginia Line*, 13-14.

[25] Washington's Order from Merrick House, December 25, 1776, in Howard Fast, *The Crossing*, 205; Washington's General Orders, in Smith, *Trenton*, 32; Brown (ed.), *Monroe*, 25; Cresson, *Monroe*, 27; Ketchum, *Winter Soldiers*, 293; Extract from a Letter from an Officer of Distinction [Lord Stirling], January 1, 1777, in Force (ed.), *American Archives*, 5th Series, III, 1442; Extract from Sergeant Joseph White's Narrative, in Stryker, *Trenton and Princeton*, 479; James Wilkenson, *Memoirs of My Own Times*, I, 128-130; Hanser, *Lt. Monroe*, 151-154; Ward, *George Weedon*, 75-76.

[26] George Washington to John Cadwalader, December 27, 1776, in Fitzpatrick (ed.), *Writings of Washington*, VI, 446; Stephen Moylan to Robert Morris, December 27, 1776, in Force (ed.), *American Archives*, 5th Series, III, 1446; Brown (ed.), *Monroe*, 25-26; Cresson, *Monroe*, 29-30.

[27] Ketchum, *Winter Soldiers*, 309; Smith, *Trenton*, 26; Davis, "Washington on the Delaware" *Pennsylvania Magazine*, IV (1880), 156-157; Stryker, *Trenton and Princeton*, 213; Brown, (ed.), *Monroe*, 25-26; Sellers, *Virginia Line*, 15; Ward, *George Weedon*, 78 and 84.

[28] George Washington to George Weedon, January 9, 1777, in Fitzpatrick (ed.), *Writings of Washington*, VI, 482; Lee, *Memoirs*, I, 400; Ketchum, *Winter Soldiers*, 297.

chapter II

THE MAKING OF A CAVARLYMAN: 1777-1779

On January 27, 1777, General Washington promoted Captain William Washington to the rank of major and transferred him to Colonel Stephen Moylan's 4th Continental Light Dragoons. Moylan commanded one of the four regular cavalry regiments authorized by the Continental Congress in 1777. The other three regiments were Colonel Theodoric Bland's 1st Regiment, Colonel Elisha Sheldon's 2nd Regiment and Colonel George Baylor's 3rd Regiment. Each regiment consisted of six troops and had an authorized strength of 280 men, a full strength that was never attained. "Dragoons" had traditionally been mounted infantrymen who rode to the battlefield and fought on foot, but the term was applied to light or medium cavalry by this time. They fought as cavalrymen on horseback with sabers and pistols and performed vital reconnaissance missions. Several state, militia, "legion" and other independent mounted units also fought at various times in the war. William was the third highest officer of the regiment, ranking behind Colonel Moylan and Lieutenant Colonel Anthony White. General Weedon had recommended William for an immediate lieutenant colonelcy, but General Washington considered that, although merited, such quick rank might "(considering the connexion between us), be looked upon as the effect of partiality."[1] William Washington would have to wait another year for a chance at an independent cavalry command.

4th Regiment of Continental Light Dragoons, 1777-1778
Company of Military Historians

General Washington had requested that Congress authorize, finance and raise a cavalry corps as early as July, 1776, but it took the bitter lessons of the retreat through New Jersey to convince the legislators of the need for cavalry in the Continental Army. Early in 1777, the Congress responded with an unrealistic call to the states for 3,000 cavalry. Although four regular regiments were eventually raised, these seldom numbered more than 150 men each.[2]   American leaders, particularly General Washington, have often been criticized for their failure to recognize the value of cavalry during the War of the Revolution. Historian Charles Francis Adams, the most avid proponent of this view, initiated this criticism. This view has been frequently repeated and remained relatively unchallenged for nearly a century. Washington's dismissal of a regiment of Connecticut mounted militia in July, 1776—shortly before the Battle of Long Island—is the usual basis for the criticism. While Washington can be justly criticized for poor tactics in that battle, his reasons for sending the problem militia horsemen home seem justified. He not only asserted that they were too expensive to maintain and could not easily be brought into battle on islands, but more importantly, he objected to their elitist demand to be exempt from guard and fatigue duties. The general rightly feared that any such special treatment afforded them would provide a bad example and source of discontent among the rest of his less than harmonious army.[3] To have permitted this particular unit to remain as preferred troops would have invited disaster to the morale and discipline of the democratic-minded and ill-organized Continental Army of 1776. General Washington faced tremendous problems at this time in maintaining any army at all, let alone a select cavalry corps composed of untested militia.

Adams' additional criticism that Washington learned nothing about cavalry from the 1776 and 1777 campaigns is also unfounded. The general wrote Congress in December, 1776, that "From the Experience I have had this campaign, of the Utility of Horse, I am convinced there is no carrying on the War without these and I would therefore recommend the

Establishment of one or more Corps." Nearly a year later, he significantly reported that "We have found so many advantages from the Cavalry [the four small regiments of light dragoons that were raised in 1777] in the course of this Campaign, that I am determined to augment them as much as possible against the next, and enable them to take the Field in a respectable manner."[4]   The reality of recruiting, equipping and maintaining a large, disciplined cavalry force mounted on good horses proved extremely difficult to achieve during the Revolution, however.   Although Washington obviously recognized the importance of cavalry, he could hardly be expected to devote too much time and scarce resources to one branch of the service without endangering the existence of the rest of the Continental Army. The challenge of keeping up the cavalry is best exemplified by William Washington's three-year tenure as a cavalry officer in the middle states, 1777-1779.

Major Washington joined Moylan's command near Philadelphia in late February, and in March, the Congress appropriated $3,000 to the 4th Dragoons for recruiting and equipping the regiment.   This paltry sum soon proved inadequate, and the legislators had to allocate an additional $22,000 to the regiment between April 8 and May 16. Most of the money went for horses and equipment, the men being paid very little. William, for example, received $60 per month. In addition, cavalry officers were required to furnish their own uniforms, arms, accouterments, horses, saddles and other horse equipment.[5] Because of the shortage of clothing throughout the army, the regiment actually wore red coats captured from the British. Their appearance alarmed General Washington, who feared that his own men would accidentally shoot the cavalrymen. To avoid such a mishap, the dragoons often had to wear hunting frocks over their uniforms until they received green coats two years later in 1779.[6] The general was further distressed when he learned that Colonel Moylan was recruiting enemy deserters and foreigners in Pennsylvania in violation of his "native-born Americans only" rule for the Continental Dragoons. As a consequence, Washington seldom trusted or favored the 4th Dragoons, preferring instead Colonel Bland's

1st Dragoons, who were supposedly recruited from native-born Americans of class in Virginia. In May, Congress entrusted William Washington with another $25,000 to specifically recruit and equip three troops (half of the regiment) in Maryland. While on this detached mission, he missed the skirmishing and maneuvers in New Jersey that opened the new campaign in June 1777.[7]

Throughout the month of June, Howe and Washington maneuvered indecisively in New Jersey in anticipation of a British attack on Philadelphia.[8] Washington, who desperately needed cavalry for reconnaissance duty, sharply ordered Moylan to bring his 4th Dragoons to the main army "armed or not" by mid-June. Howe inexplicably returned to his base of operations in New York on June 30, and both sides remained relatively inactive throughout July. Major Washington rejoined Moylan in July with only a small number of Marylanders, and he was no doubt discouraged when he found the rest of the regiment to be in a ragged and hungry state. All four regiments struggled with equipment replacement problems and the continual need for feed and fodder for such large numbers of horses. Moylan wrote the Commissary on July 7 that his men suffered from an almost complete lack of provision.[9]

On July 19, the regiment complied with orders to follow the main army north to New Windsor by way of the Clove (the Ramapo Valley gap through the Palisades or Hudson Highlands). However, they were delayed by an unfortunate incident during the night of the 20th. As the dragoons rode through Englishtown, about twenty of the more desperate men detached themselves and decided to ride directly to Philadelphia to demand their back pay from Congress! Lieutenant Colonel White and Major Washington then had to lead two troops of twenty men each in pursuit of the disgruntled troopers. White and Washington captured the band after a forty-mile chase and brought them back for trial as deserters. They were immediately taken from their mounts under arrest, and after they were found guilty, quickly dismissed from the cavalry. General Washington, as occasionally was his practice, pardoned the men from their death sentence for desertion and mutiny. The embarrassed regiment was thus reduced to about eighty men, less than one third of its authorized strength. Nonetheless, they remained in the field with the army, and by July 22, the 4th Dragoons were scouting the Amboy shore of New Jersey watching for the arrival of a large British fleet which had recently sailed from New York.[10]

On July 25, in anticipation of a British advance up the Delaware River Valley on Philadelphia, General Washington ordered Moylan's 4th, Bland's 1st and Sheldon's 2nd Dragoons all to assemble near the American capital. The dragoons rode in support of Colonel Daniel Morgan's Rifle Corps and the divisions of Generals Stirling, John Sullivan, Adam Stephen and Benjamin Lincoln. Washington remained in doubt throughout August as to where the British might strike. This may have been the first opportunity for William to meet Morgan, with whom three years later he would serve so gallantly in the South. Unfortunately during this anxious time, the 4th Dragoons had to perform the odious policing chore of apprehending stragglers and deserters. Moreover, the cavalry corps also suffered from the army's malady of desertion and occasional mutiny. The problem finally became so widespread in the cavalry units that a "general court martial of the horse" was held on August 22. Regimental officers tried many of their own men in numerous cases. These difficulties notwithstanding, the four depleted cavalry regiments mustered to form the vanguard of the army when it marched through Philadelphia on August 23, after Washington had learned that Howe had landed his army at Elkton on the Chesapeake Bay.[11]

On the following day, Washington ordered all cavalry units to Wilmington, Delaware to scout the British advance and act as military police to discourage stragglers from the main army. On September 3 through 8, the 4th and 2nd Dragoons skirmished with the advance elements of Howe's army. The opposing armies eventually clashed on the banks of the Brandywine Creek west of Philadelphia on September 11. The British severely defeated the Americans, and with the exception of Bland's 1st Dragoons (who failed for half of the day to detect Howe's flanking attack until it was too late), the cavalry played no significant part in the battle. The 4th Dragoons were attached to Stirling's Division during the battle, and they scouted continuously on the west side of the Schuylkill River for a few days after the battle as well. Brigadier General Casimir Pulaski, the recently appointed commander of all the American cavalry, reinforced Moylan in a futile attempt to delay the British advance on Philadelphia. The effort by such a small cavalry force was insignificant, and the Americans could do little more than watch as the British army marched unopposed into the city on September 26.[12]

General Washington desperately tried to reverse the effects of the Battle of Brandywine. On October 4, he attacked the British forces north of Philadelphia at Germantown, but was again defeated. During the battle, the 4th Dragoons fought on the American right center position under Sullivan, but heavy fog prevented their playing an effective role. However, their protective screening of the retreating American infantry prevented the British from effectively pursuing after the battle had ended in their favor. The regiment fought again at the inconclusive skirmishes near White Marsh on December 4, shortly before the Continental Army went into winter quarters at Valley Forge.[13] Young Washington was with his regiment at the battles of Brandywine, Germantown and White Marsh. He was quickly learning a difficult strategic reality of the Revolutionary War for the Americans—their need to quickly rebound and fight again in some fashion after being tactically defeated by the British army. Before the American army went into winter quarters at Valley Forge, however, several problems developed which severely hampered the growth and effectiveness of the American cavalry.

Throughout the campaign of 1777, General Washington had permitted the cavalry to impress horses for remounts from Tories or neutrals when it appeared the animals might otherwise have fallen into British hands. Several cavalrymen apparently abused this privilege to the point of outright looting, thus forcing the general to temporarily suspend permission to impress horses.   The cavalry corps then immediately suffered from a severe shortage of good remounts. When Pulaski assumed the difficult task of commanding all four of the dragoon regiments, he immediately faced resentment as a "foreigner" by many of the American officers who were forced to serve under him. Particularly piqued was Moylan, who as senior colonel among the four regimental commanders, thought he was next in line for such a promotion. He and Pulaski quickly became involved in a bitter feud that only exacerbated the morale problems of the cavalry.[14]

While the rest of the army settled down near the end of December for the severe winter at Valley Forge, General Washington sent all four cavalry regiments to Trenton for what he hoped would be a winter of training, refitting and recruiting.   In addition, he ordered these troops to gather intelligence and guard against any British raids and foraging expeditions from their new base in Philadelphia.   Pulaski admirably attempted the almost impossible task of molding the four regiments into a cohesive cavalry corps in the European battlefield tradition. His often-grandiose projects failed largely as a result of his poor understanding of English, the deplorable condition of the army's finances and his inability to get along with the American officers.[15] Although it is not known if the usually amiable Washington engaged in this infighting, his sense of loyalty probably made him more sympathetic towards his own regimental commander, Colonel Moylan.

The cavalry officers spent most of the winter and early spring of 1778 trying to locate remounts and otherwise refit their ragged and mostly dismounted troopers. Colonels Bland and Baylor rode to Virginia in March to procure horses for all four regiments.   By the end of the month, however, the Moylan-Pulaski fracas finally ended when the proud Pole resigned to recruit his own "legion." A legion at this time was a mixed force of dragoons and light infantry formed into a single unit.   General Washington thereupon placed Moylan in command of all the cavalry as the senior colonel, but without his much-coveted promotion to brigadier general. The general had intentionally spared the cavalry from the severe privations of Valley Forge in hopes that they would be in better condition for the coming spring campaign.[16] He soon questioned the wisdom of that decision.

In April, General Washington complained to Moylan that too many officers, in their selfish desire for "aggrandizement," had undermined his purpose for stationing the cavalry at Trenton and only "shameful neglect" of the men resulted. He again repeated his desire that only native-born Americans of class be recruited for the cavalry to avoid repeating the past years' problems. It is clear that Major William Washington was not one of these offending officers, because he was in Maryland and northern Virginia purchasing horses and equipment for the cavalry. In one instance, his zealous devotion to duty caused some trouble in Virginia. The 4th Dragoons were assigned the area north of the Susquehanna River all the way to the Hudson for horse procurement purposes, but in May, William was riding as far south as Fredericksburg (near his home in Stafford County). While there, he purchased swords at Hunter's Manufactory and several pairs of boots. Having been away from his family for almost two years, he no doubt took time to visit his Stafford County homestead. While in the vicinity, he made the mistake of buying a few horses at £150 apiece. Colonels Bland and Baylor had been assigned this region to procure horses in, and unbeknownst to William, they had previously set a purchase price of £130 per remount. Bland became enraged and complained to Baylor that horse prices had become inflated throughout Virginia as a result of Major Washington's transgression.[17] Relieved that the two colonels pursued no official action against him with Moylan, he quickly returned to his regiment's assigned area of horse procurement.

William may not have rejoined the 4th Dragoons in time for the June campaign in New Jersey. Now commanded by General Henry Clinton, the British army evacuated Philadelphia in late June and began an overland march through New Jersey for New York. While shadowing the enemy's march in late June, Moylan's 4th Dragoons, supplemented to a strength of 150-300, created many obstacles for Clinton's army when the troopers "demolished all the bridges they could." General Washington led the rebuilt Continental Army and various militia units in pursuit and forced the Battle of Monmouth on June 28. In the battle's early stages, the 4th Dragoons rode reconnaissance for the main army and were attached to Colonel Daniel Morgan's command covering the distant right wing of Washington's army. Morgan did not arrive in time to take part in resulting large-scale battle fought in the middle of one of the hottest days remembered at the time. The fight ended in a draw, though somewhat favoring the Americans. After the battle the British resumed their march back to New York, arriving in the city in early July. Moylan's horsemen followed Clinton's column at a safe distance. Washington then established his headquarters at White Plains, and the American army occupied the area north of the city on both sides of the Hudson River. The combatants had almost returned to positions similar to their situation two years previous in the summer of 1776.[18]

On July 7, General Washington ordered Moylan to bring all of the cavalry to the east side of the Hudson in an effort to contain British foraging parties and provide intelligence. The 4th Dragoons were now remounted and well accoutered, for Major William Washington had returned to his unit from his successful procurement mission! Importantly, General Washington now tapped his dependable kinsman to act as liaison officer between himself and Moylan. He needed a trusted officer to coordinate cavalry operations on both sides of the Hudson and keep him apprised. The opposing cavalry units frequently skirmished over livestock and forage in the "no man's land" of Westchester County south of White Plains.[19]

General Washington had to formally establish a written list of cavalry officers on August 7 to determine once and for all the order of seniority and rank. A number of these officers, not unlike many of the rest of the officers in the Continental Army, frequently argued over rank and seniority at no small detraction to the war effort. William Washington found himself listed as the senior major among the four dragoon regiments.   Throughout the rest of August and well into September, the strategic stalemate around New York persisted, the only activity being skirmishes between opposing detachments.   Most of the Continental Dragoons, except Baylor's 3rd, were, in General Washington's words, posted "in front near our old [1776] position at the White Plains."[20] One of the most bloody of these engagements indirectly resulted in William's promotion and his taking command of one of the four regiments.

The 3rd Dragoons

When General Charles Cornwallis led a large British expedition out of New York along the west side of the Hudson River in late September, General Washington dispatched newly uniformed and equipped Colonel Baylor's 3rd Dragoons to scout the enemy's movements. On the night of September 26, Baylor's command was completely surprised as they slept in barns at Tappan. A large infantry detachment led by General "No Flint" Charles Grey almost annihilated the corps, and nearly half of the dragoons were killed, wounded or captured during a bayonet attack. Moreover, the British captured most of the unit's horses, and Baylor himself was severely and almost mortally wounded. Many Americans considered this reverse, in Charles Pettit's words, "a kind of Masacre [sic] as little or no Resistance could be made." At the time of this action, William was temporarily commanding the 4th Dragoons, riding to join General Stirling. A useful number of Tappan survivors could not be mustered until late November, at which time General Washington ordered the dependable Major Washington to "contingently take command" of the decimated 3rd Dragoons at Bristol and take them into winter quarters. William led the dispirited band of less than 100, mostly horseless, cavalrymen into winter quarters at Frederick and Hagerstown, Maryland.[21] He would have been apprehensive at the awesome task of rebuilding the decimated and demoralized regiment, but William Washington, duty-focused as always, was up to the challenge.

3rd Regiment of Continental Light Dragoons, 1778-1783
Company of Military Historians

On November 20, Congress promoted William Washington to lieutenant colonel of the 3rd Continental Dragoons in place of Lieutenant Colonel Bird, who had resigned. He was also instructed to take full and complete command of the regiment, because the badly wounded Colonel Baylor was unable to take the field. On November 30, General Washington informed William that he had "the pleasure of transmitting your Commission which had just come to hand before in a Letter from the President [of Congress]." The general further instructed his new lieutenant colonel of cavalry to remain at Frederick and Hagerstown for the winter in hopes of rebuilding the 3rd Dragoons to fighting strength.[22] Lieutenant Colonel William Washington, two years after his gallant charge at Trenton, now held an independent command of cavalry— small as it was for the moment. He now faced the formidable task of restoring "his" regiment to effectiveness.

Throughout the winter of 1779, William doggedly recruited, trained and attempted to refit the 3rd Dragoons in anticipation of the spring and summer campaigns. In February, his men still suffered from clothing shortages, although new uniforms were constantly promised him. General Washington advised William that "if they can make a shift with their old Cloaths while in Winter quarters, they will find more benefit from the new next Campaign." At this time, William also learned that General Washington was considering sending him and his dragoons to South Carolina in the near future, but not until after Pulaski's Legion had moved south. By the end of March the redoubtable William had recruited his unit up to an effective strength of 140 men. The dragoons, including many new recruits from Maryland, required training in horsemanship and the discipline of cavalry tactics. Moreover, they still lacked sufficient horses and uniforms, a situation which their commander constantly attempted to remedy. The shortage of horses for the 3rd Dragoons was partially relieved by Congressional orders that extra horses and remounts of the 1st Dragoons be transferred to the 3rd. Still not satisfied with what he considered to be such a small number of cavalrymen riding south as two small regiments, the general warned William that he might have to delay the 3rd Dragoons for the coming winter in Wilmington, Delaware to recruit more men and purchase more horses.   Nonetheless, Lieutenant Colonel Washington was anxious to begin his long ride south (where he knew he might locate more men and especially good horses), and he led his 150 proud dragoons through Philadelphia by the end of August.[23]   However, a variety of circumstances delayed William Washington in the North after all until the following spring.

Since more cavalry was badly needed in the South Carolina theater of operations and a significant campaign failed to materialize in the North in 1779, General Washington had ordered both the 1st and 3rd Dragoons to ride directly to South Carolina in accordance with a Congressional directive of May 7.   Pulaski, who had raised an independent cavalry and light infantry "legion" after his resignation as cavalry commander in 1778, led the only large mounted force (which later included the 1st Dragoons) in the South in 1779.[24]

On August 28, General Washington instructed General Stirling to intercept William Washington in New Jersey and temporarily attach the 3rd Dragoons to his division, which had no mounted troops.   The next day, Washington ordered William to remain with Stirling until the British intentions for the rest of the campaign year were more evident.   While attached to Stirling's division, William provided mounted escorts for French dignitaries traveling to Philadelphia through New Jersey.   The French had come into the war against the British shortly after the end of the 1777 campaign around Philadelphia and the American victory at the Battle of Saratoga. In September, William dispatched an escort for Minister Luzerne by detaching a troop of dragoons under Captain Churchill Jones on the 22nd to take the Frenchman from Pompton to Philadelphia.   The minister was quite impressed with the smart appearance of the helmeted 3rd Dragoons in their white regimental coats faced in light blue.[25]

Much to his dismay, action-oriented William Washington was destined to remain with Stirling for the remainder of the year to "be usefully employed in the whole or in part for your [i.e., Stirling's] mutual security."   William assuredly was not averse to serving the commander under whom he had fought in 1776, but he knew that the 3rd Dragoons would constantly be broken into detachments for numerous, petty duties. He knew that this practice would tend to lower the cavalrymen's morale and also limit much-needed training exercises that emphasized cohesiveness of the entire unit.   Young Washington's patience was surely tested by this turn of events, because he was anxious to take the field in the South where his dragoons could be more usefully employed. An example of the desultory nature of the assignment was the September 7 order he received to provide an escort for French Minister Gerard. On the 13th, when he had assembled his troopers for this duty, he received a cancellation order. William eventually decided to send most of the 3rd Dragoons as far south as Petersburg, Virginia, where their training continued under his subordinate officers.   He also encountered delays in receiving the regiment's cash allotment for payroll and expenses from Congress, because that group of micro-managers thought he had requested too many items for his officers in relation to those itemized for the rank and file. Typical of the detached uses of cavalry in the north was Washington's October 9 order to William to detach a "trusty Non-Commissid Officer and a Dragoon or Two" to escort a dangerous deserter to Philadelphia. Yet another complication arose in November, when he was temporarily attached to William Maxwell's command at Westfield, New Jersey, where a possible British raid was expected from Staten Island. The action failed to materialize.[26]

General Washington was not totally unaware of the cavalry's difficulties, however; and on November 5, he wrote Virginia Governor Thomas Jefferson for more direct assistance. Complaining that Virginia had unfairly excluded the 1st and 3rd Dragoons from receiving state recruiting bounties paid to enlistees and clothing allotments for the units, because they were not on their original 1776 military establishment, the general aptly pointed out that many of those 1776 regiments no longer existed. Therefore, he argued, Virginia would not necessarily be subject to additional expense by supporting these badly needed cavalrymen, who were in fact mostly Virginians! Unconvinced by this logic for some time, Jefferson apparently made no effort to respond to Washington's pleas. Like most governors, Jefferson had many other, more pressing problems at the time. While the 3rd Dragoons were attached to Maxwell's light infantry command near Westfield, New Jersey to protect forage for the army, Generals Washington and Nathanael Greene determined that there was insufficient forage there for the 3rd to subsist. Greene observed that he was "afraid the Horse will be more distressing than useful...[but] it cannot be long until they will be ordered to Winter quarters." The active dragoon horses ironically may well have consumed much of the forage they had been sent to protect![27]

On November 19, General Washington finally ordered William to resume his march to South Carolina, complimenting and encouraging him thusly: "I pursuade myself that your activity and dispatch (without injuring your Horse) will be equal to the importance of the call." The general also instructed him to stop in Philadelphia and directly appeal to Congress for more money for the cavalry. The very next day, however, Washington ordered him to halt and make a complete written return of the number of men in the 3rd Dragoons and to particularly note enlistments that were about to expire. After receiving this return on December 2, he then instructed William to take with him only those men who had at least six months remaining in the army. Moreover, Captain George Lewis' troop, comprising General Washington's bodyguard, was not to ride south with the rest of the unit. The troop detached for this service soon acquired the nickname "Lady Washington's Own" for the 3rd Dragoons. Along with his orders, the general enclosed a letter to Congress, which William was to personally deliver. General Washington pointed out in his letter that of 125 men of the 3rd Dragoons able to ride south, 55 were mounted on wagon horses unsuitable for combat or extensive reconnaissance, and that more money must be appropriated to purchase good cavalry remounts. Washington also warned that any more delays would result in the regiment having to spend the winter in Virginia, which would postpone their much-needed arrival in South Carolina until the spring of 1780. The general also advised Congress that cavalry strength in the South "will be productive of many good consequences, particularly those of giving immediate Checks to the insurrections of the disaffected, and securing the Country from the incursions of the Enemy's Cavalry." Congress responded by directing Lieutenant Colonel Washington to resume his ride south, assuring him that they would try to forward the additional funds later.[28]

By December 13, an undaunted William Washington was again crossing the Delaware River at Trenton as he set out with his little band of horsemen. Typical of the five remaining troops, Captain John Stith's 2nd Troop mustered 32 effectives (17 "present," 13 "detached" and 2 "absent"). The troop included its captain, one lieutenant, one cornet, two sergeants, three corporals, one trumpeter, one farrier and twenty-two privates. Washington next rode through Wilmington, Delaware on the 17th, making steady progress toward his objective. He quickly crossed through Maryland and into Virginia. Governor Jefferson was aware of his presence in Virginia by the end of December. He passed close enough to his home in Stafford County to briefly visit his family. On February 3, after encountering "bad roads, the lack of food, the crossing of many rivers, and the sparse population of the districts traversed," William's contingent was reported near Halifax, North Carolina. By February 5, 1780, the intrepid troopers halted after their 500-mile trek near Campbellton (Cross Creek), North Carolina. Washington would push on another 200 miles through the wet Carolina winter for Charleston.[29] Although his future may have seemed uncertain and challenging as he rode through the Carolinas, both the cavalry and romance would soon play a major part in the war and William Washington's personal life in those distant places!

NOTES: CHAPTER II

[1] Jacket No. 14, Revolutionary War Rolls, RG 97, National Archives; Fred Anderson Berg, *Encyclopedia of Continental Army Units*, 27-32. For a thorough history of Revolutionary War cavalry units, see Burt G. Loescher, *Washington's Eyes: The Continental Light Dragoons*; Philip Katcher, *Uniforms of the Continental Army*; and Randy Steffen, *The Horse Soldiers, 1776-1943, Vol. I: The Revolutionary War, The War of 1812 and The Early Frontier: 1776-1850*; George Washington to George Weedon, March 27, 1777, in Fitzpatrick (ed.), *Writings of Washington*, VII, 321-322; Gregory J.W. Urwin, *The United States Cavalry: An Illustrated History*, 9-29.

[2] George Washington to President of Congress, July 22, 1776, in Ford (ed.), *Writings of Washington*, IV, 287; George Washington to the Massachusetts Council, February 11, 1777, in Fitzpatrick (ed.), *Writings of Washington*, VII, 136.

[3] Charles Francis Adams, *Studies Military and Diplomatic, 1775-1865* (New York: The MacMillan Company, 1911), 59-113 passim. Adams' assertions were later disputed by Frederick Bauer, "Notes on the Use of Cavalry in the American Revolution," *Cavalry Journal*, XLVII (1938), 138-140. Adams' conclusions survived and were repeated in Ward, *War of the Revolution*, I, 228-229. George Washington to President of Congress, July 17, 1776, in Ford (ed.), *Writings of Washington*, IV, 261.

[4] Adams, *Studies*, 68 and 88; George Washington to President of Congress, July 22, 1776 and to William Heath, December 29, 1777, in Fitzpatrick (ed.), *Writings of Washington*, VI, 350 and X, 218.

[5] Ordered, February 27, 1777 and March 14, 1777, and Resolved, April 8, 1777 and May 16, 1777, in Worthington Chauncey Ford (ed.), *Journals of the Continental Congress*, VII, 169, 178, 238 and 365; Steffen, *Horse Soldiers*, I, 5; Charles H. Cureton and Marko Zlatich, "4th Regiment of Continental Light Dragoons, 1777-1778," *Military Collector & Historian*, XXXVII, No. 3 (1985), 138-139.

[6] George Washington to James Mease, April 17, 1777 in Fitzpatrick (ed.), *Writings of Washington*, VII, 421; Charles M. Lefferts, *Uniforms of*

the American, British, French and German Armies in the War of the American Revolution, 1775-1783, 18; Katcher, Uniforms of the Continental Army, 37-38; Steffen, Horse Soldiers, I, 8-13 passim.

[7] George Washington to John Sullivan, May 29, 1777 and June 7, 1777, in Fitzpatrick (ed.), Writings of Washington, VIII, 136 and 187-188; Jacket Nos. 13 and 14, Revolutionary War Rolls, RG 97, National Archives; Benjamin Tallmadge, Memoir of Col. Benjamin Tallmadge (New York: Thomas Holman, 1858), 19. Tallmadge served as an officer in Sheldon's 2nd Dragoons.

[8] Information on the campaign of 1777 in New Jersey and Pennsylvania is from Ward, War of the Revolution, I, 325-383; general information on the role of the 4th Dragoons in the campaign is from Loescher, Washington's Eyes, 101-108.

[9] Robert Harrison to John Sullivan, June 12, 1777, in Otis G. Hammond (ed.), Sullivan Papers, I, 384; Berg, Encyclopedia, 31; William Douwes, "Logistical Support of the Continental Light Dragoons," Military Collector & Historian, XXIV, No. 4, 101-106 passim; Stephen Moylan to Commissary of Supply at Englishtown, July 7, 1777, MS, The Emmett Collection, New York Public Library.

[10] George Washington to Stephen Moylan, July 19, 1777, in "Correspondence of Stephen Moylan," Pennsylvania Magazine of History and Biography, XXXVII (1913), 343; Stephen Moylan to George Washington, July 21, 1777, in Martin J. Griffin, Stephen Moylan, 54; George Washington to President of Congress, July 23, 1777, in Fitzpatrick (ed.), Writings of Washington, VIII, 473.

[11] George Washington to Stephen Moylan, July 24, 1777, in "Moylan," Pennsylvania Magazine, XXXVII, 344; General Orders, Roxboro, August 8, 1777 and Crosswicks, August 6 and 19, 1777, George Washington to the Board of War, August 22, 1777, and General Orders, Germantown, August 23, 1777, in Fitzpatrick (ed.), Writings of Washington, IX, 36, 29, 99, 124, and 125.

[12] Samuel Steele Smith, The Battle of Brandywine, 7-19 passim; Jay Eben, Dragoon Sketchbook: 1776-1798, 10; General Orders, Derby, August 24, 1777, and George Washington to Stephen Moylan, September 13,

1777, in Fitzpatrick (ed.), *Writings of Washington*, IX, 129 and 214; Richard K. Showman (ed.), *The Papers of Nathanael Greene, Vol. II, 1 January 1777 - 16 October 1778*, 159; Ward, *War of the Revolution*, I, 356.

[13] John Sullivan to Mesbech Ware, October 25, 1777, in Hammond (ed.), *Sullivan Papers*, I, 544; General Orders, White Marsh, December 4, 1777, in Fitzpatrick (ed.), *Writings of Washington*, X, 138-139; Showman (ed.), *Papers of Nathanael Greene*, II, 174; Eben, *Dragoon Sketchbook*, 10; Loescher, *Washington's Eyes*, 106.

[14] Circular to Dragoon Commanders, October 25, 1777, in Fitzpatrick (ed.), *Writings of Washington*, IX, 432. For a discussion of the Moylan-Pulaski feud, see Bauer, "Notes on Cavalry," 140; Griffin, *Stephen Moylan*, 55-70 passim; Clarance A. Manning, *Soldier of Liberty, Casimir Pulaski*, 222-230 passim; Urwin, *United States Cavalry*, 17-18.

[15] General Washington's Instructions to Count Pulaski, December 31, 1777, and George Washington to William Livingston, December 31, 1777, and to Count Pulaski, February 14, 1778, in Fitzpatrick (ed.), *Writings of Washington*, X, 232-236 and 457. For the winter operations of 1778, see Manning, *Pulaski*, 229ff and Ward, *War of the Revolution*, II, 543-569.

[16] Douwes, "Logistical Support of the Continental Light Dragoons," *Military Collector & Historian*, 101-105 passim; George Washington to George Baylor, March 4, 1778, and to Stephen Moylan, March 20 and 25, 1778, in Fitzpatrick (ed.), *Writings of Washington*, XI, 22-23, 114-115 and 147; Loescher, *Washington's Eyes*, 109-110.

[17] George Washington to Stephen Moylan, April 11, 1778, in Fitzpatrick (ed.), *Writings of Washington*, XI, 244-245; George Washington to Theodoric Bland, April 18, 1778, in Charles Campbell (ed.), *The Bland Papers: Being a Selection of from the Manuscripts of Colonel Theodoric Bland, Jr.*, I, 83; George Washington to a Committee of Congress, January 28, 1778, in Ford (ed.), *Writings of Washington*, VI, 309; Stephen Moylan to George Washington, May 5, 1778, in Griffin, *Stephen Moylan*, 68; Receipt signed by William Washington, MS, Jacket 14, Revolutionary War Rolls, RG 97, National Archives; Theodoric Bland to George Baylor, June 6 and 17, 1778, Military Papers, Baylor Family Papers, MS, University of Virginia Library, Charlottesville.

[18] Information on the British evacuation of Philadelphia and the Monmouth campaign is from Samuel Steele Smith, *The Battle of Monmouth* and Ward, *War of the Revolution*, II, 570-586. For the role of the 4th Dragoons in the campaign, see Eben, *Dragoon Sketchbook*, 10; Loescher, *Washington's Eyes*, 111; George Washington to Phileman Dickenson, June 22 and 24, 1778, and to Charles Scott, June 24, 1778, in Fitzpatrick (ed.), *Writings of Washington*, XII, 107-108, 111-113 and 114; and Bernard A. Uhlendorf (ed.), *Revolution in America: Confidential Letters and Journals, 1776-1784, of Adjutant General Major Baurmeister of the Hessian Forces*, 183-184; Showman (ed.), *Papers of Nathanael Greene*, II, 455.

[19] George Washington to Theodoric Bland, July 22, 1778, in Campbell (ed.), *Bland Papers*, I, 98; George Washington to Stephen Moylan, July 7, 25 and 30, 1778, in Fitzpatrick (ed.), *Writings of Washington*, XII, 162, 228 and 248-249.

[20] George Washington to President of Congress, August 3, 1778, in Ford (ed.), *Writings of Washington*, VII, 139; George Washington to Theodoric Bland, August 3, 1778, General Orders, White Plains, August 7, 1778, and to President of Congress, September 25, 1778, in Fitzpatrick (ed.), *Writings of Washington*, XII, 278, 288 and 490; George Washington to Nathanael Greene, September 22, 1778, in Showman (ed.), *Papers of Nathanael Greene*, II, 525.

[21] Otho Williams to George Washington, September 25, 1778, and George Baylor to George Washington, October 19, 1778, in Sparks (ed.), *Letters to Washington*, II, 211-213 and 222-224; Charles Pettit to Nathanael Greene, October 1, 1778, in Showman (ed.), *Papers of Nathanael Greene*, II, 534; George Washington to Lord Stirling, October 4, 1778, to William Washington, November 5, 1778, and to the President of Congress, November 27, 1778, in Fitzpatrick (ed.), *Writings of Washington*, XIII, 25, 208n and 351; Loescher, *Washington's Eyes*, 69-75 passim; War Office, November 25, 1778, in Ford (ed.), *Journals of Congress*, XII, 1228: Urwin, *United States Cavalry*, 21-22.

[22] Resolution, November 20, 1778, in Ford (ed.), *Journals of Congress*, XII, 1147-1148; George Washington to William Washington, November 30, 1778, in Fitzpatrick (ed.), *Writings of Washington*, XIII, 359-360.

[23] George Washington to William Washington, February 9, 1779, to the Board of War, March 20, 1779, to Thomas Burke, March 29, 1779, and to William Washington, July 8, 1779, in Fitzpatrick (ed.), *Writings of Washington*, XIV, 88, 266 and 302-303 and XV, 385; Thomas Balch (ed.), *Papers Relating Chiefly to the Maryland Line During the Revolution*, 44; Clyde A. Risley and Marko Zlatich, "3rd Regiment of Continental Light Dragoons, 1778-1783," *Military Collector & Historian*, XLIV, No. 3 (1992), Plate No. 689; Resolution, May 5, 1779, in Ford (ed.), *Journals of Congress*, XIV, 560; James Abeel to Governor Livingston, August 21, 1779, in *The New Jersey Gazette*, Vol. II, No. 87; August 25, 1779, in Stryker (ed.), *Archives of New Jersey*, Second Series, II, 572.

[24] George Washington to Richard Henry Lee, April 30, 1779, and to William Washington, May 21, 1779, in Fitzpatrick (ed.), *Writings of Washington*, XIV, 489 and XV, 121-122; Ward, *War of the Revolution*, II, 618-620; Manning, *Pulaski*, 288-304.

[25] George Washington to Lord Stirling, August 28 and September 1, 1779, and to William Washington, August 29 and September 5, 1779, in Fitzpatrick (ed.), *Writings of Washington*, XVI, 199, 202, 216, and 230; *The Pennsylvania Packet*, September 23, 1779, in Stryker (ed.), *Archives of New Jersey*, Second Series, III, 640; Loescher, *Washington's Eyes*, 76-78.

[26] George Washington to Lord Stirling, September 29, 1779, and to William Washington, September 7 and 13, 1779 and October 9, 1779, and to William Maxwell, November 5, 1779, in Fitzpatrick (ed.), *Writings of Washington*, XVI, 359, 244, 278, 445-446 and XVII, 76; Balch (ed.), *Maryland Line*, 44; James Hunter to George Baylor, October 12, 1779, Military Papers, Baylor Family Papers, MS, University of Virginia Library, Charlottesville.

[27] George Washington to Thomas Jefferson, November 5, 1779, in Julian P. Boyd (ed.), *Papers of Jefferson*, III, 156-157; Tench Tilghman to Nathanael Greene, November 3, 1779 and Nathanael Greene to Moore Furman, November 3, 1779, in Richard K. Showman (ed.), *The Papers of Nathanael Greene, Vol. V: 1 November 1779 - 31 May 1780* (Chapel Hill: University of North Carolina Press, 1989), 8-9 and 23.

[28] George Washington to William Washington, November 19 and 20 and December 2, 1779, and President of Congress, December 2, 1779, in Fitzpatrick (ed.), *Writings of Washington*, XVII, 135, 149-150 and 211-213; Loescher, *Washington's Eyes*, 78; Resolution, December 6, 1779, in Ford (ed.), *Journals of Congress*, XV, 1351.

[29] *The New Jersey Journal*, December 14, 1779, in Stryker (ed.), *Archives of New Jersey*, Second Series, IV, 92; Jacket Nos. 13, Revolutionary War Rolls, RG 97, National Archives; Caesar Rodney to Thomas Rodney, December 17, 1779, in George Herbert Ryden (ed.), *Letters to and from Caesar Rodney, 1756-1784*, 331; Balch (ed.), *Maryland Line*, 44; Thomas Jefferson to James Innes, December 28, 1779, in Boyd (ed.), *Papers of Jefferson*, III, 246; Uhlendorf (ed.), *Revolution in America*, 333; James Emmett to Governor Caswell, February 6, 1780, in Walter Clark (ed.), *The State Records of North Carolina*, XV, 333.

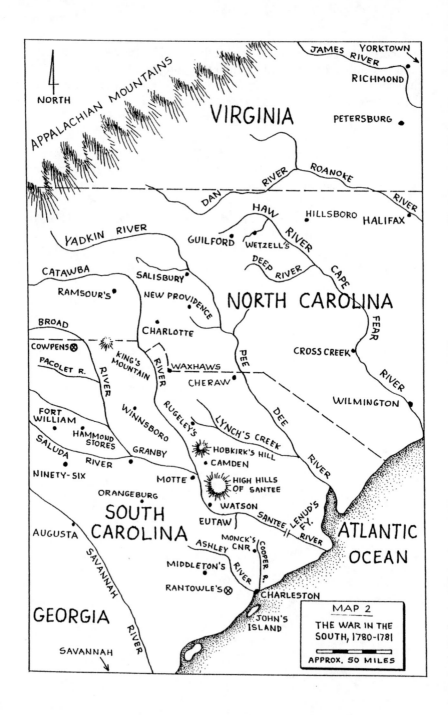

NORTH

APPALACHIAN MOUNTAINS

VIRGINIA

JAMES RIVER

YORKTOWN

RICHMOND

PETERSBURG

ROANOKE RIVER

DAN RIVER

RIVER

HILLSBORO

HALIFAX

YADKIN RIVER

GUILFORD

HAW RIVER

WETZELL'S

DEEP RIVER

CATAWBA

SALISBURY

RAMSOUR'S

NEW PROVIDENCE

NORTH CAROLINA

CAPE

FEAR

BROAD

CHARLOTTE

CROSS CREEK

COWPENS ⊗

KING'S MOUNTAIN

RIVER

WAXHAWS

PEE

RIVER

PACOLET R.

CHERAW

WILMINGTON

RIVER

RUGELEY'S

DEE

FORT WILLIAM

WINNSBORO

LYNCH'S CREEK

HAMMOND STORES

SALUDA RIVER

GRANBY

HOBKIRK'S HILL

CAMDEN

RIVER

NINETY-SIX

MOTTE

HIGH HILLS OF SANTEE

ORANGEBURG

SOUTH CAROLINA

WATSON

EUTAW

SANTEE RIVER

LENUD'S F.Y.

ATLANTIC OCEAN

AUGUSTA

MONCK'S CNR.

ASHLEY

COOPER R.

MIDDLETON'S

RIVER

RANTOWLE'S ⊗

CHARLESTON

GEORGIA

SAVANNAH RIVER

JOHN'S ISLAND

SAVANNAH

MAP 2

THE WAR IN THE SOUTH, 1780-1781

APPROX. 50 MILES

chapter III

A CAVALRY COMMANDER: 1780

Military activity in the South had been at a standstill after Clinton's abortive attack on Charleston in 1776, except for skirmishes between relatively small, local groups of Tories and Whigs. This inactivity would not last. By 1778, the British had reestablished control over most of Georgia and prepared to reopen the war in the South now that the war in the North was at a stalemate. Encouraged by the dramatic Franco-American failure to capture Savannah in October 1779, Clinton sailed for Charleston from New York in December with a fleet and army of more than 13,000 men. As Clinton sailed south—and by way of contrast—William Washington had been leading his small regiment of cavalry on a parallel land course through the Carolinas to join General Benjamin Lincoln. Pulaski and many of his cavalrymen were killed in a valiant, futile charge against British fortifications around Savannah. Lincoln, the American commander in the South, had concentrated his 5,000 troops in and around Charleston.[1]

Young Washington wasted little time in the Cross Creek area, a place where latent Tory sympathies simmered. He left by mid-February and soon linked up with Major John Jameson, who was commanding the remnants of the 1st Continental Dragoons north of Charleston. Together, the two regiments mustered about 200 effectives. Although the 1st Dragoons had been in the South since 1779, their new colonel, Anthony Walton White, did not arrive to take command until April 1780 after General Washington transferred him from the 4th Dragoons. Under Lieutenant Colonel Benjamin Temple, the

1st Dragoons' eighty or so troopers had participated in Pulaski's ill-fated cavalry charge at Savannah. Thereafter, they were stationed near Augusta, until they moved to a post 24 miles north of Charleston at Bacon's Bridge under Major Jameson in February 1780. Some historians unaware of White's transfer and other information that has become available have erroneously placed the 4th Dragoons in the Carolinas in 1780-81 as well.[2]   Other regular American cavalry units already operating in the South included Peter and Daniel Horry's South Carolina Light Dragoons and the remnants of Pulaski's Legion, now commanded by Major Pierre Vernier.

William had sent Major Richard Call ahead with an advance detachment to link up with Major Jameson's 1st Dragoons in mid-February, and from February 29 through March 7 the two units were at or near Charles Elliott's plantation, then known as "Sandy Hill." Call scouted British movements near Stono Ferry as their large army advanced on Charleston. While there, the dragoons also found time for such recreational activities as hunting, drinking, dancing and playing cards. When they received word that British forces had routed Horry and Vernier on the night of March 6, Washington moved the dragoons to Bacon's Bridge by the 10th. William had personally joined in the operations around Charleston by then and exerted a vigorous command at a time when American cavalry units were acting independently and with little coordination against similar British units. On March 8, a mixed force of British cavalry and light infantry (or Hessian Jaegers) under Captain Nash attempted a surprise attack on the 3rd Dragoons at Wambaw (Bull's Plantation). Washington, no doubt recalling the lessons of Tappan, was on alert and extricated his cavalrymen from the ambuscade without loss.[3]

Banastre Tarleton

General Lincoln formed all of the available cavalry units into a 500-man force, augmented by a number of local militia companies, and gave the overall command to General Isaac Huger, a South Carolina infantry officer. Huger's mission was to maintain a northern line of supply to the city and provide an avenue of escape for Lincoln's main army in Charleston. As soon as Clinton began active operations to take the city in March, he assigned General Cornwallis the task of countering Huger. Cornwallis turned to his own able, daring and often brutal cavalry commander, Lieutenant Colonel Banastre Tarleton, to do this job. Small in stature, which belied his reputation, the 26-year old Tarleton commanded the British Legion, a 500-man Tory unit of dragoons and light infantry. A troop of fifty men of the British 17th Light Dragoons was also attached to Tarleton's Legion, but because many of the cavalry horses were lost at sea during the voyage south, only 150 to 200 men from both units could be effectively deployed at this time.[4] For the next twelve months, William Washington and Banastre Tarleton frequently faced each other in cavalry skirmishes and full-fledged battles.

During the rest of March, the American cavalry continued the thrust and parry operations against the British while maintaining the thin supply and communications line into the city. From diary entries of an officer of the 1st Dragoons, it is clear the American light horse became much more active when William arrived. In a move south on March 12 near Drayton's Hall, Washington and Jameson led the advance guard to reconnoiter the enemy's lines near Charleston. On March 15, William was scouting British movements near Church Bridge, and he learned that on either the 20th or 23rd, Tarleton had defeated a group of "Patriot" horse at Thomas Bee's plantation near Pon Pon on the Edisto River, killing 10 and capturing 40 along with a number of horses. Tarleton was providing the vanguard for British General Patterson's troops, which had marched up from Savannah to the Stono River to meet Clinton.

On the 27th William encountered hitherto triumphant Tarleton for the first time—at Rantowle's some miles northeast of a bridge that spanned a tributary of the Stono River. William first attacked Colonel John Hamilton's North Carolina Royalist Regiment of Tory infantry, killing seven and capturing the colonel and seven more men, without loss to the 3rd Dragoons. When Tarleton arrived on the scene with his cavalry and attempted to rescue the prisoners, Washington charged him in turn and successfully drove the Legion back within sight of a large body of British regulars. Only a lack of infantry support prevented William from further exploiting his temporary advantage. He almost captured Henry Clinton, who had joined Tarleton's advanced party. Washington successfully broke off this running engagement at little cost to his own command and withdrew to Bacon's Bridge. Tarleton characteristically blamed a subordinate for this embarrassing reverse.[5]

The location of this action was, interestingly, near Sandy Hill plantation, where William would make his post-war home within two years after meeting and eventually marrying Jane Elliott—the owner's only daughter and heiress! He probably made her acquaintance sometime between February 29 and March 7, when, as noted earlier, his unit was encamped near Charles Elliott's plantation. According to family tradition, William arrived at Sandy Hill to warn Charles Elliott of the British raiding parties. It is clear that both the 1st and 3rd Dragoons spent time near the plantation in late February and early March. Charles' family then residing with him included Jane Riley Elliott and her stepmother, Ann Ferguson Elliott.

Charles Elliott (1737-1781) had been elected as one of six representatives of St. Paul's Parish in August 1775 who were asked to build a stockade fort for the Patriot cause. A staunch supporter of resistance to English taxes since 1768, this wealthy landowner's extensive holdings included several thousand acres of plantation property and a house on Frier Street in Charleston. He lent his home state £4,000 to help equip troops in 1775 while he was serving in the First and Second Provincial Congresses. Elliott was also a member of a volunteer company formed in October of 1775, and served as one of St. Paul's Parish's six members of the South Carolina General Assembly from April 1776 through February 1780. In early 1780, he served on a committee charged with augmenting the Charleston garrison by raising fatigue and artillery support battalions composed of local black slaves.

"Eutaw Flag" of Colonel Washington's Cavalry
Washington Light Infantry

Daughter Jane and Charles, Jr. (his only son, who had died young) were Charles' children by his first marriage to Jane Stanyarne. There were no other Elliott children. The large Elliott plantation at Sandy Hill was ten miles west of Charleston and about seven miles from Rantowle's Ferry. A 19th-century account described a "stately mansion" on a bluff above a stream leading into the Stono River also known as "Hyde's Park or Elliott's Savannah" embracing "many thousand acres." When young Jane Elliott encountered Lieutenant Colonel Washington, she remarked "that she would look out for news of his flag and fortune." The dashing six-foot cavalryman was very impressive in his white regimental coat with blue facings and cuffs, leather breeches and black leather billed jockey cap with a red turban and drooping fox tail crest. However, he apparently lamented the lack of a standard for his regiment while in her presence. The quick-thinking seventeen-year-old cut an eighteen-inch square of crimson damask from a drapery in her room, not uncommon in such mansions. She then fashioned the material into a lance pennon by making a sleeve and binding the edges so a fringe could be added. To the flattered Virginian, she then exclaimed, "Here is your flag, colonel! Take this, colonel, and make it your standard." William attached the banner to a hickory pole and later had it ornamented with a fringe. The flag also had a horseshoe-shaped wreath pattern opening away from the flagstaff. Thus, Washington's 3rd Dragoons had a standard they would carry through the war's end, and their commander was very impressed by this patriotic young lady! Six months later, the battle flag became famous as "Tarleton's Terror" after the battle of Cowpens, and later as the "Eutaw flag" after the September, 1781 battle of Eutaw Springs. After Jane and William met in the early spring of 1780, it would have also been possible that a wartime romance ensued which was marked by at least one or two hurried encounters in April or May before Charleston fell and the region was plunged into civil war.[6]

On March 20, Washington again led the dragoons closer to Charleston. He rode down to Drayton's to scout the enemy's lines and by the 22nd the cavalrymen were at Church Bridge at

St. Andrews Creek.   On the 26th Washington took both dragoon regiments and Vernier's detachment to Bacon's Bridge "all the way buy paths & throh rice fields" in an effort to elude ambush.   William employed the tactic of sending a detachment near the enemy to entice them into a careless pursuit into his own ambuscade, but the enemy did not take the bait.   When the British suddenly threatened to cut off the Americans from the rear in the vicinity of Rutledge's Plantation, Washington boldly fought his way out, as an officer of the 1st Dragoons described in an account typical of these sudden and violent cavalry skirmishes:

> *Colo. Washington with his Regimt. & Vanears faced about & charg'd the Enemy, & after a few minutes the Enemy retreated, with the loss of twenty kil'd wounded & taken, we had three men wounded, one very bad, the others slightly, the Enemy had a very bad Cossway to Cross where only one at a time could come over, we took the advantage of this place and charg'd them before they had more than sixty or seventy over.*[7]

On April 5, Tarleton hoped to avenge his earlier reverse at Rantowle's by surprising Washington's command at Middleton's plantation near the 23 Mile House.   William became apprehensive about his security during the night when two of his men deserted, and he quietly moved his men undetected a few miles to the north.   The next morning, when the British retired upon discovering that their prey had eluded them, the dashing Washington returned and led his men in a successful charge against Tarleton's rear detachment, taking several prisoners.[8] Washington, recalling Baylor's 1778 surprise at Tappan, was not about to have his valuable dragoons suffer a night surprise attack, and he was quickly learning and using the hit-and-run tactics needed for successfully campaigning against a numerically superior enemy in the Carolinas!

When Clinton continued to press the siege of Charleston throughout early April, Huger took personal command of all troops outside the lines north of the city and decided to concentrate all of the American cavalry together with some militia infantry at Monck's Corner. From this major supply base north of the now beleaguered city, he hoped his force would possibly threaten the enemy's rear. Cornwallis immediately seized this opportunity to perhaps destroy the troublesome American cavalry in a single blow. He dispatched two of his ablest commanders, Tarleton with his cavalry and Colonel James Webster with a brigade of British regular infantry, to do the job.

Huger had carelessly posted all of the cavalry in front of Biggin Bridge on the stream to the east of camp without any infantry support or pickets in advance of this encampment. Tarleton, upon learning of Huger's faulty dispositions from a captured or runaway slave (or by other accounts a "spy"), rode ahead of the main British column toward the unsuspecting Americans on the night of April 13. The guards were alert through midnight, and some of the dragoons were getting dressed and bridling their horses at 3:00 A.M. the next day when Tarleton struck. Although outnumbered, his "Green Dragoons" achieved complete surprise. According to the American officer of the day, "the advance guard of the British horse had passed in persuit of our picquet who was flying before them, it being an alarm in earness and no likelyhood of our men forming." The British Legion completely routed the American cavalry as most could not mount and form up, and Monck's Corner quickly fell to the British when the militia also fled. The action was a terrible blow to the American cavalry in the South. In addition to destroying Lincoln's last line of escape from Charleston, over thirty dragoons were killed (including the gallant Vernier), seventy men and fifty supply wagons were captured and more than 200 fully equipped cavalry horses were lost to the enemy. Tarleton, who had lost only two men in the action, could now remount most of his men on superior horses.

For a few minutes in the action, Washington was taken prisoner, but he managed to escape in the darkness on his fast horse, which his captors had failed to take from him. He was lucky to have survived, because the gallant Vernier and others were slain after apparently asking for quarter. Although Tarleton and others thought that Washington, Jameson and Huger escaped on foot in the nearby swamps, Hessian accounts of William's escape on horseback seem more believable. By the evening of the 14th, about sixty mounted survivors assembled approximately fifteen miles north of Monck's Corner where 100 Virginia Continental Infantry also joined them. This small combined force hid in the woods from Tarleton for several days. On the 17th, a detachment of dragoons briefly returned to Monck's Corner in a futile search for more survivors.[9]

While Lincoln continued to hold out in Charleston through the rest of April, the American cavalry began to regroup north of the Santee River under the overall command of Colonel White, who had just arrived in South Carolina on April 23 in time to take command of the 1st Dragoons. White and Washington knew each other from their days together in the 4th Dragoons in the North, and they wasted little time finding remounts for almost 250 cavalrymen who remained from the 1st and 3rd Dragoons, Pulaski's Legion and a South Carolina squadron. Major Jameson commanded the latter two corps. The officers took time over the next three days to hold a court martial for Mr. Hugh Jones, whom they suspected of helping Tarleton surprise them at Monck's Corner. Washington presided over the trial, which resulted in Jones' rather lenient sentence of prison "during the stay of the British Troops in Georgia and the two Carolinas." He might well have been executed on the spot. Colonel Abraham Buford's 3rd Virginia Continentals provided some infantry and artillery support to White's command when they also arrived in the vicinity. Washington's 3rd Dragoons were severely decimated, however. Of an original command of more than 100, slightly more than a dozen troopers remained mounted and equipped to fight. All of the troopers subsisted at this time on limited quantities of parched corn and bacon. Although the State of North Carolina had recently allocated $25,000 to rebuild his regiment, William had not yet had the time to extricate his men from South Carolina and effectively use this money, even though Huger ordered him to do so. The combined cavalry corps moved to Georgetown for a few days, but by May 3 White decided to move west and north of Charleston.[10]

On May 6, White—as senior commander—led the 200 or so mounted and dismounted remnants of the American cavalry across the Santee at Dupui's Ferry. On the following morning the Americans surprised and captured a foraging party comprised of seventeen light infantrymen and an officer detached from Tarleton's command at Wambaw, a few miles south of Monck's Corner. Informed by local Loyalists of the pesky American cavalry's return, Tarleton determined to cut White off before he could re-cross the Santee at Lenud's Ferry. Although the Americans arrived at the ferry well before Tarleton could approach, an overconfident White was flushed with his recent success at Wambaw. He posted a small guard and foolishly permitted most of his force to dismount and graze their horses while waiting for Buford's infantry on the other side of the river to begin the time-consuming ferrying of the cavalrymen and prisoners across to the north side. There was only one boat available. The cavalrymen could have crossed immediately by swimming their horses across the river, but White apparently believed the horses needed to feed and rest. Washington objected to this action and urged that they cross immediately. White, asserting his seniority, overruled William. The men dismounted and crowded together to watch the ferry take the prisoners across to Buford. Arriving at mid-afternoon after a twenty-mile ride in the hot sun that left twenty horses dead, Tarleton completely surprised the Americans. The "Green Dragoons" cut down 40 American cavalrymen, captured 70 others and took over 100 horses. Once again, an American officer described the scene:

> When the alarm pistol was fired and in an Instant we see the approach of the British Horse in full Speed; every man took his own way they coming on us so suddenly & our horses being a feeding, but few of the horse made there escape on horseback...I endeavored to bridle a horse standing just by, but the noise of horses straining, hollowing of there men and firing, it was impossible to bridle him.

To add insult to injury, the British prisoners overthrew their rebel guards and rowed back to the side of the river now controlled by Tarleton. William may not in fact have been present, given that he apparently wrote a letter dated May 5 or thereabouts from Wilmington. However, British accounts mention Washington's presence, and in particular Washington's, White's, Jameson's and a handful of other cavalrymen's escape by swimming across the Santee to a point where Buford's infantry was deployed. The British also observed that many rebels were drowned in Hell Hole Swamp, where they had fled when the charge began. This action effectively put an end to any significant regular cavalry force in the South for several months. The Americans were simply too weak. Washington and White now had fewer than forty effective mounted dragoons remaining![11] On May 10, Lincoln finally surrendered Charleston and his entire army, leaving South Carolina wide open to the British. Hearing of the surrender, Washington and Buford quickly decided to retreat as far north as Hillsboro, North Carolina.

Washington and White apparently left as many as fifty mounted dragoons with Buford, while William personally took the 75 dismounted troopers on to Wilmington, North Carolina (thus the May letter referenced earlier). William received a new horse before leaving South Carolina; it was a gift from Thomas "Gamecock" Sumter. This famous South Carolina partisan leader remained behind in South Carolina with Francis "Swamp Fox" Marion to harass the British troops for some time.[12] Perhaps Jane Elliott and William Washington were also dismayed that the fortunes of war that summer would keep them apart them for what turned out to be more than a year, although it then looked to many like the British had won the war in South Carolina.

Waxhaws: "Tarleton's Quarter"

General Cornwallis, whom Clinton had left in command of the British forces in the South upon his return to New York in May, quickly sent Tarleton chasing after Buford and young Washington, hoping to stamp out any further resistance. Tarleton led his 200 cavalry on a desperate two-day pursuit covering 150 miles. He caught up with the Americans at Waxhaws on May 29. Buford had little time to form his 350 infantry, so he sent his unprepared artillery to the rear and ordered his infantry to hold their fire until the charging British and Tory cavalry were only ten yards away. These tactical errors assured Tarleton's vigorous charge of success, and the inevitable happened after an ineffective volley. The British Legion cut down most of the Americans, and many were sabered outright although they asked for quarter. Fewer than 100 Americans escaped, including Buford and about forty of the fifty mounted 3rd Dragoons. From that time on, "Tarleton's quarter" was a synonym for the slaughter of surrendering men.[13]

Throughout the months of May, June and July, Cornwallis completed the British occupation and subjugation of South Carolina by establishing fortified posts at Camden, Charleston, Cheraw, Georgetown and Ninety-Six. Only the hot weather discouraged him from immediately invading North Carolina as well. British demands for oaths of allegiance and Tory vengefulness began to stir up forces that contributed the only resistance to the British in South Carolina for a time—partisan warfare waged by bands of irregulars commanded by Francis Marion, Andrew Pickens and Thomas Sumter. Sumter's operations particularly proved a great annoyance to Cornwallis in June and July.[14] The rebels were further encouraged by the news that General Johann de Kalb had arrived in North Carolina in late June, with 1,000 Maryland and Delaware regular infantry, to relieve the situation in the South. The only effective cavalry force with de Kalb was the mounted component of Colonel Charles Armand's American Legion of sixty dragoons and sixty light infantrymen.[15]

William Washington had remained in Wilmington through the rest of May and early June. He then moved to Halifax, where he hoped to rebuild his regiment with help promised from North Carolina. His men suffered miserably from nakedness, hunger, too few horses fit for service and no doubt a sense of defeat and desperation. His regimental quartermaster was almost arrested by local civil authorities when he impressed corn from a barn belonging to North Carolina notable Alexander Lillington.[16] The shortage of proper arms, equipment and horses that resulted from the disasters at Monck's Corner and Lenud's Ferry also prevented his own command as well as that of White from taking the field in June and July. Encouragingly, Governor Thomas Jefferson promised seventy replacements from Virginia for the 3rd Dragoons in June, and on June 19, Congress "recommended" that North Carolina and Virginia remount, equip and provide new recruits for both the 1st and 3rd Dragoons until they were brought up to a strength of 150 men each.[17]

By the end of June, William and White had joined forces at Halifax, North Carolina near the Virginia border to better coordinate recruiting and re-supply efforts in the region. As was so often the case in the War of the American Revolution, the best military intentions were seldom realized, and the rebuilding efforts proved frustratingly slow. The cavalry proved to be a tremendous expense. Virginia alone spent $700,000 from May through July on these two dragoon regiments. Although American currency was greatly depreciated at this time, the amount was still substantial. Yet neither regiment was considered fit for campaign duty by the end of July, when General Horatio Gates took command of the American troops in the South. He had commanded the victorious American army at the Battle of Saratoga in 1777, where cavalry had neither been deployed nor necessary. The experienced de Kalb informed Gates that the two regiments were not yet ready for service.[18]

Gates has often been criticized for failing to recognize the importance of cavalry in the South and to assist Washington and White with their recruiting efforts during the August campaign, which ended in the crushing American defeat at Camden.   General Otho Williams and Colonel Henry Lee, contemporaries who both despised Gates, were most critical. Williams claimed that the general "held cavalry in no estimation in the southern field." However, correspondence between Gates and two cavalry officers—especially White, the senior cavalry officer at the time—reveals the general to have been more aware of the value of cavalry than his critics portray him.   Major Richard Call, now William's Virginia cavalry recruiter, wrote Gates on July 22 that it would take Washington and White (both of whom were in Virginia recruiting) at least six weeks to place a respectable cavalry force in the field. Gates had written to White in Petersburg on July 20 that he "look[ed] up to the Cavalry for many services, in a Campaign," and that the cavalry should immediately join him at Hillsboro. Gates' error was more his faulty assumption that the cavalry could quickly refit and rejoin the army, than his lack of interest in their usefulness—and possibly his lack of resources to re-equip them. But White responded to the general by complaining that the cavalry should not take the field before the units were completely refitted and remounted. He also warned that most of the dragoons would not reenlist if they suspected they would be deployed as infantry, and that if any of the cavalry "were called into the field in their present Situation, nothing but their ruin can Insue." Gates had little choice but to accept his senior cavalry commander's counsel and to urge that the cavalry join the main army when they were ready.[19]

Camden

Gates proceeded to recklessly hurry his army through North Carolina on his way to rescue South Carolina from Cornwallis. The British general severely and easily defeated him at the Battle of Camden on August 16. Also at the battle, Armand's Legion proved to be no match for Tarleton's British Legion. Although deserving criticism for faulty campaign strategy and battlefield tactics in the Camden debacle, Gates was not unaware of the usefulness of cavalry. Henry Lee's later criticism of Gates' failure to take Washington and White with him to Camden notwithstanding, Gates simply did not have enough dependable horse troops in his army. He attempted to augment Armand's 60-man squadron and compensate for the absence of White and Washington by instructing Hawkins Martin to raise three troops of volunteer (i.e., militia) cavalry in the Carolinas. The Battle of Camden, coupled with Sumter's defeat by Tarleton on August 18, at Fishing Creek, further secured the British hold on South Carolina and now left North Carolina open to invasion by Cornwallis. During this desperate time for the Americans, only the partisan operations of Francis Marion kept the Revolution militarily alive in South Carolina.[20]

During the Camden campaign, William Washington had remained with White in Virginia, where both officers continued their frustrating attempts to rebuild the 1st and 3rd Dragoons. Virginia issued a substantial amount of clothing at this time, including up to 200 new white regimental coats for the 3rd Dragoons. Grumbling that Virginia was bearing the burden of recruiting and supplying these regiments, and that North Carolina was contributing very little, Governor Thomas Jefferson belatedly informed Gates in August that the cavalry would receive 243 new horses, while cautioning that the process would take considerable time.[21]

At Hillsboro, North Carolina, in an effort to regroup his forces after the Camden disaster, Gates gathered the remnants of his shattered army, about 700 men of his original 4,000. On August 31, White wrote to Gates that the cavalry would be joining the army as soon as their inferior swords could be replaced. Throughout September, the cavalry began arriving in Gates' camp, but in small detachments as they became equipped and remounted in Virginia. By the end of the month, William took over field command of both regiments, because White was sick with fever. One observer described Washington's command as consisting of about ninety men mounted on unshod horses and using rawhide bridles, and that the rest of the dragoons were ill in Halifax. This was the second time that the dedicated Washington had to rebuild the 3rd Dragoons, but appearances concealed the fact that he had transformed his small force into what was soon to become the cutting edge of the army in the South. At this point the two regiments were combined into a single command under Washington—with Captain John Watts commanding a troop of 1st Dragoons. White was either still sick with fever or held in disfavor over his handling of the cavalry at Lenud's Ferry and afterwards, so he and most of the surviving 1st Dragoon officers returned to Virginia to buy horses, recruit and rebuild the 1st Dragoons. In early October, William was given official command of both the 1st and 3rd Dragoons combined in the field, after White left for Virginia and eventually Philadelphia.[22]

Gates occupied himself by reorganizing the little American army in anticipation of a British thrust into North Carolina. In October, newly arrived Brigadier General Morgan—also of Saratoga fame and a proven battlefield commander—was given command of a select force of light troops consisting of Washington's 100 dragoons, 60 riflemen and three 100-man Continental light infantry companies from Virginia, Maryland and Delaware. By October 13, Morgan had advanced his corps to Rowan, North Carolina to observe and impede if possible the anticipated British invasion of the state. Cornwallis wasted little time and began his expected advance in late September, but he was slowed temporarily by stubborn resistance of partisan forces led by William Davie and William Davidson. More importantly, the British general received a decisive, unexpected setback when a large force of frontiersmen from beyond the Blue Ridge Mountains and the mountainous areas of Georgia, the Carolinas, and Virginia surprised his westernmost column of 1,100 Loyalists under Major Patrick Ferguson. Ferguson's corps was surrounded and defeated, in decimating detail, at King's Mountain, South Carolina on October 7. This reverse, which chilled recruiting efforts among residents loyal to the British, forced Cornwallis to temporarily abandon his invasion plans. By mid-October, he established his headquarters at Winnsboro, South Carolina, from where he could proceed into North Carolina when he was ready.[23]

In late October, Morgan's light corps was operating near New Providence, North Carolina, observing British outposts and discouraging Tory militia from assembling to support Cornwallis. Cavalry, as Tarleton had so effectively demonstrated in the Charleston campaign, was particularly effective in breaking up militia musters, and Morgan frequently employed William Washington for this type of mission. In late October, this self-styled "Flying Army" consisted of Washington's dragoons, three companies of riflemen and the Maryland and Delaware light infantrymen. During the first week of November, Morgan and Washington were also effectively supporting Davie's foraging operations near Charlotte and Cheraws. Morgan sent William with his dragoons and the Delaware light infantry from New Providence toward Camden to reconnoiter and procure forage. The detachment returned to New Providence unmolested after a 100-mile circuit that ranged as far as Hanging Rock.[24]

The cool, wet Carolina winter proved annoying to William, his dragoons and the rest of Morgan's men, because they had yet to receive their winter clothing. Morgan's immediate superior, General William Smallwood—a survivor of Camden— urged Gates to send any available winter clothing to Morgan's field force as soon as possible. However, the bureaucratic Board of War seemed more interested in receiving a return as to the number of the men and horses in the Continental cavalry and a description of the "present state" of the troopers' clothing and equipment and supplies they had drawn since September, 1779! By month's end, however, Morgan had rejoined the main army at Hillsboro for a council of war called to decide how to oppose Cornwallis by taking up an advanced position at Charlotte or Waxhaws. William, although he was the most junior officer present, convinced his fellow officers, according to Gates, "that at or Near Charlotte should be the present position for the Army, to which every other member of The Council assented." This position was more favorable as a base from which to observe Cornwallis and conduct harassment operations, since the Americans were still far too weak to meet the British in open battle. That this junior officer's opinion was so respected is testimony to his reputation as a trusted and respected field commander.[25]

The "Quaker Gun"

On November 28, Gates instructed Morgan to scout the Waxhaws area for much-needed forage and to ascertain the strength of the British post at Camden. Morgan, Washington and Davidson set out the same day, spurred on by the news that Tory Colonel Henry Rugeley had mustered between 100 and 200 Loyalists at his fortified farm a few miles north of Camden. When the Americans reached New Providence, Morgan detached William and his 100 dragoons to ride ahead at full speed and try to take Rugeley's party by surprise. William arrived at the place on December 1 or 2, only to find the Loyalists ensconced in a fortified barn surrounded by a ditch and abattis. Gambling on the inexperience of his opponent, young Washington resorted to an ingenious ruse. While most of his dragoons dismounted and surrounded the barn, he directed a small party of men in fashioning a mock cannon from a pine log and mounting it on a nearby carriage (or three prongs) out of view of the enemy. William had it brought into sight of the barn with great fanfare as if to fire this "Quaker gun" and summoned the defenders to surrender or risk being blown to pieces. The deception worked; the fake cannon, looking very much like a field piece, "had the same effect as if it was the best piece in Christendom" and convinced the Tories to give up without firing a shot.[26] Embarrassed by yet another unexpected strike against one of his outposts, Cornwallis confided to Tarleton that Rugeley would never be promoted to brigadier general! When General George Washington eventually learned of his cousin's exploit, he considered it worthy of "great commendation" and declared that it gave him "inexpressible pleasure to find that such a spirit of enterprise and intrepidity still prevails."

William herded his prisoners back to Charlotte after rejoining Morgan on December 4. The proud cavalryman rode into Gates' camp just in time to greet the newly arrived commander of the Southern army, General Nathanael Greene. Morgan's superior, General Smallwood, enthusiastically described William's victory to Greene: "The Colonel's Address and Stratagem on this occasion deserves Applause; having no Artillery, he mounted a Pine Log, and holding out the appearance of an attack with Field Pieces, carried his Point by sending in a Flag [of truce] and demanding an immediate surrender." Greene, in turn, described the success to Francis Marion and Thomas Jefferson, but cautioned the Governor, hoping "that these little flashes of Success will not relax the Exertions of the State [of Virginia] to give us Support."[27]

Hand-picked by General Washington to succeed Gates as commander in the South, Greene clearly recognized the importance of cavalry when he took command on December 3. He never doubted that the cavalry "must be our greatest security till we can form a respectable body of infantry."[28] Under this general's dedicated and inspiring leadership, William Washington's career as a cavalry commander would blossom.

NOTES: CHAPTER III

[1] Information on the war in the South prior to and including the Siege of Charleston in 1780 is from John Buchanan, *The Road to Guilford Courthouse: The American Revolution in the Carolinas*, 25-57; Nat and Sam Hilborn, *Battleground of Freedom: South Carolina in the Revolution*, 3-96-114; Henry Lumpkin, *From Savannah to Yorktown: The American Revolution in the South*, 1-49; Dan L. Morrill, *Southern Campaigns of the American Revolution*, 3-73; John S. Pancake, *This Destructive War: The British Campaign in the Carolinas, 1780-1782*, 1-72; Ward, *War of the Revolution*, II, 655-703.

[2] James Emmett to Richard Caswell, February 6, 1780, in Clark (ed.), *Records of North Carolina*, XV, 333; Thomas Jefferson to George Washington, June 11, 1780, in Boyd (ed.), *Papers of Jefferson*, III, 433. The error of placing the 4th Dragoons in the South prior to 1782 appeared in Ward, *War of the Revolution*, II, 698 and 701. For more accurate information, see John T. Hayes (ed.), *A Gentleman of Fortune: The Diary of Baylor Hill, First Continental Light Dragoons, 1777-1781*, Vol. 3, 18-82; Heitman, *Historical Register*, 585; Loescher, *Washington's Eyes*, 12-13; Urwin, *United States Cavalry*, 22-25.

[3] Hayes (ed.), *Diary of Baylor Hill*, Vol. 3, 36-44; Captain Johann Hinrich's Diary, in Bernard A. Uhlendorf (ed.), *The Siege of Charleston*, 197.

[4] For more on Tarleton, see Robert Duncan Bass, *The Green Dragoon; the Lives of Banastre Tarleton and Mary Robinson* and Banastre Tarleton, *A History of the Campaigns of 1780 and 1781 in the Southern Provinces of North America*.

[5] William Washington to Isaac Huger (?), March 15, 1780, EM7647, MS, Emmett Collection, New York Public Library; Loescher, *Washington's Eyes*, 78-79; Warren Ripley, *Battleground – South Carolina in the Revolution*, 43; Tarleton, *Campaigns*, 8-9; *The Pennsylvania Packet*, April 25 and May 2, 1780, in Frank Moore (ed.), *Diary of the American Revolution*, II, 271; Bass, *Green Dragoon*, 73; Balch (ed.), *Maryland Line*, 44; Lee, *Memoirs*, I, 117; *Monument to Washington*, 16; David Ramsay, *Ramsay's History of South Carolina*, I, 189.

[6] Walter B. Edgar (ed.), *Biographical Directory of the South Carolina House of Representatives*, I, 220-221; Elizabeth F. Ellet, *The Women of the American Revolution*, II, 89; Hayes (ed.), *Diary of Baylor Hill*, Vol. 3, 35-39; William Edwin Hemphill (ed.), *Journals of the General Assembly and House of Representatives, 1776-1780*, 30, 117, 262, 269-279, and 304-319 passim; Gherardi Davis, *Regimental Colors in the War of the Revolution*, 17 and Plate XIII; Peleg D. Harrison, *The Stars and Stripes and Other American Flags*, 56; Hilborn, *Battleground of Freedom*, 176; Newton B. Jones, "The Washington Light Infantry Company at the Bunker Hill Centennial," *The South Carolina Historical and Genealogical Magazine*, LXV, 196; Katcher, *Uniforms of the Continental Army*, 37; Edward W. Richardson, *Standards and Colors of the American Revolution*, 52 and Plate 45; Alexander S. Salley (comp.), *South Carolina Provincial Troops, June-November, 1775*, 120 and 138; Frank Earle Schermerhorn, *American and French Flags of the Revolution, 1775-1783*, 80-82; Steffen, *Horse Soldiers*, I, 6; Washington, "William Washington," 105; Mabel L. Webber (ed.), "Records from the Elliott-Rowland Bible," *The South Carolina Historical and Genealogical Magazine*, XI, No. 1, 60-66; Cowpens Committee, *Proceedings*, 119 and 123.

[7] Hayes (ed.), *Diary of Baylor Hill*, Vol. 3, 48-56; Eben, *Dragoon Sketchbook*, 9.

[8] Bass, *Green Dragoon*, 74; Eben, *Dragoon Sketchbook*, 9; Loescher, *Washington's Eyes*, 79; Moses Long to [?], April 5, 1780, in William Gilbert Simms, *South Carolina in the Revolutionary War*, 112; Urwin, *United States Cavalry*, 22-24.

[9] Hayes (ed.), *Diary of Baylor Hill*, Vol. 3, 68-79; Bass, *Green Dragoon*, 74; John W. Fortesque, *A History of the British Army*, Vol. III: 1763-*1793*, 315; Hayes (ed.), *Diary of Baylor Hill*, Vol. 3, 65-71; Loescher, *Washington's Eyes*, 13 and 80; Lumpkin, *Savannah to Yorktown*, 48; Captain Johann Ewald's Diary and General Johann von Huyn's Diary, in Uhlendorf (ed.), *Charleston*, 61 and 387; Ripley, *Battleground*, 50-52; C. Stedman, *The History of the Origin, Progress, and Termination of the American War*, II, 183; Tarleton, *Campaigns*, 16-17; *Monument to Washington*, 16; Urwin, *United States Cavalry*, 25.

[10] Hayes (ed.), *Diary of Baylor Hill*, Vol. 3, 80-83; William Washington to Abner Nash (?), May 5, 1780, in Clark (ed.), *Records of North Carolina*,

XIV, 807; Balch (ed.), *Maryland Line*, 44; Loescher, *Washington's Eyes*, 80.

[11] Hayes (ed.), *Diary of Baylor Hill*, Vol. 3, 85-88; Balch (ed.), Maryland Line, 44; Bass, *Green Dragoon*, 76-77; Fortesque, *History of the British Army*, III, 316; William Johnson, *Sketches of the Life and Correspondence of Nathanael Greene*, I, 285; Lee, *Memoirs*, II, 19; Loescher, *Washington's Eyes*, 81; Ripley, *Battleground*, 53-55; John Lewis Gervias to [?], May 13, 1780, in Simms, *South Carolina in the War*, 152; Stedman, *American War*, II, 184; Tarleton, *Campaigns*, 19; Balch (ed.), *Maryland Line*, 44; William Washington to Abner Nash (?), May 5 (?), 1780, in Clark (ed.), *Records of North Carolina*, XIV, 807; Ewald's Diary and von Huyn's Diary, in Uhlendorf (ed.), *Charleston*, 81 and 285; William B. Wilcox (ed.), *The American Rebellion: Sir Henry Clinton's Narrative of his Campaigns, 1775-1782*, 168-169.

[12] Loescher, *Washington's Eyes*, 82; Ann King Gregorie, *Thomas Sumter*, 72-73.

[13] Bass, *Green Dragoon*, 80; Loescher, *Washington's Eyes*, 82; Lumpkin, *Savannah to Yorktown*, 50; Tarleton, *Campaigns*, 29-30; Ward, *War of the Revolution*, II, 705-706.

[14] Gregorie, *Thomas Sumter*, 80-100 passim; Ward, *War of the Revolution*, II, 707-711; Russell F. Weigley, *The Partisan War: The South Carolina Campaign of 1780-1782*, 10-18.

[15] Information on the months immediately after the fall of Charleston in May is from Buchanan, *Road to Guilford*, 58-141; Hilborn, *Battleground of Freedom*, 115-130; Lumpkin, *Savannah to Yorktown*, 50; Morrill, *Southern Campaigns*, 75-84; Pancake, *Destructive War*, 79-94; Ward, *War of the Revolution*, II, 704-716.

[16] John Williams to Abner Nash, June 1, 1780, and Alexander Lillington to Abner Nash, June 4, 1780, in Clark (ed.), *Records of North Carolina*, XIV, 830 and 837; Balch (ed.), *Maryland Line*, 45; Benjamin Hawkins to Abner Nash, June 6, 1780, in Clark (ed.), *Records of North Carolina*, XIV, 839.

[17] Thomas Jefferson to Samuel Huntington, June 9, 1780, in H. R. MacIlwaine (ed.), *Official Letters of the Governors of Virginia, Vol. II: The*

Letters of Thomas Jefferson, 126; Resolutions, June 6 and 19, 1780, in Ford (ed.), *Journals of Congress,* XVII, 492 and 527.

[18] Nicholas Long to Abner Nash, June 27, 1780, in Clark (ed.), *Records of North Carolina,* XIV, 862; Boyd (ed.), *Papers of Jefferson.* III, 494; Johann de Kalb to Horatio Gates, July 16, 1780, in Clark (ed.), *Records of North Carolina,* XIV, 503.

[19] Greene, *Life of Greene,* III, 116; Ward, *War of the Revolution,* II, 719; Narrative of Otho Holland Williams, in Johnson, *Greene,* I, 506; Lee, *Memoirs,* II, 160; Richard Call to Horatio Gates, July 22, 1780 and Anthony White to Horatio Gates, July 26, 1780, in Clark (ed.), *Records of North Carolina,* XIV, 507-508 and 510-512; Horatio Gates to Anthony White, July 20, 1780, in Thomas Addis Emmett (ed.), "The Southern Campaign, 1780; Gates at Camden," *The Magazine of American History,* V (1880), 287; Horatio Gates to Thomas Jefferson, July 22, 1780, Richard Caswell, July 25, 1780 and Anthony White, August 4, 1780, in Emmett (ed.), "Gates at Camden," 291 and 298.

[20] Horatio Gates to Hawkins Martin, August 15, 1780, in Emmett (ed.), "Gates at Camden," 302; Lee, *Memoirs,* 171 and 191. Information on the Camden campaign and Marion's subsequent operations is from Buchanan, *Road to Guilford,* 142-193; Hilborn, *Battleground of Freedom,* 131-144; Lumpkin, *Savannah to Yorktown,* 57-90; Morrill, *Southern Campaigns,* 85-99; Pancake, *Destructive War,* 91-107; Ward, *War of the Revolution,* II, 717-737; Robert D. Bass, *Swamp Fox: The Life and Campaigns of General Francis Marion,* 32-99; Hugh F. Rankin, *Francis Marion,* 59-134; Weigley, *Partisan War,* 21-22.

[21] Risley and Zlatich, "3rd Regiment," *Military Collector,* XLIV (1992), No. 3, Plate No. 689; Thomas Jefferson to James Madison, July 26, 1780, in Boyd (ed.), *Papers of Jefferson.* III, 507 and 527.

[22] Anthony White to Horatio Gates, August 31, 1780, Ja. Christopher Senf to Horatio Gates, September 28, 1780, Proceedings of the Board of War, October 2, 1780, Peter Devreux to Horatio Gates, October 4, 1780, and Anthony White to Horatio Gates, October 18, 1780, in Clark (ed.), *Records of North Carolina,* XIV, 583, 656, 410, 664 and 702; Loescher, *Washington's Eyes,* 13-14 and 82-83; Johnson, *Greene,* I, 313 and 508.

[23] James Iredell to Hannah Iredell, October 8, 1780, in Higginbotham (ed.), *Papers of Iredell*, II, 176; Proceedings of the Board of War, October 13, 1780, in Clark (ed.), *Records of North Carolina*, XIV, 423; Ward, *War of the Revolution*, II, 734-735; Blacknell P. Robinson, *William R. Davie*, 65-70. Information on the King's Mountain campaign is from Buchanan, *Road to Guilford*, 194-241; Hilborn, *Battleground of Freedom*, 145-154; Lumpkin, *Savannah to Yorktown*, 91-104; Morrill, *Southern Campaigns*, 101-112; Pancake, *Destructive War*, 108-121; Ward, *War of the Revolution*, II, 736-747.

[24] William Smallwood to Daniel Morgan, November 3, 1780, in Gaillard Hunt (ed.), *Fragments of Revolutionary History*, 7; William Seymour, "A Journal of the Southern Expedition, 1780-1783," in *The Papers of the Historical Society of Delaware*, XV, 8-9; Ward, Christopher L., *The Delaware Continentals: 1776-1783*, 363; Otho Williams to Alexander Scammell, November 13, 1780, in Works Progress Administration (comp.), *Calendar of the General Otho Holland Williams Papers in the Maryland Historical Society*, 28.

[25] William Smallwood to Horatio Gates, November 16, 1780, Council of War, November 25, 1780, and Memorandum by Horatio Gates, 1780, in Clark (ed.), *Records of North Carolina*, XIV, 742 and 755 and XV, 161; Benjamin Stoddert to Nathanael Greene, November 23, 1780, in Richard K. Showman (ed.), *The Papers of Nathanael Greene, Vol. VI: 1 June 1780 - 25 December 1780*, 501.

[26] Horatio Gates to Daniel Morgan, November 28, 1780, in Hunt (ed.), *Fragments*, 13; William Smallwood to Horatio Gates, November 29, 1780, in Clark (ed.), *Records of North Carolina*, XIV, 764; Charles Cornwallis to Henry Clinton, December 3, 1780, in Wilcox (ed.), *Clinton's Narrative*, 479; Nathanael Greene to Thomas Jefferson, December 6, 1780, in Boyd (ed.), *Papers of Jefferson*, IV, 184; James Graham, *The Life of Daniel Morgan*, 249; Lee, *Memoirs*, I, 245-247; Seymour, "Journal," 10; Tarleton, *Campaigns*, 182; Otho Williams to Elie Williams and John Dunlap, December 31, 1780, in *Williams Papers*, 32 and 33.

[27] Lord Cornwallis to Banastre Tarleton, December 4, 1780, in Tarleton, *Campaigns*, 205; Lord Cornwallis to Henry Clinton, December 4, 1780, in Tarleton, in Clark (ed.), *Records of North Carolina*, XV, 302-307; George Washington to Nathanael Greene,

January 9, 1781, in Fitzpatrick (ed.), *Writings of Washington*, XXI, 87; Balch (ed.), *Maryland Line*, 45; William Smallwood to Nathanael Greene, December 6, 1780; Nathanael Greene to Francis Marion, December 4, 1780; and Thomas Jefferson, December 6, 1780, in Showman (ed.), *Papers of Greene*, VI, 538-539, 520 and 531.

[28] Nathanael Greene to Mordecai Gist, November 20, 1780, and President of Congress, November 2, 1780, in Greene, *Life of Greene*, III, 59 and 43; Ward, *War of the Revolution*, II, 748-749.

chapter IV

THE SWORD OF THE ARMY: COWPENS AND GUILFORD

When Nathanael Greene took command of the Southern Army in early December, he fully recognized the futility of directly resisting Cornwallis' impending invasion of North Carolina. His ragged, hungry army of about 1,500 men (including militia) would simply be unable to do more than maneuver and harass. Cornwallis commanded an excellent field army of 2,500 men supported by an additional 8,000 garrison troops—all composed primarily of veteran British, Hessian and Tory regulars. But Greene decided upon a daring gamble. Dividing his own little army into two parts, he hoped to confuse Cornwallis and possibly force the British commander into foolish decisions. The general believed that his unorthodox strategy of dividing the army, in his own words, "makes the most of my inferior force." By December 20, he had separated the army into two small divisions and began leaving Charlotte. Greene's decision to abandon this now vulnerable base was inevitable, and his army could subsist and travel more easily in smaller units. While awaiting the British invasion, the North Carolina militia had managed to deplete the local countryside of most supplies and forage, leaving little for the subsistence of Greene's army. Not until Greene persuaded Davie to give up command of his small partisan corps and assist his Commissary General, Lieutenant Colonel Edward Carrington, did the American supply situation begin to improve.[1]

Greene and Huger took 1,000 regulars and militia with all of the artillery northeast to Cheraws to establish a base of operations on Cornwallis' right flank.   Morgan led the remaining 600 regulars west toward the Catawba River to threaten and annoy the Englishman's left flank and, as Greene ordered, "give protection and spirit to that part of the country, to annoy the enemy in that quarter [and] do every thing in your power to distress the enemy and afford protection to the Country."   This division consisted of the army's most mobile and dependable light troops, which included William Washington's 80 dragoons, Colonel John Eager Howard's 320 Maryland and Delaware regular infantry and Captains Tate's and Triplett's 200 Virginia militia (all former Continental regular infantry).   Greene hoped that local militia would augment this force wherever Morgan moved.[2]

Greene realized that this campaign of the war in the South would be one of swift and deadly maneuver and that he would have to rely heavily on his cavalry. However, at this critical time only Washington's small band of regular cavalry could initially be counted on for this purpose. Reluctantly, Greene had ordered a unit of Virginia cavalry, led by Major Thomas Nelson, back to Virginia when Washington advised him that they were unfit for service because of their "near nakedness." Other troopers had been discharged or were scattered throughout North Carolina waiting for clothing and accouterments. In addition to Nelson's corps, the remnants of Armand's Legion also had to return to Virginia. These disparate units were also consuming the provisions and forage needed for the troops that were actually capable of taking the field.[3]

The cavalry, not unlike the rest of the army, was also plagued by desertion at this desperate and hungry time. On December 7, twelve men of the 1st Dragoons were apprehended when they deserted. Greene, following General Washington's preferences expressed in 1777 and 1778, also desired only native-born Americans for cavalry duty. He found that "foreigners," like the men comprising the remnants of Pulaski's and Armand's Legions, deserted more frequently and carried off valuable horses and equipment when they did so. Greene also desired "the better sort of men," because he knew that much depended at times on the reliability of observations made and information given by a single dragoon in the field. Most of William's men were native-born Americans from Maryland, Virginia and the Carolinas. Of his five senior officers, three were from Virginia and one each was from North and South Carolina. Greene also complained to Congress that too many of the cavalrymen were scattered all over the state of North Carolina waiting for clothing and accouterments, a situation that left William with less than 100 fully effective dragoons at any given time. It was also at this difficult period that an altercation erupted between Washington and White, leading Washington to actually order his fellow officer's arrest. White of course responded by demanding a court martial, but Greene had no time to deal with this problem just then and he allowed White's arrest to be temporarily set aside.[4] In spite of these numerous hardships and distractions, William Washington, now recognized as a fearless and experienced cavalry officer who personally led his charges, often proved that he could make the most of his small force. What he lacked in numbers, he compensated for with speed, surprise and daring!

On December 15, when he divided the army, Greene ordered William, who was scouting southward again towards Hanging Rock, to "join Morgan" with all of the army's cavalry. He later advised Morgan to keep Washington's cavalry in good order and to let the militia horse do all of the fatigue and forage duty, so as to prevent the valuable regulars from becoming worn down and leave the entire army without a force of disciplined, sword-armed cavalry on which to depend. William's dragoons constituted the only American force able to contend with Tarleton's "Green Dragoons" in the coming campaign. The other small force of troopers of the 1st Dragoons under the command of Griffin Faunt le Roy were near Cheraws, where they lacked both horses and apparently unit discipline and could not "take the field in six weeks." White was far to the north in Salem, North Carolina with another small force. Morgan's division marched west out of

Charlotte on December 21, and after a desperate sixty-mile march over rain-soaked clay roads, they encamped along the Pacolet River on Christmas Day. Approximately 300 Georgia and Carolina militia reinforced Morgan during the next week. He immediately augmented Washington's cavalry with two small troops of about twenty-five men each of Georgia and Carolina mounted militia commanded by Colonel James McCall and a Major Benjamin Jolly. William issued his extra sabers to these troopers to facilitate their service as heavy shock cavalry.[5] The occasion soon arose when Morgan employed William Washington's cavalry force to annoy Cornwallis' left flank.

A band of 250 Georgia Loyalists led by Colonel Thomas Waters had crossed the Savannah River and burned Patriot homes between Ninety Six and Winnsboro in mid December, and according to Morgan, "were insulting and Plundering the good people [there]." The raiders were operating in the Whig country near Fair Forest Creek when Morgan arrived north of that area. On December 24, while following the path of destruction wrought by this "Party of Plunderers," William sent a dispatch to Greene declaring that "The Distress of the Women and Children stripp'd of every thing by plundering Villains cries aloud for Redress."

On December 27, Morgan dispatched Washington with his cavalry and McCall's mounted militia (reinforced up to a strength of 200 horsemen for this mission) to destroy and disperse Waters' marauders. The next day, after a forty-mile ride through farmland devastated by the Tories, the Americans caught up with their prey at Hammond Stores, twenty-six miles east of the strategic British post at Ninety Six. Catching their quarry dismounted and preparing their noon meal, the Americans briefly held the advantage of surprise. Waters hurriedly formed his men in line on the crest of a hill. William quickly formed into line on another hill facing their enemy, with his regular dragoons in the center and the mounted militia—many of whom were armed with rifles—on the flanks. He called for the militia to fire a volley while he ordered his bugler riding next to him to sound the charge for his

Continental Dragoons. Collin, the young African American who would provide his commander with more than trumpeting at a later battle, loudly heralded the cavalry to the charge. Major Thomas Young, the commander of the South Carolina mounted militia at the battle recalled the action:

> *When we came in sight, we perceived that the Tories had formed a line on the brow of the hill opposite us. We had a long hill to descend and another to rise. Col. Washington and his dragoons gave a shout, drew swords, and charged down the hill like madmen. The tories fled in every direction without firing a gun. We took a great many prisoners and killed a few.*

Although Washington's men had to canter down one hill and charge up another, the Tories immediately broke under this well-coordinated assault. The pursuing Americans cut down most of their enemies when they attempted to flee to nearby woods during the melee. Waters managed to escape with only 60 survivors. Washington's cavalrymen took 40 prisoners and 50 horses, but 150 Tories were killed or sabered beyond hope of recovery. Morgan noted in his report on the action, "What makes this success more Valuable...it was attained without the loss of a man." Morgan also observed the successful tactic of supplementing regular dragoons with militia cavalry for a specific action. The militia, being from Georgia and South Carolina like their enemies, was no doubt in a vengeful mood because of the depredations these Tories had wrought in the friendly civilian settlements in the area (and previously in their Georgia homesteads). They were probably responsible for the brutality of the pursuit.[6] Such was the nature of this often civil war dimension of the Southern campaigns, which were characterized more by raids, sudden charges and surprise ambuscades than by more formal, set piece battles typical of the eighteenth century.

Flushed with victory and displaying his sometimes-impetuous nature, William Washington wanted to strike yet another blow while still deep in enemy territory before returning to Morgan's main force. On the 29th, he detached Cornet James Simons with ten dragoons and Captain Joseph Hayes' 40 mounted militia to attempt a surprise of Tory General Robert Cunningham's 150 men. Only fifteen miles from Ninety Six, this force had fortified Williams' Plantation and was well stocked with food and forage stolen from the local inhabitants. The Tories, upon being summoned to surrender and having heard about the fight at Hammond Stores, feared a similar fate and hastily evacuated their fort. While delaying an American attack as they pretended to consider Simons' surrender terms, they escaped into the nearby woods. The rebels were content to burn the fort down and return to Washington.[7] General Morgan was anxious over Washington's prolonged absence, and he was both pleased with the cavalry's exploits and relieved when the young paladin rode victoriously back into camp on the 31st. General Otho Williams at Greene's headquarters, however, was still arguing with Steuben in Virginia about the lack of satisfactory written returns enumerating the cavalry and its equipment, the former finally asserting that "the corps are on detached commands." While harping at Greene for the paperwork, Steuben managed to offer a congratulatory note to Greene on "the two affairs of Genl Sumter and Lt Colo Washington which tho so little decisive will at least serve to encourage the Troops and intimidate those of the Enemy." Greene finally advised the Baron that the returns would not be very useful whenever they were completed, since he had sent Washington 150 miles east to Kershaw's Ferry, on the other side of the Pee Dee River, and White's remnants were also dispersed.[8] The cavalry had indeed been very much "detached!"

Cornwallis, on the other hand, had had enough of this annoying activity on his western flank. He reacted to Washington's daring raids by sending his own cavalry commander, Tarleton, to pursue him. The elusive Washington had vanished by the time Tarleton arrived on the scene, however. The first two weeks of January, 1781 were marked by the almost quiet, yet desperate, searching and scouting activity by both sides as Cornwallis prepared to invade North Carolina and to also send Tarleton farther west to drive off or destroy Morgan and Washington. As British General Clinton later recalled, "Colonel Washington's move being reported to Lord Cornwallis with some exaggerations, His Lordship suspected that Morgan's whole detachment had marched to Ninety-Six, and accordingly ordered [Tarleton] to compel him to fall back." Greene and Morgan still remained one hundred and fifty miles apart.[9]

On New Year's Day, 1781, a sergeant of the 3rd Dragoons arrived in Washington's camp bearing a request from Greene's adjutant, Colonel Otho Williams, for a written return of men and equipment in the cavalry commander's corps. William responded briefly with as accurate a return as was then possible, considering what he called the "Disguised Situation of our Assignment." Apprehensive that the British might learn his exact strength, William wrote that of his original regiment of 1779, only one-fourth remained and that the rest had been discharged or lost during the Charleston campaign. On January 3, he received a welcome, albeit small, reinforcement of a corporal, seven privates, and nine remounts. Finally becoming impatient and embittered by desertions at this precarious time, Washington uncharacteristically had to set a severe example for his men by having a deserter tried and shot on January 4—the very day the man was apprehended! This incident tends to discredit Henry Lee's later observation that William's system of discipline was sometimes lax.[10]

Cowpens

Greene welcomed an elite unit of badly needed reinforcements on January 13: Lieutenant Colonel Henry "Light Horse Harry" Lee's Legion of 100 regular cavalry and 180 light infantry, all of whom were experienced in partisan hit-and-run tactics. Cornwallis also awaited reinforcements at Winnsboro: General Alexander Leslie's 1,500 regulars who were marching up from Charleston. But before Leslie arrived, the British commanding general decided to stop Morgan's harassing activities on his left flank by detaching Tarleton to track the rebels down with a force of about 1,000 regulars and light troops, including his dreaded "Green Dragoons." Greene's strategy was working! Cornwallis had now divided his army into three parts (including Leslie's detachment) in order to protect his western flank and invade North Carolina. Tarleton set out in early January to "push him [Morgan] to the utmost," while Cornwallis laboriously moved to the north to cut off Morgan's force from North Carolina. Leslie finally arrived at Camden to counter any moves against Cornwallis' lines of communication and right flank by Greene and Huger. On January 13, Greene sent an urgent dispatch to Morgan, warning him of Tarleton's impending attack and expressing his hope that the Americans would "have a decent reception for him." Morgan dispatched a courier on January 14 to find Washington, who was having his horses re-shod at Wooford Iron Works, and to "tell Billy that Benny [Tarleton] is coming and that he [Washington] must meet me tomorrow evening...on the east side of Thicketty Creek."[11]

Morgan initially withdrew before Tarleton's rapid advance, but on the 16th, he decided to stop and fight rather than risk getting caught by the "Green Dragoons" in the midst of crossing the Broad River. As to Morgan's decision to fight, Washington reportedly said, "No more burning, no flying: but face about and give battle to the enemy, and acquit ourselves like men in defense of their baggage, their lives, and the interests of the Country." Morgan chose a position about five miles south of the Broad locally known as the Cowpens, so named because farmers rounded up their cattle in the vicinity. A small rise dominated the sparsely wooded area flanked by wet cane bogs that could prevent wide flanking movements by Tarleton's cavalry. Morgan, counting on a frontal attack so characteristic of Tarleton, prepared a masterful defense-in-depth battle formation: about 150 picked Georgia and North Carolina riflemen three hundred yards south of the rise facing the enemy, more than 300 North and South Carolina militia infantry under Pickens about one hundred and fifty yards south of the rise behind the first line, 320 Maryland and Delaware regular infantry under Howard in the center and on the left of the rise itself, and 200 Virginians under Tate and Triplett on

Howard's right and left respectively.   He positioned Washington with his 80 dragoons and at least 45 mounted militia in a swale hidden behind the rise and part way up a smaller knoll.   In the portion of his battle report describing how his cavalry were placed behind the infantry, Morgan stated that the Washington's dragoons "were so posted at such a distance in their rear as not to be subjected to the Line of Fire directed at them [the infantry], and to be so near as to be able to charge the Enemy, should they be broke."   Trusting Washington's judgement to act on his own initiative, his only instructions were that he "be able to charge them should an occasion offer."[12]   Morgan, realizing that militia could not be expected to stand up and fight in the open for any length of time against formed regulars, instructed his first two lines to deliver only two accurate volleys at killing range and then withdraw to the rear of the regulars to regroup.   The regulars on the rise would bear the brunt of the fighting, while William's cavalry comprised the reserve.   Morgan thus deployed a defense in depth designed to wear down the advancing British.

On the morning of the 17th, after a four-hour night march, Tarleton crossed the Pacolet.   His advanced scouts informed him that the Americans were drawn up for battle just ahead. Morgan's men had just finished their early breakfast and were taking their assigned positions when Washington's advanced pickets from three miles out rode in closely followed by the British advanced guard.   Tarleton, no doubt anticipating a somewhat large-scale repeat of his victory at Waxhaws, quickly deployed his troops for an immediate frontal attack.   His first line from left to right was composed of 50 Legion cavalry, 200 inexperienced recruits of the 7th Foot (Royal Fusiliers), a three-pound cannon, about 200 seasoned Legion infantry, another three-pound cannon, over 100 skilled British light infantry and 50 elite troopers of the 17th British Light Dragoons.   The second line consisted of 200 veterans of the 1st Battalion, 71st Highlanders and the remaining 200 Legion cavalry.[13]

The battle commenced at 7:00 A.M., when Morgan's first line of sharpshooters repulsed Captain Richard Hovenden's troop of Tarleton's Legion dragoons who were sent to probe the American position. The riflemen emptied nearly fifteen saddles and, along with other factors, this accurate volley would contribute to most of the Legion cavalry's timidity during the rest of the battle. Tarleton then ordered a general advance by his entire first line. The first American line quickly fell back, all the while keeping up a steady sniping at the advancing ranks of red-coated British and green-coated Legionnaires. The British light artillery fire went high over the American infantry, forcing Washington to move his cavalry slightly to the right. When Tarleton's force advanced to within fifty yards of the second American line, Pickens' men delivered two devastating, well-aimed volleys, which took a particularly heavy toll among officers and sergeants. The militia were all highly motivated this day no doubt by their knowledge that they were now fighting to defend their homes from Tarleton's eventual plundering—not unlike the militia's spirit at King's Mountain three months earlier. Although the British line staggered for a few moments, it soon redressed ranks and resumed the advance. By 7:15, Pickens' men began their planned, but hasty, withdraw to the left rear of the army just as Morgan had instructed. Lieutenant Henry Nettles, commanding the 17th Light Dragoons on the British right wing, interpreted the militia's retreat as a rout and charged them. But as soon as the 17th closed with the militia, they were met by William Washington's cavalry, which had sallied from behind the rise to cover the militia's withdrawal and protect the American left flank at this critical point in the battle. The Americans achieved a complete surprise and reportedly inflicted eighteen casualties. According to one of the militiamen, William's cavalry

> *was among them [the British cavalry] like a whirlwind, and the poor fellows began to keel from their horses without being able to remount. The shock was so sudden and violent they could not stand it and immediately betook themselves to*

flight. There was no time to rally and they appeared to be as hard to stop as a herd of Choctaw steers going to a Pennsylvania market. In a few moments the clashing of swords was out of hearing and quickly out of sight.[14]

William was able to bring superior numbers—Tarleton's total cavalry force outnumbered Washington's by two to one—to bear at a critical point on the battlefield where he could outnumber the British (see Map #3A emphasizing the cavalry action). Washington wisely allowed only one small troop under Lieutenant Bell to pursue the defeated enemy cavalry and pulled the rest of his corps back behind the main infantry position. After the militia escaped to a position behind the knoll followed and protected at some distance by the victorious American cavalry, Pickens and Morgan began rallying them for hopefully more action.

Despite the setback on their right flank, the British infantry line continued to advance up the slope of the rise, where they engaged the third American line in a lively firefight. At 7:30, Tarleton sent the 71st Highlanders to support Captain David Ogilvie's troop of 50 Legion Dragoons in outflanking the American right wing. The American company on the extreme right began a retrograde shift to their right rear to meet this threat, but the rest of the American line interpreted this movement as an ordered retreat and faced about and marched down the reverse slope of the rise (in good order). McDowell's skirmishers held out in their detached position on the extreme American right and delayed Ogilvie's flanking movement for a few minutes. Morgan, fearing defeat, asked Howard if the men were in fact beaten. Howard replied that they were not, and Morgan then ordered the men to continue for a few more yards, turn about, and fire on the pursuing British.[15]

Morgan indicated that Washington's initial charge against the enemy dragoons was "with such Firmness that instead of attempting to recover the Fate of the Day [later in the battle], which one would have expected from an officer of his [Tarleton's] Splendid Character, broke and fled." Now Washington led his main force from behind the knoll to meet

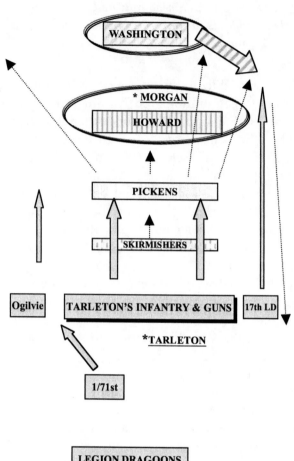

WASHINGTON

* MORGAN

HOWARD

PICKENS

SKIRMISHERS

Ogilvie

TARLETON'S INFANTRY & GUNS

17th LD

*TARLETON

1/71st

LEGION DRAGOONS

MAP 3-A
BATTLE OF COWPENS
JANUARY 17, 1781
INITIAL ACTION

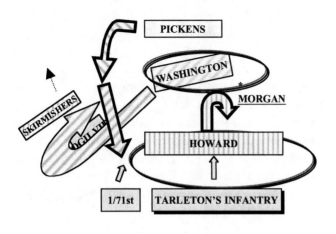

PICKENS

WASHINGTON

SKIRMISHERS

MORGAN

*

HOWARD

1/71st   TARLETON'S INFANTRY

Guns

BELL

TARLETON *

LEGION DRAGOONS   17th

MAP 3-B
BATTLE OF COWPENS
JANUARY 17, 1781
FINAL ACTION

Ogilvie's flanking charge. An officer who rode in this charge recalled, "We made a most furious charge, and cutting through the British Cavalry, wheeled and charged through them in the rear." The leaderless reserve Legion cavalry failed to counter this move and support Ogilvie. Tarleton was closer to his first line, and his able second, Major George Hanger, was ill back in Cornwallis' camp. Washington's daring maneuver, along with the earlier losses suffered at the hands of American riflemen, so cowered the reserve force of spectator "Green Dragoons" that they remained inactive for the rest of the battle (see Map #3B emphasizing the cavalry action).[16]

Washington's second charge ended about 7:40, when all of the British infantry began running down the rise in pursuit of the American regulars. Howard later recalled that Washington's dragoons were still posted (perhaps after returning from their second charge) behind his infantry. He further recalled that "Washington did not encounter the artillery. He moved from our rear, to attack Tarleton's horse, and never lost sight of them until they abandoned the ground." As he viewed the scene of the enemy's charging infantry from a position either to the rear of the British infantry or off to the American left after completing his charge(s), Washington sent word to Morgan and Howard: "They're coming on like a mob. Give them one fire, and I'll charge them!"[17]

At 7:45, Howard's line of regulars faced about and poured a withering volley into the over-confident, now disorganized mass of pursuing British and Tory infantry. The Americans followed their stunning volley with a bayonet charge, and Washington's cavalry charged the British from the rear. One of McCall's militia cavalrymen riding with the dragoons later recalled: "At this moment the bugle sounded. We, about half formed and making a sort of circuit at full speed, came up in the rear of the British line, shouting and charging like madmen...and the day was ours." This charge against the 71st Highlanders also placed Washington between the dispirited reserve dragoons and the two British infantry regiments. Pickens also rejoined the fight and surrounded the Highlanders while Washington rode on. The combined shock was too much for Tarleton's foot soldiers;

the 7th Foot immediately surrendered, the Legion and light infantry broke and ran for the rear (only to be vigorously pursued by William's cavalry), and after a few minutes, the stubborn Highlanders also surrendered.   Henry Lee later commented on this phase of the battle, observing that the Americans did not avenge the Waxhaws massacre while Washington's cavalry was rounding up prisoners from the Legion and British infantry: "Lieutenant-Colonel Washington, who commanded the horse on that day with so much glory, while he pushed the just claim of vengeance, preserved his laurels pure and spotless."[18]

Tarleton—who at this same time had just had his horse shot from under him by Pickens' sharpshooters—returned to his reserve force of "Green Dragoons" and ordered them to charge and save the day. Only about 50 responded, and most of these were the remnants of the 17th Light Dragoons. Thus, nearly 200 panicked Legion cavalry "forsook their leader, and left the field of battle," according to Tarleton. The "Green Dragoons" were not accustomed to making frontal attacks, preferring to attack the exposed flanks or the backs of their enemies as they retreated. General Clinton later noted that "all of the cavalry, except the detachment from the 17th Light Dragoons and chief of the officers, forsaking their leader, fled with precipitation from the field of battle." Yet another British officer later observed that "the legion-cavalry, though three times the number of those of the enemy, contributed nothing...250 horse which had not been engaged, fled through the woods with the utmost precipitation." British military historian Sir John Fortesque considered them to be "ill disciplined at the best of times and spoiled by easy successes...not the men to face so desperate a venture...looking to the behavior of the Legion, there can be little doubt but that the better men won the day."[19] The Briton charged forward anyway to try to rescue his artillery, but before he could reach them the Delaware regulars had come up to the guns and captured them. His small corps briefly crossed sabers with Washington's cavalrymen who were riding up to support the Delawares, but the British soon retreated.   Impetuous William, anxious to capture the retreating British commander, soon out-distanced most of his men in headlong pursuit—his fourth charge in less than an hour! Tarleton, seeing an opportunity to cut down the isolated rebel cavalry commander, turned about with two officers and galloped toward Washington bent on personal combat.

William first encountered the officer on Tarleton's right, and unfortunately broke his inferior sword near the hilt while slashing at the Briton and striking his sword. As that officer rose in his stirrups to return the blow, Collin, William's 14-year old bugler and attendant shot him. The other British officer struck at Washington, but recently arrived Sergeant Major Perry of the American dragoons parried the blow. Tarleton himself now closed with his famous oversized saber to finish Washington, but the charmed dragoon commander parried the blow with his broken sword! Tarleton wheeled about and fired his pistol, missing William but wounding his horse. By this time, the rest of Washington's cavalry approached, forcing Tarleton to flee after his own men. This duel would eventually be dramatized in no less than four 19th-century paintings (1845-1898)! William gathered and reformed his horsemen, secured a remount, and resumed the chase. When the Americans captured Tarleton's well-provisioned baggage, Cornet Simons recalled the contrasting privations of the campaign in that he "had not for months seen candles, coffee, tea, sugar, pepper or vinegar." Although Washington's cavalry made several more enemy dragoons prisoner in a twenty-mile pursuit to the banks of the Pacolet, the Americans took a wrong fork in the road when misled by the wife of a farmer whom Tarleton had taken with him as a guide. Tarleton made good his escape. During this pursuit, Tarleton captured Major Young, who had become isolated from the rest of Washington's force. The major later recalled that Tarleton expressed considerable surprise at the small size of Washington's cavalry force and in particular the willingness of the militia cavalry to fight in the pitched battle.[20]

The stunning American victory at Cowpens was one of the most complete of the war, especially considering that it was one of the conflict's few standup, formal encounters. The British

"Battle of Cowpens" by William Ranney. *Eastern National*

"Col. William Augustine Washington at the Battle of Cowpens" by S.H. Gunbar. *National Archives*

"Battle of Cowpens" by Alonzo Chappel. © *Collection of the New-York Historical Society*

"Combat between Colonels Washington and Tarleton"
Lodge's Story of the Revolution, Vol. II

lost 300 killed or wounded and 600 prisoners, and only about 180 dragoons escaped and rejoined Cornwallis' army. The American losses amounted to but twelve killed and sixty wounded. Congress ordered gold medals struck for Morgan and silver ones for Washington and Howard in appreciation of their battlefield prowess. Greene wrote to Henry Lee that "Lt. Colonel Howard and Washington were the heroes of the day." Throughout the Colonies, the battle proved to be a great morale boost at a desperate time in the war for the Americans, just as the victory at Trenton had been. And in both instances, William Washington had distinguished himself by personally leading critical charges to help win the day.[21]

Aware that Cornwallis' army would rapidly march to block any move to the north, Morgan wasted little time basking in his victory. He collected his prisoners, crossed the Broad River by the morning of the 18th and headed for the Catawba River, hoping to put as many obstacles between himself and the British as possible.

In an unusual coincidence, the day before William fought his death-defying duel with Tarleton, Jane Elliott's 44-year-old father died at Sandy Hill when he "fell a victim to disease ere the war had been waged in Carolina." He was buried in the old Elliott family cemetery at Live Oak the day after his daughter's crimson flag flew across the Cowpens battlefield with William Washington's cavaliers! In the meantime, by the 19th, Washington had rejoined Morgan after giving up his pursuit of Tarleton. Morgan detached him to escort the burdensome prisoners up the Catawba to Island Ford to ensure that they would not be rescued and rearmed by Cornwallis. William at this time set the imprisoned British Dr. Jackson free to tend the wounded among the prisoners. The rest of the Americans passed through Ramsour's Mills and crossed the Catawba at Sherill's (AKA Sherrald's or Sherrard's) Ford on the 22nd.[22]

Tarleton reached Cornwallis' new camp on Turkey Creek on the 18th and reported his defeat. The British general now found himself in a position similar to that of the preceding autumn right after the Battle of King's Mountain, when he had to abandon an invasion of North Carolina. This time, however, all of the material was assembled and Leslie's reinforcements had arrived. The British general was too committed to turn back, and he wanted to avenge the recent reverses by forcing a battle with Greene or Morgan. Cornwallis delayed his advance until the 19th, giving Morgan time to put two large rain-swollen rivers between the opposing armies. On the 21st, Cornwallis marched to the Broad River, where he remained for two days. No doubt his temporary lack of an aggressive cavalry force severely hampered his getting timely intelligence about the movements of Morgan and Greene. On the 25th he moved on to Ramsour's Mills, only to learn that Morgan was two days' march away on the other side of the Catawba. Here the American general had halted and awaited further orders from Greene. Washington and Pickens, after sending their dejected prisoners on to Salisbury with Triplett's Virginians, rejoined Morgan on the 23rd and 25th, respectively. Cornwallis now reckoned that the only way to catch the elusive Americans was to strip his own army of heavy baggage and make it a light corps. His army spent two days at Ramsour's Mills burning tents and wagons, and disposing of provisions deemed not absolutely essential. Although he was under orders to consolidate conquered territory as he advanced, Cornwallis set out on January 27 to chase the rebel army in what would become one of the most famous marches of history.[23]

Guilford Court House

Greene and Huger reacted swiftly to the unexpected Cowpens victory and the ensuing British maneuvers. On the 25th, the American commanding general ordered a withdrawal of troops from and wholesale evacuation of supply bases in North Carolina. Carrington hurried ahead to assemble all boats available on the Dan River along the Virginia border. Huger took the main army up the Pee Dee and Yadkin River valleys with the intention of joining Morgan near Guilford Court House, while Greene himself rode directly across country with only a small escort to join Morgan and personally coordinate his plans. Before departing, he settled White's court martial by reversing the initial "Court" judgment, which had been temporarily in White's favor—not Washington's. Although he now backed Washington in this matter, he ended the feud when he adroitly "released the Colonel from his arrest; and he sets out tomorrow to the Moravian Towns from whence he will send forward fifty more horse; after which he goes onto Virginia to compleat [sic] his regiment."[24]

Greene arrived on the 30th at Morgan's camp, where Morgan and North Carolina General Davidson were collecting the area militia for a possible stand against Cornwallis along the Catawba River. The next day, Greene, Morgan, Davidson and Washington all met at Beattie's Ford for a council of war. In true partisan style, the four leaders sat on a log discussing possible strategies for about twenty minutes. They decided that Davidson's militia would contest and delay the British crossing as long as possible while Greene, Morgan and Washington hurried their regular forces north to join Huger. Greene hoped that the North Carolina militia would then turn out in sufficient numbers to help him to more directly confront the British invasion. He ordered White to send all dragoons fit for duty to join Washington at Sherrald's Ford, North Carolina as soon as possible. He also attempted to bolster his cavalry by requesting a 100-man detachment from the North Carolina militia, which was to be "well-mounted and properly officered troops to serve with Col. Washington." On February 1, after Morgan had left, Davidson died leading his militia in a brief, spirited fight at Cowan's Ford. Later that same day, Tarleton followed up the British success by leading his still intact cavalry to Torrence's Tavern, where he dispersed the remaining North Carolina militia. These twin reverses—particularly Davidson's death—dashed Greene's hopes for militia support for some time. Only after the American army reached Virginia, he reckoned, could they regroup in sufficient strength to reenter North Carolina. Once again, only the partisan forces of Marion, Pickens and Sumter remained in the Carolinas to contest the British occupation. Washington's dragoons were reduced to only 60 men, compared to Tarleton's still powerful force of over 200. Therefore, Greene did not dare reenter North Carolina across the Yadkin until he had more cavalry.[25]

On February 3, General Charles O'Hara of the Guards led the British van to the banks of the Yadkin east of Salisbury, only to find the Americans and all available boats on the other side of the rain-swollen river.   Commanding the rear guard, Washington had been the last to cross, and he and his dragoons swam their horses over.   Cornwallis then marched some twenty miles through the mud to Shallow Ford, hoping to cross there and catch Greene before he could move his slower moving stores across the Dan.   But Greene had anticipated such a contingency, and his supplies were safely across the Dan by the 8th.   The same day, Huger joined Morgan at Guilford. Greene now realized that the final seventy miles to the Dan would be an all-out race, so again he divided the army.[26]

Greene created a select force of 700 light troops under Colonel Otho Williams to act as the rear guard division, while the rest of the army marched ahead for the Dan.   Greene at first offered the command of the light troops to Morgan, but he declined the post because of illness and returned to his Virginia home.   The light division consisted of 280 Maryland and Delaware regular infantry under Howard, 180 light infantry of Lee's Legion, 60 Virginia riflemen and about 200 cavalry from Lee's Legion and William Washington's dragoons. Greene wrote to George Washington on February 9 that "I have formed a light army composed of the 1 and 3d Regts and the Legion [Lee's] amounting to 240, to harass the enemy in their advance, check their progress."   Washington, Lee's senior in rank, briefly commanded all of the cavalry.   Lee later commended William, noting that "Lieutenant-Colonel Washington contributed his full share to the execution of the success of Williams."[27]   During the weeklong chase from Guilford County to the Dan River, William's cavalry force constantly skirmished with Cornwallis' advanced units, and Tarleton usually kept a safe distance from the formidable Americans. The "Green Dragoon" apparently did not wish to clash head-on again with William Washington's sabers so soon after Cowpens! By February 14, the entire American army was safely across the rain-swollen Dan. The cavalry was the last to cross, and Cornwallis, exhausted by the frustrating chase, was forced to halt his army for rest and re-supply.

The famous "Race to the Dan" for several hundred miles in winter weather also exhausted the light troops, who "were very much fatigued both by travelling and want of sleep...had not scarce time to cook our victuals, their [the British] whole attention being on our light troops." The grueling campaign had also taken a heavy toll among the American cavalry horses. Greene, with Virginia Governor Thomas Jefferson's permission, temporarily permitted Washington to impress Virginia horses for the cavalry in this emergency. The farmers whose horses were to be pressed into service were to be issued certificates of value for their animals. As had occurred in Pennsylvania in 1777, individual dragoons and officers soon violated the spirit of this type of order. Desperate soldiers indiscriminately impressed prized stallions and breeding mares and assigned them low values on the certificates they gave to the owners. The resulting public outrage seriously hampered Greene's efforts to quickly remount his cavalry. He had to order Washington and Lee to return any stallions; "otherwise the people will think they are plundered." Greene continued to plead with von Steuben and others in Virginia to send additional fully mounted and equipped cavalrymen. Governor Jefferson finally relented by giving Greene "regular blank power" to impress horses. Because the North Carolina militia cavalry the general had requested several weeks earlier had all deserted, he cautioned the North Carolina Legislature that they "should not put arms into the hands of doubtful characters." He also pleaded with that body for more horses and stressed the need to prevent the British from capturing local horses in Virginia. At the same time, he took this vital matter into his own hands by authorizing William to go ahead and impress good dragoon horses so that all of his men would have mounts. The general did order Washington and his officers to "treat the Inhabitants with tenderness" when doing so, however. Although the dragoons were to give certificates to the owners, he also told William to brand the animals as army horses. Washington and Lee eventually remounted about 180 of their regular dragoons on good horses for field duty, and by February 20, the two dashing commanders were scouting across the Dan River in advance of Greene's reentry into North Carolina. The Americans were not about to let the British rest for long and consolidate their hold on that state![28]

Greene hoped to quickly attack Cornwallis in his weakened and somewhat exposed condition before he could encourage very many Loyalist militia to support him, but American reinforcements failed to arrive in time. Cornwallis withdrew from the Dan River vicinity to Hillsboro, where he erected the Royal Standard and indeed attempted to recruit local Tories to supplement his army. Greene reacted swiftly to discourage Tories from joining Cornwallis by sending out the rest of Colonel Williams' light troops to support Lee and Washington in harassing British or Tory detachments. Lee detached his dragoons and joined Pickens, who had recently arrived on the scene with 700 newly raised militia of his own. On the 25th, Lee and Pickens, the former impersonating Tarleton (both Lee's and Tarleton's Legions wore green jackets), encountered Colonel John Pyle's 400 North Carolina Loyalists near the Haw River. Lee would later claim that he had intended to identify himself and demand Pyle's surrender as the dragoons rode past the dismounted Tories drawn up as if for inspection. However, some of Pickens' militia were prematurely sighted in hiding and a general melee ensued. With swords already drawn as if in salute as part of the American ruse, Lee's cavalry was the better prepared for close combat. They commenced a general slaughter, killing or wounding over half of the surprised Tories without any significant loss to themselves. This defeat, coupled with Tarleton's own mistaken attack on another band of Loyalists and Cornwallis' inability to restrain his men and the camp followers from plundering friend, foe and neutral alike in the surrounding area, brought British recruiting efforts in North Carolina to a sudden standstill.[29]

Greene re-crossed the Dan into North Carolina with his main army on February 22, and he now had with him about 1,500 regulars and 800 Virginia militia. Colonel Williams' still detached light division kept Cornwallis confused by maneuvering between him and Greene, while the latter gathered even more reinforcements. The American cavalry also effectively contained British foraging operations. Each time Tarleton attempted to close with Colonel Williams and hold him in place, he was either evaded or repulsed. These cavalry skirmishes were sudden and deadly, often taking place in the darkness of night or the shadows of dusk or dawn.

On March 1, Colonel Williams encamped near Alamance Creek, where Lee, Pickens and Colonel William Preston's 300 newly raised mountaineer riflemen joined him. Greene camped at Speedwell Iron Works on the Reedy Fork. William warned off the eager North Carolina militia from risking a dusk attack on the British position on the evening of the 1st. Major Joseph Graham, commanding the mounted militia, had been ordered by Pickens to probe the British positions across the Alamance. He later recalled that he encountered Washington first, who advised him that "it was not safe to proceed any farther, for said he, 'there is a skygale ahead yonder,'" pointing to the light of the enemy's encampment, which appeared as if the woods were on fire." Graham also observed how "Pickens, Lee, Williams and Washington kept up their game of checkers...continually changing their quarters, and appearing to act separately, but yet connected in their plans." On the 2nd, Tarleton attempted to surprise Colonel Williams, but Washington (whose command now included Major Joseph Graham's troop), Lee and Preston repulsed the Englishman.[30]

Cornwallis dispatched Webster's entire brigade on the 5th and 6th in yet another attempt to catch Williams, this time at Wetzell's Mills on the Reedy Fork. They were discovered by a patrol of Washington's vigilant cavalry, and Williams escaped with his main force, leaving Washington, Lee and Preston to harass Webster. This hotly contested delaying action resembled a pitched battle at times, but the American cavalry effectively prevented any British pursuit when the Americans broke off the engagement. According to Williams, the enemy "pursued some distance but receiving several checks from small covering parties and being cow'd by our Cavalry He thot proper to halt." Graham's account provides a detailed view of

the tactics Washington, Lee and Tarleton employed in this type
of running engagement:

> Colonel Tarleton and corps were within one hundred yards of
> the front of their infantry, and though so many opportunities
> offered for attacking scattering parties of militia coming in on
> the flanks, he never attempted to charge or pursue them. The
> appearance of Lee and Washington before him must have
> prevented him from improving such advantages as frequently
> offered in the course of the day. Washington and Lee
> superintended the rear alternately in person. The pursuit
> continued in this manner for ten miles [to Whitsell's Mill].
> Washington's cavalry and Graham's reduced squad of
> militia dragoons, one hundred yards on the right, and rather
> in the rear of Williams' line [i.e., Lee with his Legion
> Infantry and Preston's riflemen at the Mill]. A column of
> the enemy's infantry, which had not yet been brought into
> line, came on to the ford, and Tarleton with his cavalry came
> through. On the rise of the hill, he sounded his bugle. As
> soon as it was heard, Colonel Washington yet in his position
> on the right, about forty poles from Tarleton, sounded his
> bugle also, and Major Rudolph, at the head of Lee's corps
> [Legion Cavalry] on the left sounded his. Upon this,
> Washington and Lee's cavalry went off at a canter, meeting
> each other in the road, about twenty poles from Tarleton's
> front. As they met, they wheeled up the road in a gallop
> (though in good order), after Colonel Williams. Tarleton was
> halted on the hillside, and suffered them to pass without
> moving. The infantry on the opposite hill kept firing until
> they were out of view. When Washington and Rudolph came
> to Williams' rear, they turned out of the road, about sixty
> steps on each side, along his flanks. His men were marching
> briskly, and the cavalry officers gave orders that if the
> infantry was charged by the enemy in the rear they should
> wheel and take him in each flank. Washington himself and
> eight of his troopers took the rear. At such parts of the road as
> a view could be had, two of them were stationed, who, on
> seeing the front of the enemy, galloped up and reported...three
> or four miles.

During the night of the 6th, Washington's cavalry intercepted and surprised a party of 25 Tories taking beef cattle to Cornwallis. The dragoons killed all but three of the Tories—the violence of these "civil war" clashes seemingly escalating. The captured cattle were indeed a welcome prize for Greene's always-hungry army, and this vigorous campaign also left Williams' force tired and hungry. The men had not had a cooked meal in three days and Williams felt his force could not rapidly move again "until the horses of Col. Washington's dragoons have been reshod."[31]

Once during these fast-paced days of early March, William displayed behavior bordering insubordination. When Colonel Carrington ordered him to provide an escort of seven dragoons for prisoner exchange negotiations with the British, William refused. No doubt recalling the petty details which had so dispersed his regiment in New Jersey two-years prior—and the proximity of the still-potent and lurking cavalry force of Tarleton—Washington downright refused to recognize Carrington's authority in the general's stead (as only Greene's Quartermaster). He also remonstrated that his horses needed to be re-shod before continuing any field operations. Finally, Greene wrote his cavalry commander a strong reprimand on March 9, in which he assured him that all orders from his staff had his approval and that they were to be strictly obeyed. He directed Washington to quickly get the horses re-shod and join the main army by the next day.[32]

When William rode into Greene's camp on March 10, the general was again busy reorganizing the army—in preparation for a major battle with Cornwallis. Long-awaited reinforcements had arrived and the militia mustered in force: 500 Virginia regular infantry under Colonel Richard Campbell, 1,000 North Carolina militia under Generals John Butler and Pinketham Eaton and 1,700 additional Virginia militia under Generals Robert Lawson and Edward Stevens. Greene formed two powerful flank units composed of his best light troops. The left, commanded by "Light Horse Harry" Lee, consisted of his 75 Legion cavalry, 82 Legion infantry and Colonel William Campbell's 200 Virginia riflemen. The right, led by William

Washington, consisted of his 86 dragoons, Captain Robert Kirkwood's 110 crack Delaware light infantry and Colonel Charles Lynch's 200 Virginia riflemen. Greene soon detached his two cavalry commanders to "either separately or conjunctively as you [Washington and Lee] may agree, to give the enemy all the annoyance in your power." He wrote to von Steuben on the 11th that "I am superior in Cavalry and therefore can approach them [the British army] without risqueing more than circumstances may make necessary." On the 11th, William sent word to his commanding general that the British were then on a "direct Route to Bell's Mill." On the 14th, the entire army encamped at Guilford Court House while the two flank detachments continued to scout Cornwallis' expected advance. By nightfall, Lee relieved William in the Deep River area, but not before the two cavalry commanders cooperated in taking twenty prisoners and forcing Tarleton's "Green Dragoons" back to the protection of the main British column. A Virginia militia officer described this encounter in a letter to his wife; "Lee and Washington took twenty prisoners yesterday and the day before. Tarleton is evidently afraid of these two formidable partisan officers."[33]

Greene chose the ground at Guilford for this forced battle because of its suitability for a defense-in-depth formation. He was hoping for a repeat of Cowpens, but on a much larger scale. Cornwallis would march from the west along the only direct road, which would take his army through a defile and then into a wooded area of steadily rising ground approaching the courthouse. In the front center of the battlefield on either side of the road were two cleared fields enclosed by a rail fence. A dense oak woods lay some three hundred yards behind the fields as the road continued eastward. Five hundred yards to the northeast of this woods a clear ridge rose to the right of the courthouse.[34] Greene's numerically superior army of 4,500 men was comprised of 1,600 regular infantry (only half of whom were veterans), 2,600 militia infantry and volunteer riflemen (often of unknown staying power in a pitched battle), 60 artillerists with four six-pound cannons and about 160 regular cavalry. He deployed the troops in three lines similar to Morgan's formation at Cowpens, but spread much further apart and not in a position to quickly support each other. The resulting battle would later in fact become three engagements. The unpredictable North Carolina militia took up a position behind the rail fence on the eastern side of the fields supported by two cannons on the road. On their right flank stood Washington's light corps of observation and on their left Lee's similar force offered support. In the oak woods to the rear of the North Carolinians, the Virginia militia took cover. The third line consisted of the regular infantry (i.e. "Continentals") supported by the remaining two field pieces deployed on the high ground north of the court house—Huger's Virginia brigade on the right and Colonel Williams' Marylanders on the left. Greene remained with this line as his post throughout the battle.

Cornwallis' veteran army of 2,000 elite and regular troops approached the American position on the morning of the 15th. After a pre-dawn skirmish at New Garden between Tarleton and Lee, who had temporarily gone forward to guard against a surprise night attack, the British emerged from the defile in view of the Americans.

As Greene had hoped, his enemy deployed into line for a general frontal assault. The first line consisted of four regiments formed into two small brigades: the Hessian Regiment von Bose and the 2nd Battalion, 71st Highlanders (sister unit to the 1st Battalion that surrendered at Cowpens) on the right of the road under General Leslie and Webster's command of the 23rd Foot (Royal Welsh Fusiliers) and the 33rd Foot on the left. Cornwallis positioned three cannons on the road that separated the two infantry brigades. The Light Infantry of the Guards and the Hessian Jaegers supported Webster's left and rear near a more wooded edge of the battlefield (opposite Washington's light corps). General O'Hara commanded the reserve comprised of the 1st Battalion of the Guards behind Leslie and the 2nd Battalion and Grenadiers of the Guards positioned behind Webster. Tarleton's cavalry formed a reserve column on the road far to the rear of the army, resting their horses somewhat from the previous night's patrols and skirmishes.

The battle opened with a largely ineffective artillery duel in the center that lasted about half an hour, after which the British line began a general advance. As the British crossed the open ground in disciplined linear formation, the North Carolinians timidly contested them with desultory fire but were themselves soon routed when the redcoats responded with a volley and their dreaded bayonet charge. Greene never expected them to hold very long, because few had bayonets, and he had requested only two volleys from these untrained men (as Morgan had done at Cowpens with similar troops). Washington covered their retreat by bringing Lynch's riflemen into action against Webster's left flank, delaying him for a time with a galling fire from cover and higher ground. He personally stayed with Lynch, leaving his cavalry and Kirkwood's Delaware infantrymen in reserve (see Map #4A emphasizing Washington's action). But the British officer extended his line by calling the Jaegers and Light Infantry to counter the riflemen's accurate fire. Under Webster's determined advance, the riflemen broke and Washington rejoined his cavalry.[35]

Lee opposed Leslie in a similar fashion on the British right wing, and he forced the British to commit the 2nd Guards. Leslie and Lee gradually became separated from the main battle, fighting their own running action for most of the day. When the majority of the North Carolina militia finally gave way and fled in panic, William Washington withdrew his corps to a position to favorably support the Virginia militia— Cornwallis' next obstacle. Webster followed and attacked this line, and a bitter struggle ensued as the Virginians fired from the cover of trees and held their ground for some time. O'Hara then came up with the Grenadiers and 1st Guards, permitting Webster to employ his own woods fighters—the Jaegers and Light Infantry—in a successful flank attack against the militia's right. When the Virginians began to grudgingly retreat, Washington and Kirkwood briefly covered them until the militia eventually quit the field. Washington then withdrew

Courthouse

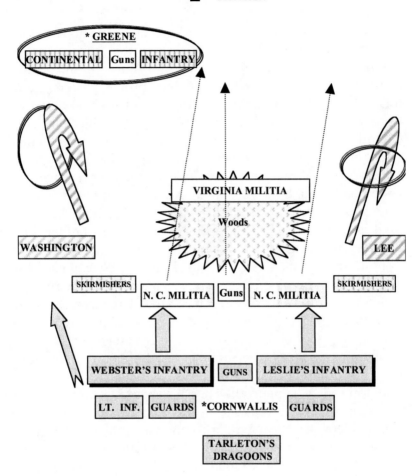

* GREENE

| CONTINENTAL | Guns | INFANTRY |

WASHINGTON

VIRGINIA MILITIA

Woods

LEE

SKIRMISHERS   N. C. MILITIA   Guns   N. C. MILITIA   SKIRMISHERS

WEBSTER'S INFANTRY   GUNS   LESLIE'S INFANTRY

LT. INF.   GUARDS   *CORNWALLIS   GUARDS

TARLETON'S
DRAGOONS

MAP 4-A
BATTLE OF GUILFORD
MARCH 15, 1781
INITIAL ACTION

to the third and final American line of Continentals near the courthouse, where he and Kirkwood formed Greene's tactical reserve.

With O'Hara driving the rest of the Virginia militia before him, the dauntless Webster discovered that there was no opposition to his advancing on the third American line. Thus emboldened, he led his battered but spirited Jaegers, Light Infantry and 33rd Foot in a daring assault on the center of Greene's line of Continentals. He even left the 23rd Foot behind to assist O'Hara, who was still engaged in the center with some of the more stubborn Virginia militia in the woods. Greene's line of regulars proved to be a different foe than the militia had been, however. When the British and Hessians had closed to within one hundred feet, the disciplined Americans fired a devastating volley and charged with the bayonet. Webster, suffering crippling casualties and receiving a mortal wound, saw his men fall back in disorder. Ever anxious to preserve his precious regular army and unaware of the condition of the rest of Cornwallis' army, Greene recalled his men to the high ground instead of pressing this temporary advantage. Cornwallis in turn took advantage of Greene's hesitation and began regrouping his disorganized, bleeding army for what he hoped would be a final, decisive attack. Tarleton rode to support the Hessians engaged with Lee on the far right, which freed Leslie's other two regiments (the 71st Highlanders and the 1st Guards) for the coming fight in the center and left. But before the British had completely regrouped, Lieutenant Colonel Stuart led the 2nd Guards and Grenadiers in a premature attack on Greene's left flank nearest the court house. They struck the least experienced regiment of Marylanders, who routed and left two field pieces in British hands.

This action could have turned the battle into an American debacle, had not William Washington seized the opportunity to charge the exposed Guards and recapture the artillery. His dragoons, augmented by Graham's small troop of North Carolina militia horse, slashed through the startled British like a scythe, and Kirkwood's Delaware infantry and the veteran 1st

Maryland followed with a bayonet charge of their own. One of William's troopers, a seven-foot giant named Peter Francisco, single-handedly killed eleven Guardsmen. A Delaware officer who was present, recorded that the cavalry charged "so furiously that they either killed or wounded almost every man in the regiment, charging through them [the Guards] and breaking their ranks three or four different times." Lee dramatically recalled "The rush and spurring of the chargers, and the murderous slashing of the fierce dragoons." A Hessian officer observed that the Guards "suffered much from Colonel Washington's and Lee's [whose unit was not actually on this wing] Cavalry." Cornwallis later described the fate of the Guards as "thrown into confusion by a heavy fire, and immediately charged and driven back into the field by Colonel Washington's dragoons, with the loss of the six pounders they [the Guards] had taken." Indeed, the victorious Americans retook their cannons, killed Stuart and routed the elite Guards with great slaughter (see Map #4B emphasizing Washington's action).[36]

Once Washington's cavalry passed through the Guards, the impetuous paladin noticed an officer surrounded by his staff only a couple hundred yards distant. Seeing a chance to capture the enemy commander, William spurred his charger toward Cornwallis. Only a pair of freak accidents saved the British general. As young Washington dashed forward, his helmet fell to the ground when the chinstrap broke. He instinctively halted to retrieve this item so necessary to a charging cavalryman, and at the same moment the officer leading the rest of his command was shot. The man's horse galloped out of control to the right followed by the entire unit, who thought the turning movement was intended. Discovering his isolated position (and perhaps recalling his brush with Tarleton's officers at Cowpens), Washington judiciously returned to his command and led his dragoons in yet another attack on the Guards.[37]

At this desperate moment of the battle Cornwallis finally resorted to the brutal expedient of ordering his artillery to fire grapeshot at short range into the melee in which the Guards

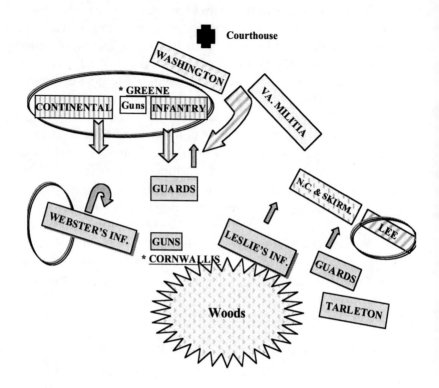

Courthouse

WASHINGTON

VA. MILITIA

* GREENE

CONTINENTAL   Guns   INFANTRY

N.C. & SKIRM.

LEE

GUARDS

WEBSTER'S INF.

GUNS

LESLIE'S INF.

* CORNWALLIS

GUARDS

TARLETON

Woods

MAP 4-B
BATTLE OF GUILFORD
MARCH 15, 1781
FINAL ACTION

had become so entangled. The murderous cannon fire stopped the impetus of the American attack, but it also killed many of the Guards. Greene, now confident that he had inflicted severe losses on the British, broke off the battle and retreated in good order. Cornwallis claimed a great victory by remaining on the battlefield, but it was in fact a Pyrrhic one. He lost over 500 men killed or seriously wounded—over one fourth of his army. The Americans lost only 250 killed or wounded, and as Greene had expected, the militia failed to rally and return to the army. The courageous British infantry had tactically won a hard-fought battle against superior numbers, but the heavy losses and his exposed position in the interior of North Carolina soon forced Cornwallis to abandon the invasion of that state.

William Washington's part in the battle is best described by Greene's praise the after the action: "The horse, at different times in the course of the day, performed wonders. Indeed, the horse is our great safeguard, and without them the militia could not keep the field in this country." In another report, the general noted that the "corps of observation, under Washington and Lee, were warmly engaged and did great execution." William lost four killed, seven wounded and another seven were missing. His losses were heaviest among his officers—one death and three of the wounded.[38]

From March 17 through 22, Cornwallis was in full retreat down the valley of the Cape Fear River headed for the Loyalist settlement of Cross Creek (now Fayetteville, North Carolina). There he hoped to be re-supplied by boat from the British-held port at Wilmington, but rebel partisans operating along the river prevented most of the supplies from getting through. Greene cautiously pursued the British to demonstrate to the countryside that Cornwallis had lost the campaign, thereby discouraging any active Tory support. He specifically deployed Washington and Lee for this purpose, ordering them to push hard on the British rear guard. On April 7, the British retreated to the safety of their post at Wilmington. Cornwallis, tired of Greene and the Carolinas, soon marched north where he would eventually be entrapped at Yorktown. He was, however, still convinced at the time that he could still win the war by invading Virginia and linking up with other British forces operating there.[39]

The American cavalry, as well as the rest of Greene's army, continued to face manpower and supply problems in April. Washington and Lee had to stop at Wilcox's Iron Works on March 30 for several days to have most of their horses re-shod, "which at this time they stood in great need of," according to a Delaware officer. Shortly after the Battle of Guilford Court House, the Virginia House of Delegates—still angry over the dragoons' harsh impressment practices—ordered that only horses worth less than $5,000 could be taken for the cavalry, and further that any horses already with the army and valued at that much or more be immediately returned to their owners. This order was probably ignored, but Greene could no longer hope for much support for his cavalry from Virginia in his next campaign. At the same time, Washington tried to obtain better weapons for his men by sending a captured British cavalry saber to Major Call for use as a model at Hunter's Manufactory in Virginia. But Call was pessimistic about filling the order, while observing that "our mounted men at present have swords but the quality of them are much inferior to the British." He also bitterly complained to Thomas Jefferson that only inferior horses and equipment could be procured, since contractors were seldom timely paid (if at all) by Virginia for supplying anything for the cavalry. Greene also lamented the decayed condition of the cavalry's nine-month old clothing "in this severe service." He hoped that White would order more dragoons to join Washington's corps, which now had enlisted "upwards of 100 men for the War [i.e., its duration]." Ironically, Tarleton would later seize all the good horses withheld by Virginians from the Continentals![40]

These reverses notwithstanding, William and his stout-hearted dragoons remained with the army when Greene marched into South Carolina for what he hoped would be the final and decisive campaign of the war in the Carolinas. Washington had clearly demonstrated his keen tactical sense of timing and personal bravery as a battlefield commander of cavalry capable of supporting the army in with numerous charges in pitched battles at Cowpens and Guilford Court House. British military historian, Sir John Fortesque, would later complement Greene's officers, "Henry Lee and William Washington, a kinsman of the great George, both of whom enjoyed great reputations as leaders of cavalry." Indeed, General Greene had come to consider Henry Lee his "eye" and William Washington his "arm" in the fast-paced warfare in the South.[41]

Guilford Courthouse, 13 March 1781. *U.S. Army Center of Military History*

Guilford Courthouse Third Line Field & Cavalry Monument. *Eastern National*

NOTES: CHAPTER IV

[1] Hugh F. Rankin, *Greene and Cornwallis: The Campaign in the Carolinas* (Raleigh: North Carolina Dept. of Cultural Resources, 1976), 3-17; Theodore George Thayer, *Nathanael Greene: Strategist of the American Revolution* (New York: Twayne, 1960), 296-297; Mildred P. Treacy, *Prelude to Yorktown: The Southern Campaigns of Nathanael Greene* (Chapel Hill: University of North Carolina Press, 1963), 61-65; Ward, *War of the Revolution*, II, 750-751; Quoted in Greene, *Life of Greene*, III, 131-132; Nathanael Greene to George Washington, January 13, 1781, MS, Nathanael Greene Papers, Library of Congress; Robinson, *Davie*, 90-105.

[2] Nathanael Greene to Daniel Morgan, December 16, 1780, MS, Greene Papers, Library of Congress and Showman (ed.), *Papers of Greene*, VI, 589; Treacy, *Prelude*, 66. Information the Cowpens campaign is from Lawrence E. Babits, *A Devil of a Whipping: The Battle of Cowpens* (Chapel Hill: University of North Carolina Press, 1998); Edwin C. Bearss, *Battle of Cowpens: A Documented Narrative and Troop Movement Maps*, (Johnson City, Tenn.: The Overmountain Press, 1996 reprint of the original 1957 National Park Service edition); Buchanan, *Road to Guilford*, 260-333; R. Ernest and Trevor N. Dupuy, *The Compact History of the Revolutionary War* (New York: Hawthorn Books, Inc., 1968), 372-388; Thomas S. Fleming, *Cowpens: "Downright Fighting"* (Washington, D.C.: National Park Service, 1988); Lumpkin, *Savannah to Yorktown*, 116-134; Morrill, *Southern Campaigns*, 121-133; Pancake, *Destructive War*, 122-140; David Schenck, *North Carolina 1780-81: Being a History of the Invasion of the Carolinas by the British Army under Lord Cornwallis*, 178-225; Ward, *War of the Revolution*, II, 755-762; Wood, *Battles*, 208-276. Babits presents the most current research on the battle and provides considerable detail regarding the participation and movements of individual units on both sides.

[3] Thayer, *Greene*, 283; Nathanael Greene to Thomas Jefferson, December 14, 1780 and January 1, 1781, in Boyd (ed.), *Papers of Jefferson*, IV, 206-207 and 288-289; List of Officers, in Graham, *Morgan*, 311; Thomas Jefferson to President of Congress, March 21, 1781, in MacIlwaine (ed.), *Letters of Jefferson*, 422; Nathanael Greene to Thomas Jefferson, December 14, 1780, in Showman (ed.), *Papers of Greene*, VI, 573; Nathanael Greene to Samuel Huntington, December 28, 1780, in

Richard K. Showman (ed.), *The Papers of Nathanael Greene, Vol. VII: 26 December 1780 - 29 March 1781* (Chapel Hill: University of North Carolina Press, 1994), 7-8.

[4] Seymour, "Journal," 10-11; Nathanael Greene to President of Congress, December 28, 1780, MS, Greene Papers, Library of Congress; Nathanael Greene to Lafayette, December 29, 1780, in Greene, *Life of Greene*, III, 70n; Anthony White to Nathanael Greene, December 28, 1780, in Showman (ed.), *Papers of Greene*, VII, 15.

[5] Seymour, "Journal," 11; Nathanael Greene to William Washington, December 16, 1780, to Griffin Faunt le Roy, December 25, 1780 and to Daniel Morgan, January 8, 1781, and Griffin Faunt le Roy to Nathanael Greene, January 7, 1781, in Showman (ed.), *Papers of Greene*, VI, 590 and 612 and VII, 70 and 72-73; Nathanael Greene to Daniel Morgan, January 8, 1781, MS, Greene Papers, Library of Congress; Graham, *Morgan*, 291-292; Ward, *War of the Revolution*, II, 752.

[6] William Washington to Nathanael Greene, December 24, 1780, in Showman (ed.), *Papers of Greene*, VI, 611; Daniel Morgan to Nathanael Greene, December 31, 1781, in Showman (ed.), *Papers of Greene*, VII, 30-31; Nathanael Greene to Francis Marion, January 7, 1781, MS, Greene Papers, Library of Congress; Nathanael Greene to Thomas Jefferson, January 9, 1781, in Boyd (ed.), *Papers of Jefferson*, IV, 322-323; George Washington to Count Rochambeau, February 14, 1781, in Fitzpatrick (ed.), *Writings of Washington*, XXI, 225-226; Graham, *Morgan*, 265-266; Johnson, *Greene*, I, 363; Lumpkin, *Savannah to Yorktown*, 121; Bobby Gilmer Moss, *The Patriots at the Cowpens* (Greenville: A Press, 1985), 48; J. B. O'Neal (ed.), "Memoir of Major Joseph McJunkin," *The Magnolia*, II (1843), 37; Rankin, *Campaign in the Carolinas*, 30-31; Ripley, *Battleground*, 127; Thomas Young, "Memoir of Thomas Young, A Revolutionary Patriot of South Carolina," *The Orion*, III, No. 2 (October 1843), 87; Seymour, "Journal," 12.

[7] North Callahan, *Daniel Morgan: Ranger of the Revolution* (New York: Holt, Rinehart and Winston, 1961), 198; Joseph Johnson (ed.), *Traditions and Reminiscences Chiefly of the American Revolution in the South* (Charleston: Walker & James, 1851), 303; Daniel Morgan to Nathanael Greene, January 4, 1781, in Showman (ed.), *Papers of*

Greene, VII, 50-51; Rankin, *Campaign in the Carolinas*, 31; Ripley, *Battleground*, 128-129.

[8] Greene, *Life of Greene*, III, 135-136; Otho Williams to Nathanael Greene, December 31, 1780, Baron von Steuben to Nathanael Greene, December 24, 1780, and Nathanael Greene to Baron von Steuben, January 7, 1781, in Showman (ed.), *Papers of Greene*, VI, 601 and 608; Otho Williams to Baron von Steuben, December 31, 1780 and January 20, 1781, in *Williams Papers*, 32 and 33.

[9] Graham, *Morgan*, 267; Thayer, *Greene*, 302; Wilcox (ed.), *Clinton's Narrative*, 245.

[10] Otho Williams to Daniel Morgan, December 30, 1780, and to William Washington, January 3, 1781, in Theodorus Bailey Myers (comp.), "Cowpens Papers, being correspondence of General Morgan and the prominent actors," Charleston *News and Courier*, Tuesday, May 10, 1881, 1; William Washington to Otho Williams, January 5, 1781, EM6567, Emmett Collection, New York Public Library; Seymour, "Journal," 13; Lee, *Memoirs*, I, 403.

[11] Thayer, *Greene*, 303; Treacy, *Prelude*, 67; Ward, *War of the Revolution*, II, 753-754; Tarleton, *Campaigns*, 211; Ward, *War of the Revolution*, II, 754; Nathanael Greene to Daniel Morgan, January 13, 1781, in Myers (comp.), "Cowpens Papers;" Morgan quoted in O'Neal (ed.), "Memoir of McJunkin," 38.

[12] Daniel Morgan to Nathanael Greene, January 19, 1781, in Showman (ed.), *Papers of Greene*, VII, 152-153; Babits, *Whipping*, 40-54.

[13] Young, "Memoir," *The Orion*, III, No. 2, 88; Tarleton, *Campaigns*, 216.

[14] Daniel Morgan to Nathanael Greene, January 19, 1781, in Showman (ed.), *Papers of Greene*, VII, 159; James Simons to William Washington, November 3, 1803, in Balch (ed.), *Maryland Line*, 45-46; Account of James P. Collins, quoted in Commager and Morris (eds.), *The Spirit of Seventy-Six*, 1156 and James M. Roberts (ed.), *Autobiography of a Revolutionary Soldier* (New York, Arno Press, Inc., 1979), 57; Babits, *Whipping*, 82-99; Bass, *Green Dragoon*, 156-158; Fortesque, *History of the British Army*, III, 366; Graham, *Morgan*, 468-469; Tarleton, *Campaigns*,

216; Rankin, *Campaign in the Carolinas*, 32-37; Ward, *Delaware Continentals*, 376; Ward, *War of the Revolution*, II, 758-760; Alice Noble Waring, *The Fighting Elder: Andrew Pickens, 1739-1817* (Columbia, University of South Carolina Press, 1962), 45.

[15] Daniel Morgan to Nathanael Greene, January 19, 1781, in Graham, *Morgan*, 468-469; Babits, *Whipping*, 106-123; Bass, *Green Dragoon*, 156-158; Lumpkin, *Savannah to Yorktown*, 130; Tarleton, *Campaigns*, 216-217.

[16] Edward Stevens to Thomas Jefferson, January 24, 1781, in Boyd (ed.), *Papers of Jefferson*, IV, 441; Graham, *Morgan*, 303; Ward, *War of the Revolution*, II, 761; Daniel Morgan to Nathanael Greene, January 19, 1781, in Showman (ed.), *Papers of Greene*, VII, 154; Uhlendorf (ed.), *Revolution in America*, 458; Young, "Memoir," *The Orion*, III, No. 3, 100; Babits, *Whipping*, 126-127. Babits' research clearly documents the second cavalry clash after Washington defeated the 17th British Light Dragoons, and this was also affirmed by Urwin, *United States Cavalry*, 26. Based mostly on the accounts of three officers present (Howard, Simmons and Young), the author of this biography also concluded that there was a second clash, and that Washington defeated a force of British Legion Dragoons at a critical point in the battle. See Stephen E. Haller, *William Washington: Cavalryman of the Revolution* (Oxford, Ohio: Miami University Masters Thesis, 1975), 69-70.

[17] Colonel Howard's Notes, in Henry Lee, *Campaign of 1781 in the Carolinas* (Philadelphia, Bradford and Inskeep, 1824), 97-98; Quoted in Greene, *Life of Greene*, III, 146; O'Neal (ed.), "Memoir of McJunkin," 38-39.

[18] Daniel Morgan to Nathanael Greene, January 19, 1781, in Graham, *Morgan*, 468-469; "Journal of Lieutenant Thomas Anderson of the Delaware Regiment, 1780-1782," *The Historical Magazine*, I (April 1867), 209; Bass, *Green Dragoon*, 158; Tarleton, *Campaigns*, 217-218; Uhlendorf (ed.), *Revolution in America*, 415; Ward, *Delaware Continentals*, 378; Young, "Memoir," *The Orion*, III, No. 3, 101; Lee, *Campaign of 1781*, viii-ix.

[19] Balch (ed.), *Maryland Line*, 46; Bass, *Green Dragoon*, 158-159; Tarleton, *Campaigns*, 218; Lumpkin, *Savannah to Yorktown*, 130;

Roderick MacKenzie, *Strictures on Lieutenant Colonel Tarleton's History* (Cornhill: Printed for the Author, 1787), 91 and 100; Ripley, *Battleground*, 136; Wilcox (ed.), *Clinton's Narrative*, 247; Fortesque, *History of the British Army*, III, 368-369.

[20] Babits, *Whipping*, 129-133; Bass, *Green Dragoon*, 159-160; Graham, *Morgan*, 306-308; Don Higgenbotham, *Daniel Morgan: Revolutionary Rifleman* (Chapel Hill: University of North Carolina Press, 1961), 141; Johnson (ed.), *Traditions and Reminiscences*, 303; Lee, *Campaign of 1781*, 95-96; Hugh McCall, *The History of Georgia* (Atlanta: A. B. Caldwell, 1909 reprint of original 1811 edition), 508-509; John Marshall, *The Life of George Washington* (Fredericksburg: Citizens Guild, 1926 reprint of the original 1805 edition), IV, 347; Moss, *Patriots at Cowpens*, 48; Rankin, *Campaign in the Carolinas*, 38; Uhlendorf (ed.), *Revolution in America*, 415; Warley, *Oration*, 11-12; Young, "Memoir," *The Orion*, III, No. 3, 102.

[21] Nathanael Greene to Henry Lee, January 26, 1781, in Showman (ed.), *Papers of Greene*, VII, 203; Order, March 9, 1781, in Ford (ed.), *Journals of Congress*, XIX, 247.

[22] Edgar (ed.), *Biographical Directory*, I, Ellet, *Women*, I, 89; Mabel L. Webber (comp.), "Death Notices from the South Carolina and American General Gazette, and its Continuation, The Royal Gazette," *The South Carolina Historical and Genealogical Magazine*, XVII, No. 4 (October 1916), 157; Bass, *Green Dragoon*, 163-164; Treacy, *Prelude*, 112-114; Ward, *War of the Revolution*, II, 763-764.

[23] Daniel Morgan to Nathanael Greene, January 23, 1781, in Showman (ed.), *Papers of Greene*, VII, 178; Treacy, *Prelude*, 117-119; Ward, *War of the Revolution*, II, 765; Weigley, *Partisan War*, 34-35.

[24] Nathanael Greene to Henry Lee and Anthony White, January 26, 1781, in Showman (ed.), *Papers of Greene*, VII, 203.

[25] Nathanael Greene to Anthony White, January 30, 1781 and to John Lutterell, January 31, 1781, in Showman (ed.), *Papers of Greene*, VII, 221-222 and 227; Graham, *Morgan*, 289-312; Thayer, *Greene*, 310-315; Treacy, *Prelude*, 125-140; Ward, *War of the Revolution*, II, 766-772; Weigley, *Partisan War*, 36-37; Ichabod Burnet to Henry Lee, February 2, 1781, in Showman (ed.), *Papers of Greene*, VII, 234.

[26] Information on the "Race to the Dan" is from Buchanan, *Road to Guilford*, 334-358; Dupuy, *Compact History*, 389-394; Lumpkin, *Savannah to Yorktown*, 163-168; Morrill, *Southern Campaigns*, 135-144; Pancake, *Destructive War*, 141-171; Rankin, *Campaign in the Carolinas*, 40-56; Thayer, *Greene*, 316-320; Treacy, *Prelude*, 143-153; Ward, *War of the Revolution*, II, 770-776; Weigley, *Partisan War*, 34-41; Schenck, *Invasion of the Carolinas*, 226-292.

[27] Nathanael Greene to George Washington, February 9, 1781, in Showman (ed.), *Papers of Greene*, VII, 268; Johnson, *Greene*, I, 462; Lee, *Memoirs*, I, 588.

[28] Seymour, "Journal," 17; Nathanael Greene to William Washington, February 16 and 17, 1781, MS, Greene Papers, Library of Congress; Nathanael Greene to the North Carolina Legislature, February 15, to Henry Lee, February 17, 1781, to William Washington, February 16 and 17, 1781, to Robert Lawson and Baron von Steuben, February 18, 1781, and Thomas Jefferson to Nathanael Greene, February 19, 1781, in Showman (ed.), *Papers of Greene*, VII, 291 and 298, 301-302, 305, 310-311, and 317; Johnson, *Greene*, I, 434 and 449.

[29] Thayer, *Greene*, 321-323; Treacy, *Prelude*, 160-163; Ward, *War of the Revolution*, II, 777-779; Lee, *Memoirs*, II, 311.

[30] William A. Graham (ed.), *General Joseph Graham and his Papers on North Carolina Revolutionary History* (Raleigh: Edwards & Broughton, 1904), 52, 329, and 341; Otho Williams to Nathanael Greene, March 1, 1781, in Showman (ed.), *Papers of Greene*, VII, 378-379; Tarleton, *Campaigns*, 235; Thayer, *Greene*, 324-325; Treacy, *Prelude*, 164-165; Ward, *War of the Revolution*, II, 780-781.

[31] Graham (ed.), *General Joseph Graham*, 54 and 342-346; Treacy, *Prelude*, 167; Ward, *War of the Revolution*, II, 781; Otho Williams to Nathanael Greene, March 7 and 8, 1781, in Showman (ed.), *Papers of Greene*, VII, 407 and 413-414; Charles Magill to Thomas Jefferson, March 10, 1781, in Boyd (ed.), *Papers of Jefferson*, V, 94.

[32] Nathanael Greene to William Washington, March 9, 1781, MS, Nathanael Greene Collection, William L. Clements Library, Ann Arbor, Michigan.

[33] Charles Magill to Thomas Jefferson, March 10, 1781, in Boyd (ed.), *Papers of Jefferson*, V, 115; March 10, 1781 entry, in Joseph Brown Turner (ed.), *The Journal and Order Book of Captain Robert Kirkwood* (Wilmington: The Historical Society of Delaware, 1910), 14; Treacy, *Prelude*, 173; Ward, *War of the Revolution*, II, 783-785; Nathanael Greene to Henry Lee, March 9 and 10, 1781 and to Baron von Steuben, March 11, 1781, and William Washington to Nathanael Greene, March 11 and 14, 1781, in Showman (ed.), *Papers of Greene*, VII, 415, 421, 427, 428 and 431; Nathanael Greene to William Washington, March 13, 1781, and William Washington to Nathanael Greene, March 13, 1781, MS, Greene Collection, Clements Library; St. George Tucker to his Wife, March 13, 1781, in Charles Washington Coleman, Jr. (ed.), "The Southern Campaigns, 1781 From Guilford Court House to the Siege of York," *The Magazine of American History*, VII (1881), 39.

[34] Information on the Battle of Guilford Court House is from Thomas E. Baker, *Another Such Victory: The Story of the American defeat at Guilford Courthouse that helped win the War for Independence* (New York: Eastern Acorn Press, 1981), 28-86; Buchanan, *Road to Guilford*, 359-383; Dupuy, *Compact History*, 394-404; Lumpkin, *Savannah to Yorktown*, 169-175; Morrill, *Southern Campaigns*, 145-157; Pancake, *Destructive War*, 172-186; Rankin, *Campaign in the Carolinas*, 64-69; Courtland T. Reid, *Guilford Courthouse National Military Park, North Carolina* (Washington, D.C.: National Park Service, 1959); Treacy, *Prelude*, 177-188; Ward, *War of the Revolution*, II, 784-794; Wood, *Battles*, 227-256; Schenck, *Invasion of the Carolinas*, 293-398.

[35] The performance of these troops is an unsolved controversy of this battle, but the most balanced account is in Treacy, *Prelude*, 181-183; Lee, *Memoirs*, II, 245; and Nathanael Greene to Samuel Huntington, March 16, 1781, in Showman (ed.), *Papers of Greene*, VII, 433-435; A. A. Gunby, *Colonel John Gunby of the Maryland Line* (Cincinnati: Robert Clarke Company, 1902), 54; Seymour, "Journal," 20; Schenck, *Invasion of the Carolinas*, 335-358.

[36] Thomas E. Baker, *The Monuments at Guilford Courthouse National Military Park* (Greensboro, North Carolina: National Park Service, 1991), 72-75; Charles Cornwallis to Lord Germain, March 17, 1781, in Clark (ed.), *State Records of North Carolina*, XVII, 1004; Fred J. Cook, "Francisco the Incredible," *American Heritage*, X, (October 1959), 92-

93; William Henry Foote (ed.), *Sketches of North Carolina, Historical and Biographical* (New York: Robert Carter, 1846), 278; Fortesque, *History of the British Army*, III, 377-378; Gunby, *Colonel John Gunby*, 50-52 and 57; Lee, *Campaign of 1781*, 174-175; Lee, *Memoirs*, II, 245; Seymour, "Journal," 21; Tarleton, *Campaigns*, 274; Uhlendorf (ed.), *Revolution in America*, 427; Charles Cornwallis to George Germain, March 17, 1781, in *Clinton's Narrative*, 499; Nathanael Greene to Samuel Huntington, March 16, 1781, in Showman (ed.), *Papers of Greene*, VII, 433-435.

[37] Balch (ed.), *Maryland Line*, 51; Johnson, *Greene*, II, 12; Lee, *Memoirs*, I, 348; Warley, *Oration*, 13.

[38] Nathanael Greene to Joseph Reed, March 18, 1781, in William Bradford Reed (ed.), *The Life of Joseph Reed* (Philadelphia: Lindsay and Blakiston, 1847), II, 350; Return of the Killed and Wounded at Guilford Court House, MS, Greene Papers, Library of Congress; Thomas Jefferson to President of Congress and others, March 21, 1781, in McIlwaine (ed.), *Letters of Jefferson*, 421; Return of Losses at Guilford Court House by Otho H. Williams, March 17, 1781, in *The (Charleston) Royal Gazette*, Wednesday, May 23, 1781, 2.

[39] Nathanael Pendleton to William Washington, March 17, 1781 and Greene to Henry Lee, March 21 and 22, 1781, in Showman (ed.), *Papers of Greene*, VII, 445, 457, and 461; Lee, *Campaign of 1781*, 218; Rankin, *Campaign in the Carolinas*, 80-84; Thayer, *Greene*, 330-331; Treacy, *Prelude*, 189-201; Ward, *War of the Revolution*, II, 795-797.

[40] Seymour, "Journal," 22; Resolved, Virginia House of Delegates, March 7 and 17, 1781, MS, Greene Papers, Library of Congress; Thayer, *Greene*, 338-339; Richard Call to Thomas Jefferson, March 29, 1781, in Boyd (ed.), *Papers of Jefferson*, V, 274-275; Nathanael Greene to the Board of War, April 4, 1781, to Henry Lee, April 12, 1781, and to Baron von Steuben, April 15, 1781, in Dennis M. Conrad (ed.), *The Papers of Nathanael Greene, Vol. VIII: 30 March 1781 - 10 July 1781* (Chapel Hill: University of North Carolina Press, 1995), 45, 86, and 99.

[41] Johnson, *Greene*, II, 42; Washington, "William Washington," 101; Fortesque, *History of the British Army*, III, 363-364.

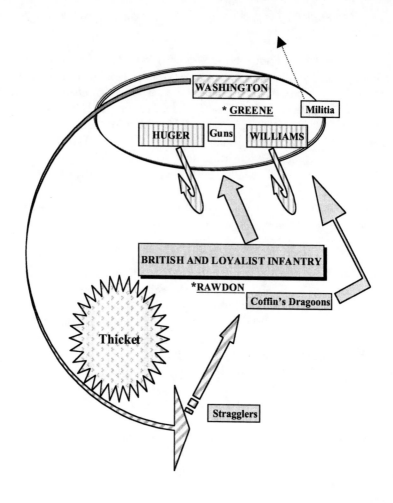

MAP 5
BATTLE OF HOBKIRK'S HILL
APRIL 25, 1781

chapter V

THE LAST CHARGES:
Hobkirk's Hill And Eutaw Springs

Only a few hundred militia rallied to Greene's main army after the Battle of Guilford Court House, but he sent them home because their enlistments were about to expire. Thus, when the general broke camp at Ramsey's Mill on April 7, 1781 to re-enter South Carolina, he commanded fewer than 1,500 men, most of whom were regulars. A day earlier, he had detached Lee's Legion and a company of Maryland infantry with an artillery piece to join forces with Francis Marion, who was operating along the Pee Dee River.

Lieutenant Colonel Francis Lord Rawdon, the British commander in the Carolinas after Cornwallis marched into Virginia, had about 8,000 British regulars and Tory veterans at his disposal. However, most of these troops were scattered throughout South Carolina and Georgia defending the numerous posts that the British had established in 1780. The partisan operations of Marion, Sumter and Pickens had forced the British to garrison these positions in strength, which left very few units available for active field duty. Greene hoped to coordinate the partisan bands with his army to eliminate the enemy posts piecemeal.[1]

By April 17, Greene was waiting for Lee, Marion and Sumter to join him at Lynch's Creek several miles north of the strong British post at Camden, South Carolina. Lee and Marion had recently reduced the British outpost at Fort Watson and were maneuvering against a force of 500 British and Tories led by

Lieutenant Colonel John Watson. Sumter, on the other hand, simply ignored Greene and went his own arrogant way for the time being. Too weak to mount a direct assault on Camden, Greene took up a strong position on Hobkirk's Hill a few miles north of the post. He then sent Kirkwood's Delaware infantry into nearby Logtown to skirmish with out-posted British and Tory troops and keep an eye on Camden.

William Washington joined Kirkwood on the 20th, leading fewer than 60 of his dragoons. Although there were 87 dragoons in William's corps at this time, shortages of horses and equipment permitted only 56 of the troopers to be mounted and ready for action. Hoping to double the number of dragoons, Greene had previously requested Anthony White in Virginia to send two officers and clothing for 50 men recently recruited from the Virginia infantry to be trained as cavalrymen. Given Tarleton's presence in Virginia, there was little response from White. The desperate general also instructed Lee and Sumter to secure more cavalry horses and at the same time deprive the enemy of dragoon and wagon horses. Nonetheless, Washington and Kirkwood launched a daring raid on April 21 around the western side of Camden, where they burned a fortified house and redoubt near the Wateree River. They also captured more than 50 cattle and 40 horses, all of which were desperately needed by Greene's ragged army.[2]

Hobkirk's Hill

This action, along with Rawdon's fears that Camden might be surrounded and reduced, convinced the British commander to risk an attack on the numerically superior Americans. On the 25th, he sallied out of Camden with 900 British and Tory troops, hoping to surprise the 1,500 Americans. He wanted to drive them from their menacing position on Hobkirk's Hill before local militia reinforced them and especially before their artillery arrived. The superior American cavalry and the partisans hampered his intelligence, so he believed the guns had not yet come up.

"Hobkirk's Hill: Charge of Colonel Washington's Cavalry" *by F.C. Yohn*

The battle opened when the Americans were initially surprised at breakfast when the large British column was first sighted.   Kirkwood, who commanded the pickets several hundred yards in front of Hobkirk's Hill, conducted a gallant delaying action that gave Greene time to form his army in an excellent position along the contours of the hill.   General Huger's 550-man Virginia Brigade of two Continental infantry regiments under Colonels Richard Campbell and Samuel Hawes was to the right of the road that bisected the hill.   On the left of the road, Colonel Williams commanded his 550-man Maryland Brigade of two Continental infantry regiments under Colonel John Gunby and Lieutenant Colonel Benjamin Ford. Colonel Charles Harrison's Virginia Artillery (i.e., the recently arrived 1st Continental Artillery), brought up three 6-pounders on the road between the two infantry brigades.   Moreover, the infantry intentionally screened the guns from Rawdon's view for some time.   Washington's under-strength corps of fifty dragoons and Colonel Jesse Read's North Carolina militia comprised the reserve directly behind the Marylanders. Kirkwood's hard-pressed Delaware infantry joined the reserve once the main American battle line was formed.

Rawdon approached the hill from the southeast and initially deployed his men into three lines.   The first line consisted of the King's Americans, the New York Volunteers, and the British 63rd Foot, in all about 400 infantry.   The second line of about 300 infantry consisted of the Convalescents and the Volunteers of Ireland.   His third line was composed of about 200 cavalry and infantry from South Carolina and New York.   Major John Coffin, an able cavalry commander, led the mounted portion of this reserve.[3]

Greene quickly observed that the British front was much narrower than his own and could be enveloped.   Instead of waiting for the British to attack him (uphill!), he unmasked his cannon and ordered the infantry to attack all along the line. He also sent Washington far around the enemy left flank to gain their rear.   The galling artillery barrage surprised Rawdon, since he still believed their guns had not yet arrived in the American camp.   He soon realized an error in his formation and quickly brought his second line up to the first so as to present a wider front just as the Americans closed for the close-in fighting.

Initially, the Americans were successful in stunning the British line by the sheer weight of their downhill charge against the thin red line. After delivering a volley and charging with the bayonet, they were on the verge of overwhelming Rawdon. However, the sudden death of an officer in Gunby's Maryland regiment caused an unexpected panic among the troops in the unit and Gunby ordered a temporary withdrawal to regroup. When Colonel Ford was also killed, his Marylanders panicked, and the entire American left flank collapsed. Chaos then spread to the Virginians, and Campbell's regiment also broke and ran at the sight of the retreating Marylanders. Only Hawes' Virginians, Kirkwood's Delaware infantry and Read's North Carolinians remained to fight and thereby cover the rear of Greene's now retreating army! The victorious British and Tories surged up the hill, and Major Coffin's Tory dragoons captured Harrison's artillery pieces.

Meanwhile, Washington had been unable to penetrate a dense thicket to the left rear of the enemy line at the critical time of Greene's charge, and he had to take a much longer route to gain the British rear. When he finally did so, he arrived in the midst of the British rear elements, consisting mainly of medical and service personnel and a number of troops who had fled from the initial American artillery fire (see Map #5 emphasizing Washington's action). Motivated by his more humane nature, he chose not to simply ride down and saber these defenseless people. He took as many prisoners as his men could manage by pulling them up on the horses behind them. Thus burdened, the American dragoons nonetheless advanced on the scene of the main battle. When Washington saw that his comrades were losing the battle, he quickly paroled all of the prisoners except four of the surgeons. Again he could have sabered the prisoners as many other commanders might have done in this often-savage war. He finally rushed to help cover the American retreat and immediately charged Coffin's cavalry. His dragoons routed the

Tories and rescued the precious American artillery pieces by dragging them away behind some of their own horses. William's corps then joined the other units covering the American retreat. This action enabled Greene to rally most of his men a few miles north of the hill and once again keep his army intact.

An American participant wrote to "Light Horse Harry" Lee that although "many of our troops behaved infamously...Col Washington made a timely charge and cut down a number of them [the enemy] besides taking about 40 prisoners." Otho Williams described William's efforts in a letter two days after the battle: "The cavalry led on by Washington behaved in a manner truly heroic. They charged the British Army in the rear, took a great number of prisoners, sent many of them off with small detachments, and when he saw we were turning our backs upon victory in front, by a circuitous manoeuvre, he threw his dragoons into our rear, passed the lines, and charged the York Volunteers (a fine corps of cavalry), killed a number, and drove the rest out of the field. Washington is an elegant officer; his reputation is deservedly great."[4]

Each army lost about 250 men killed and wounded in the Battle of Hobkirk's Hill. Although Rawdon clearly won a tactical victory by driving Greene from the battlefield, his losses forced him to return to the safety of Camden's stockade walls and earth works. Greene blamed Gunby for the defeat and had him court-martialed. The court—comprised of Huger, Harrison and Washington—commended Gunby's spirit but condemned his order to retire as "the only cause why we did not obtain a complete victory." When he attempted to follow Greene's order to turn the enemy's flank and charge their rear, Washington's time-consuming action among the enemy non-combatants may also have contributed somewhat to the American reverse. However, Greene insisted that William and his men "acquired no inconsiderable share of the honour" and that his "behavior and that of his Regiment upon this occasion did them the highest honor" in the battle. Colonel Howard, who had shared the Cowpens laurels with him, later explained this part of the Hobkirk's Hill battle, "I assert, upon the authority of Washington himself, that Greene's statement is correct. No *officer was less liable to boast than Washington, nor was there one whose veracity could be less doubted.* He did penetrate into the enemy's rear, and found them flying in confusion...found some wounded, and others without wounds, making their escape. They said, in excuse, that their army was beaten." Lord Rawdon also acknowledged that Washington's presence prevented him from exploiting his victory over Greene's infantry.[5] The American general's favorable opinion of his dependable cavalry commander was probably influenced by William's efforts at the end of the battle and his brilliant success the following day.

Young Washington returned to the battlefield the very next morning to scout the British position and determine if Rawdon intended to remain in the field and pursue the Americans. He also hoped to rescue any wounded Americans left behind. He advanced a few dragoons within sight of Camden and enticed Coffin to sally out with his 40 cavalry to catch what appeared to him to be a scouting party. He hoped to even the score with his enemy for the defeat at the close of the previous battle. The Americans feigned a hasty retreat, drawing Coffin and his men down a road bordered by dense brush and trees. Washington's men, who were concealed in ambush along both sides of the road, charged the Tories in the flank as they rode by. The ambush was a complete success. William's troopers were experienced at this type of warfare and they killed 20 Tories and chased Coffin and the survivors back to the gates of Camden. The loss of over half of his cavalry further discouraged Rawdon from offensive operations at this time. Greene exclaimed to "Light Horse Harry" Lee that "Col. Washington never shone upon any occasion more than this [Hobkirk's Hill and following action]...in the course of the day [he] made several charges, and cut to pieces their dragoons."[6]

Greene regrouped his army and encamped at Rugeley's Mill until May 3, when he decided to assist Marion and Lee in their attempts to cut off Watson's detachment before it could return to Camden. Washington and Kirkwood attacked on the south side of the Wateree River opposite Camden, and on the 4th seized and burned a redoubt consisting of a house and fortification. However, Greene's attempt to cut off Watson failed, and that officer's force marched unharmed into Camden as welcome reinforcements on the 7th.

Dispirited and disgusted after the Battle of Hobkirk's Hill, Greene again considered his situation desperate. He wrote von Steuben that the dragoons were "much broken down...ruin will follow if attacked with superior [British] horses." This shortage of horses in the main army almost resulted in a personal rift between Marion and Greene. The American general had long begged the "Swamp Fox" for help in turning over horses captured from the British and Tories to Washington and Lee. He asked the partisan to "Get all the good dragoon horses you can to mount our Cavalry...This is a great object and I beg your attention to it." In early May, Lee informed the general that he believed Marion's raiders were hoarding about 150 spare horses as their personal plunder. On the 4th, Greene accused Marion of permitting his men to plunder the countryside solely for the purpose of rewarding them. He also demanded that any extra horses be immediately turned over to the regular cavalry. Marion was infuriated and he threatened to resign, asserting that his men needed all of the horses they captured. If forced to give them up, he asserted that his mounted partisans would soon disband. Greene, somewhat embarrassed and probably more inclined to believe Marion than the occasionally bombastic Lee, apologized to this invaluable South Carolina partisan leader. Apparently, both Marion and Sumter believed that Washington and Lee were quite capable of procuring their own horses. It did not help matters that horses were virtually unavailable from Virginia, now that Tarleton's Dragoons and Colonel John Simcoe's Queen's Rangers were raiding that state's horse farms with impunity.[7]

Rawdon's situation at Camden was considerably worse than Greene's, however. His exhausted garrison troops and their depleted units were not fit for a grueling summer campaign against the dispersed, mobile forces of Greene, Marion, Lee, Sumter and Pickens, all of whom threatened his supply lines from Charleston. In addition, Coffin could muster only a small troop of cavalry after his two earlier encounters with William Washington at Hobkirk's Hill.

On May 8, Rawdon again made a lunge at what he thought was Greene's army near Sawney's Creek, but his prey had eluded him. Washington and Kirkwood put on an impressive show, acting as a diversion. A North Carolina militia officer later described Washington's performance as the rear guard, "where his [Rawdon's] advanced troops met our strong pickets and Colonel Washington's cavalry (always their terror) judiciously posted. Instantly a handsome firing took place. Lord Rawdon paused, examined with caution the ground his adversary occupied, Washington keeping himself raised in his stirrups, watching the exact moment when to strike with the saber his quondam friend Major Coffin, with the British cavalry in view." The two main armies never clashed, and Rawdon eventually marched back to Camden.

On May 10, Washington and Kirkwood returned to Camden on another reconnaissance in force only to discover that Rawdon had evacuated his army and was marching to relieve Fort Motte. Marion and Lee besieged that post, and it surrendered on the 11th—only a few hours before Rawdon's trudging relief column arrived. The Americans escaped with the garrison as prisoners, leaving Rawdon and his men exhausted and even more frustrated than ever. On the same day, Sumter and his partisan corps captured the British post at Orangeburg. On the 13th, Lee seized Fort Granby and Marion took Georgetown. After his success at Granby, Lee marched into Georgia and captured Augusta from the British and Tories. While Rawdon reeled in confusion at these strokes, he was unable to react forcefully with his small field force. The rapid reduction of Rawdon's outposts continued and Greene seized this opportunity to march his army into western South Carolina and force the evacuation or surrender of the last remaining British stronghold beyond Charleston's environs—Fort Ninety Six.[8]

Ninety Six

Greene began his march toward Ninety Six on May 15, shortly after Rawdon headed for Charleston in hopes of raising a more effective field army.   He also received word from Lafayette and von Steuben in Virginia that White's small band of 30 to 60 dragoons was desperately needed there to counter Tarleton and Simcoe "who have seized every horse he [Tarleton] would come across." Greene bitterly responded to Lafayette about the preponderance of well-mounted enemy cavalry now ravaging that state, observing that Virginia's "Inhabitants appear to be not less attached to their horses than their liberties and this attachment has embarrassed the Legislature exceedingly."   William Davie even remarked to Greene in amazement that "for a while they fondly hoped that Washington or Lee might have been spared to their assistance." Josiah Parker lamented to Greene that Tarleton had "so many fine horses tis almost impossible to say where his career will end."   Greene, however, pressed on toward his objective of reducing the British posts in South Carolina.   William Washington's cavalry and Robert Kirkwood's Delaware infantrymen formed his army's advanced guard as they marched for Ninety Six.   When they approached the fort on May 21, these enterprising officers ambushed a small party of Tories, killing four and capturing six.[9]

Greene opened a formal siege of Ninety Six the next day, but Tory Colonel John Cruger led his 500 men in such a stubborn defense against the 1,000 Americans that a stalemate resulted until mid-June.   Although Greene had field artillery, these light guns were not adequate to reduce the walls of a fort in a siege.   After capturing Augusta, Lee marched to reinforce Greene's position, arriving on June 8.   Greene then renewed active siege operations in earnest after learning from an express captured by Washington's dragoons that Rawdon was marching from Charleston with a large relief column.   The American commander detached Washington with his own dragoons and the cavalry of Lee's Legion to join forces with

Sumter and Marion to do everything in their power to delay Rawdon.

From June 14th through the 17th, Greene and Sumter exchanged numerous messages regarding the whereabouts of Rawdon's relief column, which now included a fresh cavalry force under Coffin comprised of 150 men recruited from the Royal South Carolina Regiment.   Sumter and Washington could do little more than shadow Rawdon's superior force, even though Sumter augmented William's regulars with 200 South Carolina State dragoons and mounted infantry.   Over the next several days of close fighting, Greene and Lee almost forced the fort's surrender, but the Americans had to give up on the 19th, when William Washington sent word that he and Sumter could not delay Rawdon's powerful army: "The enemy was moving this morning about 10 o'clock two Miles this side of the little Saluda...their Force is near twenty-five Hundred Men."[10]

Greene gathered his troops and immediately set out for Charlotte, North Carolina, determined to put as many rivers as possible between his weak army and Rawdon's fresh corps (as he had done when he faced Cornwallis four months earlier). Washington, Lee and Kirkwood provided the rear guard for the army.   By the 24th, the Americans had crossed the Saluda, Enoree, Tiger and Broad Rivers.   Rawdon, satisfied to rescue Cruger, abandoned his pursuit of Greene at the Enoree River and returned to Ninety Six.   His men now exhausted by the frustrating mid-summer march, he decided to abandon the post and return to Charleston.   Taking no chances, he also ordered British Lieutenant Colonel Alexander Stewart to march his newly arrived troops out of the city to meet him. When Greene learned of Rawdon's withdrawal from the interior, he returned to South Carolina and headed toward the Congaree River to resume operations against the British. While Lee and Kirkwood shadowed the front of Rawdon's column, Washington, Marion and Sumter rode ahead to interdict communications between the slower moving columns of Stewart and Rawdon.   To no avail, Greene also encouraged other commanders in the field to assist Washington in cutting off Stewart's isolated force in early July. Desperate to inflict losses on the British, Greene at one point joined most of the cavalry under his personal command to ambush Stewart. Washington strongly advocated bringing the entire army up to attack Rawdon's weaker and more fatigued force rather than chasing Stewart with mounted troops alone, "I believe Col. Lee is mistaken with respect to his numbers...their [Rawdon's] number from one thousand to twelve hundred...they have about eighty Cavalry in horrid order. I think his Lordship will run away or lose his Army if not reinforced." Greene followed Lee's advice, and Stewart eluded his pursuers. Greene's attempts to coordinate the movements of so many detachments made it impossible to prevent his enemies' junction, and the two British columns met at Orangeburg on July 10.[11]

Greene quickly reassembled his exhausted, hungry army at Beaver Creek on the 10th, and he wisely decided to encamp in the High Hills of Santee for a rest during the hot months of July and August. The partisans and light troops kept the field for a time, however. They harassed Rawdon's outposts and foraging parties near Charleston in what later became known as the "Dog Days" expeditions.

Washington's men also had to continue the campaign in spite of their worn out uniforms. In one of Greene's dispatches to Lafayette about the need for increasing both of their respective cavalry forces, the general noted that "Washington's Regiment is in distress for want of Cloathing and every necessary, and is of itself very small." Greene also observed that "Virginia certainly is able to complete one Regiment; and if after the scourging she has had [by Tarleton's Dragoons freshly mounted on Virginia horses], she neglects to do it, she will suffer unpitied in future." Even his appeals to local South Carolina Militia officers produced little assistance at this time. Nonetheless, William spent most of the last two weeks of July shadowing Stewart's command at Orangeburg after Rawdon returned to Charleston with a small force. Anticipating the possibility that Stewart might fortify Orangeburg, Washington destroyed local mills and otherwise succeeded in depriving the British of forage and supplies. In one message to Greene,

William declared that if Stewart moved he would "send immediate word," but in reference to his own supply situation he added that he would need "a few sheets of paper" to do so.[12]

In two engagements before returning to the main army encampment in late July and early August, Washington's cavalry captured 50 prisoners and disrupted most British and Tory communications around Charleston. One of his raids took him along the banks of the Cooper River, and his cavalry and Kirkwood's infantry frustrated a British foray out of Orangeburg towards McCord's Ferry on the Congaree River by moving all boats to the opposite bank. By July 30, he observed that the British had evacuated Orangeburg, leaving about 300 sick and wounded behind. However, the American cavalry had become exhausted from the strenuous campaign. Moreover, von Steuben's belated promise of 60 horses awaiting the cavalry in distant Charlottesville, Virginia was of little consolation.

Greene took the time to praise his small cavalry forces in a letter to Anthony Wayne in late July, exclaiming that "Colonels Lee and Washington are the heroes of the South and bear down all before them." He singled out William again on August 6 for inflicting forty casualties on the enemy's cavalry forces, remarking that "The enterprise of our cavalry equals any thing the world ever produced." The American cavalry continued to harass enemy foraging parties until the British pulled in all detachments and concentrated their forces at Eutaw Springs by the end of the month. Illness also plagued William's command; one of his officers, for example, had to return to Virginia because of sickness.[13]

Washington's corps continued to operate effectively with Lee, Sumter, Marion, Wade Hampton and Peter Horry in raids up to the very outskirts of Charleston. Also at this time, William was close enough to Sandy Hill to attempt a reunion with his beloved Jane. No doubt he made every effort to pay her at least one brief visit, if Jane and her widowed stepmother were in fact staying at Sandy Hill.

His health broken by the exhausting and fruitless early summer campaign, Lord Rawdon had to return to England on July 20 to recuperate. He left Lieutenant Colonels Nisbet,

Balfour and Stewart in command of the British and Tory forces in Charleston and its immediate vicinity. These two officers concentrated on supplying their garrison in July and August, rather than fielding an army. At the same time, Greene anxiously waited for more reinforcements from Virginia. Governor Jefferson was understandably reluctant to release men or supplies promised to Greene at this time, because of Cornwallis' presence in his state. An exasperated Greene desperately also pleaded with the Board of War in Philadelphia, offering a detailed and revealing description of William's regiment at this time:

> The deplorable situation which the Third Regiment of Cavalry are in for want of cloathing...Saddles and bridles, the importance they are of in the Southern operations; the certainty of their being rendered totally unfit for duty in a short time without a new supply of the above articles, has induced me to send Capt. Swan to solicit the board to have an immediate supply provided and for him to take measures to get them forward with all possible dispatch...All of the Cavalry furniture that was provided at Baltimore for the Southern Army has been stopped in Virginia and I am told given to the Volunteer horse...Col Washington had a report lately from his quarter Master...who was sent to Philadelphia to procure supplies that he had not the smallest prospect of procurring the articles he was instructed to provide. Nothing can distress us so much as the failure of our Cavalry."

Not until Thomas Nelson replaced Jefferson as governor and Cornwallis withdrew to Yorktown, did Greene again receive any assistance from Virginia. Lafayette hoped for a time that White's 200 men and horses could take the field, but a lack of clothing and accouterments prevented it. Washington's officer in Virginia, Major Call, also had authority in August to impress 200 horses. However, the other officers (no doubt including the lackluster White) who were there estimated it would be "two months" before horses, recruits and accouterments would move south! In spite of these circumstances, Greene built his army up to more than 2,000 comparatively experienced and well-rested troops by the end of August.[14]

While Greene's army was still encamped in the High Hills of Santee, Balfour ordered the execution of Isaac Hayne, an American militia colonel who had broken an allegedly forced oath of allegiance not to fight the British.   Greene and his officers were outraged, and for a time considered retaliating by hanging the next high-ranking British officer they captured. William Washington was particularly incensed and he became a spokesman for Greene's officers, urging some strong action on his part for "that sanguinary Step...unjustifiable upon any Principle of Justice...I can find no security from being subject to a similar Fate if the Fortunes of War should throw them [his fellow officers] into their Hands...[and that retaliation] is the only argument that will avail with Men whose Minds are callous to every Sentiment of Humanity."   Other events soon overshadowed the incident when Stewart marched a sizable army out of Charleston.   By August 23, he had moved his army to Eutaw Springs, but Greene's numerically superior cavalry forces "allowed him no rest night or day, continually hanging about them and harassing them, for their Cavalry is almost entirely destroyed."   In a dispatch to Congress, Greene wrote: "The Corps of Horse under Lt. Colos Washington and Lee have at different times since I wrote you last, taken 30 and 40 Prisoners, and killed and Wounded a number more, the greatest part of the whole were Cavalry."   In a remarkable incident on August 31, an American officer found eight wagonloads of clothing in Charlotte, North Carolina sent from Philadelphia for Washington's regiment.   The contractor would not venture beyond Charlotte, and Greene's officer discovered that the vests, leather breeches, boots and socks were too damaged for use.   He told Greene that he would bring the remaining items forward.[15]   Within the week, Greene brought his entire army up and prepared to attack Stewart in what would be the final pitched battle for South Carolina.

Eutaw Springs

On the warm morning of September 8—a day that would become a sweltering summer day—the confident Americans

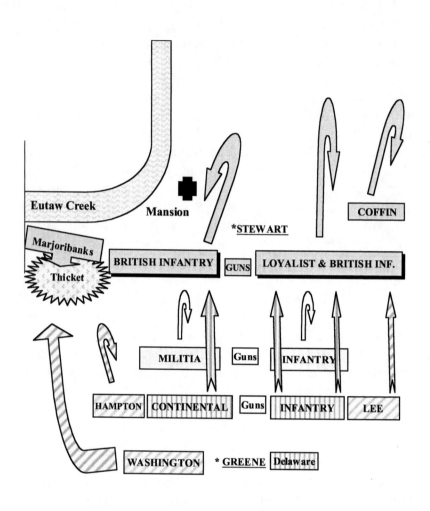

Eutaw Creek

Mansion

*STEWART

COFFIN

Marjoribanks

Thicket

BRITISH INFANTRY   GUNS   LOYALIST & BRITISH INF.

MILITIA   Guns   INFANTRY

HAMPTON   CONTINENTAL   Guns   INFANTRY   LEE

WASHINGTON   * GREENE   Delaware

MAP 6
BATTLE OF EUTAW
SEPTEMBER 7, 1781

marched seven miles from their temporary camp at Burdell's Plantation towards the unsuspecting British. However, Stewart was alerted to the danger when Lee's Legion and Colonel John Henderson's South Carolina light militia infantry attacked Coffin's light troops and stampeded them back to the main army. Sinkler's large brick mansion surrounded by a brick palisade dominated the center of this sparsely wooded battlefield. A road running parallel to the Santee River bisected the mansion grounds east of the building and branched off in two directions, one parallel with the river and the other south to Charleston. The Eutaw Creek flowed into the Santee northwest of the mansion, the area of their junction being densely thicketed with dwarf blackjack oaks and scrub impenetrable on horseback.[16]

After sending a small force of infantry to delay Greene's advance for a time, Stewart deployed his 2,000 British regulars and Tory veterans to the west of the mansion in typical linear formation. Major John Marjoribanks held the extreme right flank with 300 elite infantry comprised of six light infantry and grenadier companies. To his left stood the 3rd British Foot, a large regiment known as the "Buffs" who were newly arrived in America. Cruger's two Tory battalions from Ninety Six with three artillery pieces straddled the road and the veteran 63rd and 64th British Foot formed the left flank. Coffin's regrouped cavalry and light infantry were held in reserve behind the 64th Foot.

Greene's 2,200 regulars, veteran militia and partisan units approached in line of battle from the west on both sides of the road. His first line consisted of about 700 North and South Carolina militia infantry under the very able command of Marion, Pickens and the Marquis de Malmedy. Two 3-pounder artillery pieces bolstered the militiamen. Colonel Williams' Maryland, Campbell's Virginia and Colonel Jethro Sumner's North Carolina regular infantry brigades (Continentals) accompanied by two 6-pounders formed the second line of 1,200 men. Lee's Legion of about 200 cavalry and light infantry held the right flank, and Wade Hampton's 70 South Carolina cavalry and Henderson's 70 South Carolina infantry were on the left. Kirkwood's 100 Delaware infantry and

William Washington's 70-odd dragoons—still riding under Jane Elliott's now famous crimson battle flag—stood in ready reserve along the road behind the army.

The Americans steadily advanced in the mid-morning heat and soon engaged in a fierce exchange of musketry with the British line. To Stewart's astonishment, the enemy militia stood for some time, fighting like regulars. The two American flank detachments attacked the 3rd and 64th Foot in separate actions. Stewart resorted to the always-reliable bayonet charge to finally drive the militia and the American left flank back in disorder. Greene quickly committed Sumner's fresh North Carolina Continentals into the gap, while holding Williams and Campbell back for the decisive strike. When Sumner's men began to fall back after a spirited fight, the British line sensed victory and came on in a disorderly rush. Greene then ordered his regulars from Virginia and Maryland to fire and charge. These veterans met the British and Tories with a devastating volley followed by a successful bayonet attack that put the entire enemy line to flight. But Marjoribanks remained in his flanking position in the thicket, and Greene sent Washington— who it appears from contemporary accounts to perhaps have already joined the fight—to drive this last intact British unit off, while the rest of the Americans pursued the British and Tories past the mansion. Kirkwood's foot soldiers followed Washington's dragoons at some distance.

William, anxious for action and wishing to strike a decisive blow, impetuously galloped through the woods around the American left, hell-bent to close with the enemy. Well ahead of Kirkwood and unaware that Hampton's cavalry was also riding to his support, Washington led his gallant troopers in an unsupported frontal charge against Marjoribanks' excellent defensive position. As the dragoons approached the thicket, William realized that his men would not be able to penetrate it, and therefore ordered his command to wheel by sections to the right and ride for an open space to gain the enemy's rear. Performed within killing distance of the British muskets, this maneuver was disastrous (see Map #6 emphasizing Washington's action). The British, firing enfilade with deadly efficiency, turned this gallant cavalry unit into a screaming, disordered mass of wounded and dying men and horses. Marjoribanks followed up the volley by leading his men out of the thicket in a bold bayonet charge—killing, wounding, or capturing over half of the Americans. The officers were most exposed to the volley and only two of ten survived. Sergeant Major Perry, William's comrade during his personal duel with Tarleton at Cowpens, was wounded five times. The stunned Americans attempted to meet the charging enemy, but to no avail. William's horse was shot, and the animal fell on him and pinned him to the ground. While struggling to escape, one of the charging Redcoats bayoneted him. Only his massive size and the timely intervention of a British officer saved his life. An American participant later described the melee:

> *Washington jumped his horse into the midst of the enemy and was suddenly taken prisoner. A British soldier appearing to be in the posture of attempting to stab Colonel Washington, one of his men rushed forward and cut him down at one blow. Washington being a prisoner, and his men mingled in confusion with the enemy, and not knowing what else to do, this applicant with about twenty-five retreated and left the field.*

Three weeks after the battle, another observer described Washington's capture:

> *He flew to the Militia but not finding the British in the front, concluded that they were urging upon the militia in the rear, he passed thro' these and in a moment was incircled [sic] with the best troops of the British Army; finding it impossible to retreat he resolved to attempt to cut his way thro' the whole British Army; his horse being shot he fell under him and as he fell received a slight wound from a Bayonet; thus incumbered with the weight of his horse he was taken prisoner. One of his Captains were killed and four of his lieutenants wounded.*

Alas, William's luck had run out, and he was made a prisoner of war. The next day Greene commended his cavalry commanders for their "repeated and gallant services" and "instances of Heroism." Marjoribanks soon retreated when Kirkwood's infantry came up. He herded his prisoners and the wounded Washington towards the mansion where another British force had been holding out.[17]

Meanwhile, some of Cruger's Tories had barricaded themselves in the mansion itself during the retreat, and Greene had to draw off many of his regulars to besiege the place. While Lee with his Legion Infantry and Howard's Marylanders attacked the mansion and Kirkwood skirmished with Marjoribanks, the rest of the Americans fell into complete disarray when they discovered and plundered the rich supplies of liquor and food in the abandoned British camp. Greene was at this time preoccupied with the assault on the mansion, and Lee's cavalry was trying to drive Coffin's cavalry from the field. When Marjoribanks arrived near the mansion, he led his disciplined troops in a charge through the milling mob of Americans in the camp. This bold action routed the American infantry and cost Greene the battle (and Marjoribanks his own life). Stewart, who had rallied a number of his fugitive units, returned to the battlefield to claim victory for the British.

The three-hour Battle of Eutaw Springs exacted a horrific toll on both armies—about one-fourth of the Americans and one-third of the British were killed, wounded or missing. Stewart could not afford such losses and remain in the field very far from his safe haven in Charleston and uncertain of re-supply. He soon returned to the city, leaving Greene's army defeated, but still very much intact. Francis Marion wrote Greene on September 11 to complain about Lee's timid pursuit of Stewart, detailing an incident when the American prisoners (including William Washington) were guarded by only 50 or 60 infantry, "but to our astonishment, a retreat was ordered [by Lee]," and when two of Marion's officers requested Lee's permission to make an attempt, they "were peremptorily refused." The American general had once again failed to win a tactical battlefield victory, not unlike the actions at Guilford Court House, Hobkirk's Hill and Ninety Six. But more importantly from a strategic perspective, he inflicted enough irreplaceable losses on the British while preserving his own army to ultimately win the campaign for the Carolinas. In fact, the British now only held four coastal ports in the South: Savannah, Charleston, Wilmington and Yorktown. The war in the South was essentially over, and Cornwallis' surrender at Yorktown on October 19 left only skirmishing and observation duties for Greene's army. Ironically, Tarleton's cavalry career also ended when Cornwallis surrendered at Yorktown, within a few weeks of William Washington's capture at Eutaw Springs. After Cornwallis surrendered at Yorktown, George Lux of Baltimore wrote to Greene lamenting Washington's capture while at the same time criticizing the ubiquitous Anthony White, "especially as Col [White] is not here considered his equal in merit & I am told, he has marched down with a full Corps to join you, adorned with Tarleton's spoils." In a closing remark on the use of cavalry in this war, the British military historian Sir John Fortesque observed, "It is true that Tarleton and, *still more conspicuously, the American Colonel Washington had occasionally wrought great results by the charge of a mere handful of sabres.*"[18]

William remained a British prisoner in Charleston from mid-September, 1781 until December 14, 1782, when the British evacuated the city. On the very evening of the day William was captured at Eutaw, the gallant and dying Major Majoribanks permitted Washington to send the following message to Greene:

> *I have the Misfortune to be a Prisoner of war, I am wounded with a bayonet in my Breast, which together with the Contusion from the fall off my Horse which was killed makes me extremely sore: But I am in hope not dangerous.*
>
> *I shall be extremely obliged to forward the enclosed to Capt. Watts & permit my Cloathing [sic] to be sent in as soon as Possible being informed by Col. Stewart that I am not to be indulg'd with a Parole on any Latitude. I have been treated politely by many of the British officers.*

Stewart also assured Greene that Washington "is in no Danger from the Wound he received in the action of yesterday."[19]

"Battle of Eutaw Springs" after Alonzo Chappel. *Courtesy of South Caroliniana Library*

It appears that Washington was well respected by not only his own, but also by British officers as well. While recovering from his wounds, William was evidently accorded a high degree of trust by both Balfour and Stewart. He was also one of the highest ranking American regular army officers in captivity. Greene was quite anxious to exchange a British officer for his valuable cavalry commander, but the Americans in the Carolinas held no one of high enough rank. The British were aware of their prized prisoner and were for a time concerned about American retaliation for the previous hanging of Colonel Hayne. A Hessian officer observed in October 1781 that rebel newspapers "lament the loss of the wounded and captured Colonel Washington" and "Hence, Colonel Washington and others, will be held as principal hostages [against retaliation for Hayne's execution]."

When Washington had fully recovered by January 1782, General Leslie—the new commander of the Charleston garrison—entrusted him to perform various liaison duties when he needed to negotiate with Greene. Neither side was strong enough to act decisively against the other, and as peace negotiations began in Europe, the war degenerated into occasional skirmishes and mutual observation. Leslie sent Washington to Greene's camp in January as "the bearer of this letter" explaining the status of two American dragoons who may or may not have deserted, for example. Leslie trusted Washington to explain "every matter relative" to the incident. In February, Greene became concerned that Leslie might confine prisoners to James Island, where a large number of Loyalist refugees also resided. He informed Leslie that "Washington says he would sooner go into a Dungeon than take a Parole on that Island in its present situation." Greene's concerns over prisoners and feeding his army were by far not his only problems. Sensitive to criticism of his arguably detached actions during the heat of battle at Eutaw Springs, "Light Horse Harry" Lee became temporarily piqued that the general favored Washington. Greene placated Lee by responding, "I have a regard for Col Washington and think him a good Officer. But I don't mean to draw a comparison between you and him. Every body knows my sentiments on that head." Lee eventually calmed down and apologized to his commanding general.[20]

Although he had to remain in the city most of the time, William surely did not altogether object, because he now spent much of his time courting Jane. Sometime after her father's death in January 1781, Jane devoted herself and a portion of her inheritance to the relief of wounded American soldiers held in Charleston. She had rushed to William's bedside when she learned of her hero's capture and injury. No doubt her nursing skill and attention to his wounds may have saved his life, given the potential for deadly infections caused by bayonet wounds in 18th-century warfare.

Jane Elliott and William Washington warmed to each other, pursued a courtship and found the time and wherewithal in the enemy-occupied city to become husband and wife. Elizabeth Ellet described Jane at this time as "in the early bloom of youth, and surpassingly beautiful. Her manners were dignified, yet gentle and winning; her perceptions quick, and her nature frank and generous." Ellet also considered William "a gallant officer, imbued with the chivalric feeling of that period...[and]...It was not strange that two so congenial should love each other, and become bound by a mutual pledge to unite their fortunes." Jane was noticed by officers of both armies in Charleston, and a certain Major Barry addressed the following poem to "Jane Elliott playing the guitar":

> Sweet harmonist! Whom nature triply arms With virtue, beauty, music's powerful charms,—
> Say, why combined, when each resistless power
> Might mark its conquest to the fleeting hour?

According to Henry Lee, "Washington became acquainted with Miss Elliott, a young lady, in whom concentrated the united attractions of respectable descent, opulence, polish, and beauty. The gallant soldier soon became enamored of his amiable acquaintance, and afterward married her." They were married in the city on April 21, 1782. William no doubt loved Jane very much, but to a lesser degree he may have also weighed the future of owning and managing Sandy Hill in his "adopted" state of South Carolina. Otherwise, he would have to wait for a portion of Windsor Forest back in Stafford County, where his brother Bailey, Jr. was now managing more of the homestead for his father. Shortly after the wedding, Greene observed that "Washington is married to a lady of great merit and capital fortune...and [fat] upon the rice swamps; I think we may expect a plentiful harvest in due season"[21]

In September 1782, William and Jane spent a few days at William Gibbes' home on Kiawah Island, along with General Greene's wife and some of his fellow officers (for health reasons). While there, Captain William Pierce wrote to Greene that "Washington and [Dr. Robert Johnston], like two grumbling old women, sat over the backgammon Table, and railed at fortune for the whim of the dice...everyone here seems improved by them [the salts], and Colo. Washington looks again (to use your own Epithet sir) like the Hercules of the Day. His dear Partner [Jane] is by his side, and cherishes him with smiles." Captain Nathaniel Pendleton also observed that "We play Backgammon, at Cards; we run races on the beach, we dine and we exercise our wit...Mrs. Washington makes segars, & the Colonel smokes them; I wish they would employ themselves more in this way, and less in kissing which is not so uninteresting to the feelings of even convalescents as we are." The British finally evacuated Charleston in December and Greene triumphantly entered the city on December 14, 1782. William was again a free man after his fourteen months in captivity. Charles Elliott's will was finally approved on January 18, 1783, and Jane thus inherited her family's large, prosperous rice plantation at Sandy Hill. In the months prior to the British evacuation of Charleston, the plantation had apparently been used as a hospital by Jane's stepmother, Ann Ferguson Elliott.[22]

Tired of the war and delighted to remain in South Carolina where he had become highly regarded, 31-year-old William and his 19-year-old bride surely looked forward to a peaceful and comfortable life at Sandy Hill. This must have been an auspicious Christmas and New Year's season with the war ending, and the happy young couple could begin their new lives together as they rode west of the city to their home.

NOTES: CHAPTER V

[1] Information on Greene's campaign in South Carolina is from Hilborn, *Battleground of Freedom*, 183-212; Lumpkin, *Savannah to Yorktown*, 176-221; Morrill, *Southern Campaigns*, 158-169; Pancake, *Destructive War*, 187-221; Thayer, *Greene*, 332-395; Ward, *War of the Revolution*, II, 797-844; Weigley, *Partisan War*, 46-68.

[2] Nathanael Greene to Anthony White, April 16, 1781, to Thomas Sumter, April 15, 1781, and to Henry Lee, April 24, 1781, in Conrad (ed.), *Papers of Greene*, VIII, 104 100, and 143; Seymour, "Journal," 24; April 20, 1781, in Turner (ed.), *Journal of Kirkwood*, 16; Thayer, *Greene*, 338; Ward, *Delaware Continentals*, 428.

[3] Information on the Battle of Hobkirk's Hill, also called the 2nd Battle of Camden, is from Dupuy, *Compact History*, 405-412; Hilborn, *Battleground of Freedom*, 184-187; Lumpkin, *Savannah to Yorktown*, 169-175; Morrill, *Southern Campaigns*, 158-161; Pancake, *Destructive War*, 187-203, Ripley, *Battleground*, 161-165; Thayer, *Greene*, 344-347; Ward, *War of the Revolution*, II, 802-808; Schenck, *Invasion of the Carolinas*, 399-413.

[4] Nathanael Greene to Henry Lee, April 28, 1781, in R. W. Gibbs (ed.), *Documentary History of the American Revolution, Chiefly in South Carolina* (New York: D. Appleton and Company, 1853-1857), III, 61-62; John C. Dann (ed.), *The Revolution Remembered: Eyewitness Accounts of the War for Independence* (Chicago: University of Chicago Press, 1977), 220; Johnson, *Greene*, II, 93; Fortesque, *History of the British Army*, III, 387; John Marshall, *The Life of George Washington* (Fredericksburg: Citizens Guild, 1926 reprint of 1805 edition), IV, 6; Scheer and Rankin (eds.), *Rebels and Redcoats*, 456-457; William Pierce to Henry Lee, April 25, 1781, in Conrad (ed.), *Papers of Greene*, VIII, 146; Otho Williams to Elie Williams, April 27, 1781, in H. R. Howland, "The Second Battle of Camden, S. C.—Account of it, Written at the Time, by Gen. Otho H. Williams," *Potters American Monthly*, IV (1875), 103; Seymour, "Journal," 25.

[5] Nathanael Greene Orders, May 2, 1781 regarding the Court Martial, in Conrad (ed.), *Papers of Greene*, VIII, 187; Nathanael Greene to President of Congress, April 25, 1781, in *Spirit of Seventy-Six*, 1176;

Nathanael Greene's Orders, April 26, 1781 and Nathanael Greene to Samuel Huntington, April 27, 1781, in Conrad (ed.), *Papers of Greene*, VIII, 151, 156-157 and 159n; Howard's Note, in Lee, *Campaign of 1781*, 280; Bass, *Swamp Fox*, 181; Marshal, *Washington*, IV, 7-10; *Monument to Washington*, 24-26.

[6] Gunby, *Colonel John Gunby*, 75; Lee, *Memoirs*, II, 63; William Moultrie, *Memoirs of the American Revolution* (New York: David Longworth, 1802), II, 278; Note and Nathanael Greene to Henry Lee, April 28, 1781, in Conrad (ed.), *Papers of Greene*, VIII, 160n and 169; Seymour, "Journal," 26; Warley, *Oration*, 14-15.

[7] Nathanael Greene to Baron von Steuben, May 1, 1781 and to Francis Marion, April 27 and May 9, 1781, in Conrad (ed.), *Papers of Greene*, VIII, 184, 161, and 231; Nathanael Greene to Francis Marion, April 28, 1781, in Gibbs (ed.), *American Revolution*, III, 61; Nathanael Greene to Francis Marion, May 4 and 6, 1781, and Francis Marion to Nathanael Greene, May 6, 1781, in Greene, *Life of Greene*, III, 291-292; Edward McCrady, *The History of South Carolina in the American Revolution, 1780-1783* (New York: The MacMillan Company, 1902), 240-241; Baron von Steuben to Nathanael Greene, May 15, 1781, MS, Greene Papers, Library of Congress.

[8] For information on the partisan operations against British posts, see Hilborn, *Battleground of Freedom* 183-195; Lumpkin, *Savannah to Yorktown*, 184-192; Pancake, *Destructive War*, 191-192 and 200-203; Ripley, *Battleground*, 148-160 and 166-174; Thayer, Greene, 345-355; Ward, *Delaware Continentals*, 438; Ward, *War of the Revolution*, II, 809-815; Weigley, *Partisan War*, 45-56. For the eyewitness account, see Dann (ed.), *Revolution Remembered*, 223.

[9] Marquis de Lafayette and Baron von Steuben, May 18 and May 26, 1781; Nathanael Greene to Marquis de Lafayette, June 9, 1781; William Davie to Nathanael Greene, June 17, 1781; Josiah Parker to Nathanael Greene, June 17, 1781, in Conrad (ed.), *Papers of Greene*, VIII, 279-283, 315, 406, and 407; May 21, 1781, in Turner (ed.), *Journal of Kirkwood*, 18.

[10] Information on the campaign and Siege of Ninety Six is from Robert D. Bass, *Ninety Six: The Struggle for the South Carolina Back Country* (Lexington, South Carolina: The Sandlapper Store, Inc.,

1978); Marvin Cann, Old *Ninety Six in the South Carolina Backcountry, 1700-1781* (Troy, South Carolina: Sleepy Creek Publications, 1996); Lumpkin, *Savannah to Yorktown,* 193-205; Ripley, *Battleground,* 175-179; Ward, *War of the Revolution,* II, 816-822; Weigley, *Partisan War,* 57-63. For Greene's detachment of the cavalry, see Bass, *Swamp Fox,* 201-205; Waring, *Pickens,* 84-89; Nathanael Greene to William Washington, June 14 and 19, 1781 and William Washington to Nathanael Greene, June 19, 1781, MS, Greene Collection, Clements Library; Nathanael Greene to Thomas Sumter, June 10, 12, and 17, 1781, and Thomas Sumter to Nathanael Greene, June 14, 17, and 17, 1781, in Conrad (ed.), *Papers of Greene,* VIII, 376, 382, 405, 390, 403, and 408; Lee, *Memoirs,* II, 122 and 131-132.

[11] Nathanael Greene to William Washington, June 29 and July 3, 1781, and William Washington to Nathanael Greene, July 2 and 6, 1781, MS, Greene Collection, Clements Library; Nathanael Greene to Henry Lee, June 29, 1781, in Gibbs (ed.), *History of the Revolution,* III, 102; Lee, *Memoirs,* II, 141; Seymour, "Journal," 28-30.

[12] Dennis M. Conrad (ed.), *The Papers of Nathanael Greene, Vol. IX: 11 July 1781 - 2 December 1781* (Chapel Hill: University of North Carolina Press, 1997), xii; Nathanael Greene to James Conyers, July 17, 1781 and to Marquis de Lafayette, July 22, 1781; William Washington to Nathanael Greene, July 18 and 19, 1781, in *ibid.,* 23, 58-59 and 43 and 54.

[13] William Washington to Nathanael Greene, July 25, 1781, in Conrad (ed.), *Papers of Greene,* IX, 82; William Washington to Nathanael Greene, July 18, 19 and 30, and August 15, 1781, MS, Greene Collection, Clements Library; July 23, 1781, in Turner (ed.), *Journal of Kirkwood,* 21; John B. Irving, *A Day on the Cooper River* (Columbia: R. L. Bryan Co., 1842 monograph enlarged and edited by Louisa Cheves Storey, 1932), 43; Lee, Memoirs, II, 147; McCrady, *South Carolina in the Revolution,* 434 and 552; William Washington to Nathanael Greene, August 1, 1781, MS, Greene Papers, Library of Congress; Nathanael Greene to Anthony Wayne, July 24, 1781, and Wade Hampton to Nathanael Greene, August 5, 1781, in Conrad (ed.), *Papers of Greene,* IX, 75 and 132; Baron von Steuben to William Davie, July 27, 1781, in Hunt (ed.), *Fragments,* 158-159; Nathanael Greene to George Washington, August 6, 1781, in Sparks (ed.), *Correspondence of the Revolution,* III, 374; Ripley, *Battleground,* 236; Waring, *Pickens,* 92.

[14] Nathanael Greene to Board of War, July 27, 1781, Marquis de Lafayette to Nathanael Greene, August 12, 1781, and Ichabod Burnet to Nathanael Greene, August 20, 1781, in Conrad (ed.), *Papers of Greene*, IX, 87-88 and 173. Information on the events in the High Hills of Santee is from Thayer, *Greene*, 366-373 and Ward, *War of the Revolution*, II, 825-826.

[15] William Washington to Nathanael Greene, August 22, 1781, MS, Greene Collection, Clements Library; Nathanael Greene to President of Congress, August 25, 1781, and John Hamilton to Nathanael Greene, August 31, 1781, in Conrad (ed.), *Papers of Greene*, IX, 241 and 273; Thayer, *Greene*, 371-372; Ward, *Delaware Continentals*, 457; James Iredell to Hannah Iredell, September 3, 1781, in Higginbotham (ed.), *Papers of Iredell*, II, 287; Schenck, *Invasion of the Carolinas*, 444-462.

[16] Information on the Battle of Eutaw Springs is from Dupuy, *Compact History*, 416-420; Lumpkin, *Savannah to Yorktown*, 212-221; Ripley, *Battleground*, 199-206; Pancake, 216-221; Thayer, *Greene*, 375-380; Ward, *War of the Revolution*, II, 826-834; Weigley, *Partisan War*, 65-68.

[17] Nathanael Greene to President of Congress, September 11, 1781, and the Account furnished by Col. Otho Williams and other Officers of the Battle of Eutaw, in Gibbs (ed.), *History of the Revolution*, III, 141-152; Return of the Killed, Wounded, and Missing at Eutaw, September 8, 1781 and Declaration of Jesse Alsobrook, in Clark (ed.), *State Records of North Carolina*, XV, 637-638 and XXII, 95-96; General Greene's Orders, September 9, 1781, and Nathanael Greene to John Rutledge, September 9, 1781, in Conrad (ed.), *Papers of Greene*, IX, 307-308; William Hooper to James Iredell, October 1, 1781, in Higginbotham (ed.), *Papers of Iredell*, II, 302-303; Otho Williams to Edward Giles, September 23, 1781, in *Williams Papers*, 52; Dann (ed.), *Revolution Remembered*, 232; Fortesque, *History of the British Army*, III, 391; Lee, *Memoirs*, II, 293; Marshall, *Washington*, IV, 33-36; Accounts of the Battle of Eutaw, in the Charleston *Royal Gazette*, September 8-12, 15-19, and 26-29, 1781.

[18] Francis Marion to Nathanael Greene, September 11, 1781, and George Lux to Nathanael Greene, November 3, 1781, in Conrad (ed.), *Papers of Greene*, IX, 342 and 524; Fortesque, *History of the British Army*, III, 537.

[19] William Washington to Nathanael Greene, September 8, 1781, in Joseph W. Barnwell (comp.), "Letters to General Greene and Others," *The South Carolina and Genealogical Magazine*, Vol. XVI (July 1915), No. 3, 105.

[20] Alexander Stewart to Nathanael Greene, September 9, 1781, MS, Greene Papers, Library of Congress; John Rutledge to Francis Marion, October 16, 1781, in Gibbs (ed.), *History of the Revolution*, III, 191; Johnson, *Life of Greene*, II, 196; Uhlendorf (ed.), *Revolution in America*, 468-469; Alexander Leslie to Nathanael Greene, January 7, 1782, in Clark (ed.), *State Records of North Carolina*, XVIII, 179; Nathanael Greene to Alexander Leslie, January 7 and February 1, 1782, and to Henry lee, Jr., February 18, 1782, in Dennis M. Conrad (ed.), *The Papers of Nathanael Greene, Vol. X: 3 December 1781 - 6 April 1782* (Chapel Hill: University of North Carolina Press, 1998), 166, 295-296 and 378-379; Nathanael Greene to Alexander Leslie, February 7, 1782, MS, Greene Papers, Emmet Collection; Cowpens Committee, *Proceedings*, 118.

[21] Marriage Notice, in the Charleston *Royal Gazette*, April 27-May 1, 1782, 3; Alston Deas, "Genealogy of Lt. Col. William Washington," Unpublished Papers, South Carolina Historical Society, Charleston; Ellet, *Women*, I, 89-90; Lee, *Memoirs*, I, 402; Nathanael Greene to Otho Williams, June 6, 1782, in *Williams Papers*, 66, and to John Eager Howard, June 6, 1782, in Dennis M. Conrad (ed.), *The Papers of Nathanael Greene, Vol. XI: 7 April 1782 – 30 September 1782* (Chapel Hill: University of North Carolina Press, 2000), 294 and 300; Webber (ed.), "Elliott-Rowland Bible," 60-61. "Major Barry" may have been one of two South Carolina captains listed in Heitman's *Register*, and no British officer of that rank was found.

[22] Nathaniel Pendleton to Nathanael Greene, September 2 and 20, 1782, in Conrad (ed.), *Papers of Greene, XI*, 622 and 682; William Pierce, Jr. to Nathanael Greene, September 14, 1782, in Conrad (ed.), *Papers of Greene, XI*, 660-662; Ann Ferguson Elliott to Nathanael Greene, September 17, 1782, in Conrad (ed.), *Papers of Greene, XI*, 672; Deas, "Genealogy of Washington;" Thayer, *Greene*, 402 and 407; Webber (ed.), "Elliott-Rowland Bible," 60-61.

chapter VI

THE PEACEFUL PLANTER: 1783-1810

William Washington, Revolutionary War hero and husband of rice heiress Jane Elliott, found himself almost instantly immersed in his adopted state's post-war social, economic and political circles. He would lead a very active—although not outwardly ambitious—life of a planter and legislator for the twenty-five years that followed the end of the Revolutionary War. Motivated by the same sense of duty that guided him through six years of war, Washington willingly served his state and community in the legislature, civic organizations, his state's militia and for a brief time, the new United States Army.

Artist Charles Wilson Peale included his portrait among the Revolutionary War heroes in his National Gallery by October 1784. Washington probably made the trip to Philadelphia by way of Stafford County shortly after the British evacuation of Charleston in December 1782 and his release as a prisoner of war, most likely within the first six months of 1783 or perhaps as late as the same period of 1784. In the color painting considered to have "all the immediacy of a life portrait," William has gray-brown hair and brown eyes and wears the uniform of the 3rd Dragoons (white coat with blue facings). He apparently chose to wear a single epaulette on his right shoulder to hold his sword belt, rather than the two epaulettes of a lieutenant colonel. Peale charged "5 guineas" at the time for these 23" by 19" portraits. The painting now hangs in the Independence National Park in Philadelphia. A later painting was presented to the Mount Vernon Ladies' Association by Washington's descendants in the 1890s, but it cannot now be found.[1]

Shortly after his release by the British and their evacuation of Charleston, Washington stepped forward in March, 1783 to serve as a justice of the peace for the Charleston District at a time when the former patriots were quickly reestablishing state and local government. At the same time he became a member of the standing committee of the South Carolina Society of Cincinnati, a close-knit national organization made up primarily of former Continental Army officers. Washington, along with Charles Cotesworth and Thomas Pinckney, provided the leadership for the local chapter. The following year he joined the Charleston Library Society, no doubt out of his long affinity for classical works.[2] A staunch Federalist, he was also not averse to protecting his own and his fellow planters' powerful political positions in South Carolina. He joined his new friends and fellow Low Country "aristocrats" in taking a dim view of a radical political movement led by Isaac Peronneau in the summer of 1784. The radicals took to the streets to protest the return to Charleston of wealthy merchants and planters who had either been neutral or had sided with the British in the war. The radicals hoped to limit the power of Low Country planters and merchants, but their political efforts failed. The frustrated radicals soon resorted to mob violence, threatening the city's peace and intimidating the local militia. When the governor and his Privy Council became afraid that the rioters might overcome the town militia and seize a number of artillery pieces, they called on the one man they knew could lead a bold counter stroke—William Washington, Cavalryman of the Revolution! The Council resolved on July 12

> That as from the conduct of the Military, Government in the city seems lost, the good and virtuous citizens be invited by Government to form a volunteer corps of horse under the command of Col. Washington, his second in command Maj. Thomas Pinckney, to assemble at the State House or first at the Colonel's door on any riot or alarm given, to have special commissions on the spur of the occasion in the most

expeditious way as by letter or otherwise, in which, to leave all operations entirely to the dictates of their own prudence, discretion, and humanity; at all times providing for the security of the field pieces in the Arsenal and the public arms there and in the State House.

By September, William was to act in concert with Generals Marion and Winn who might bring their brigades into the city to "enforce the just resentment of a long provoked mild government." When street fighting erupted between the militia and Peronneau's adherents, William led this cavalry corps of "virtuous citizens" through the city and successfully dispersed the radicals with very little bloodshed. A contemporary account of events included a description of the skirmish: "A small corps of horse soon paraded: Major Pinckney [and] Col. Washington with a few gentlemen on foot, charged them sabre in hand." Members of this force roughed up and jailed a few of their opponents, and Peronneau himself was clubbed and arrested. This ended for a time this particular opposition to the Low Country's political domination in the state. Although a few months later Washington and some of his friends were subjected to a few verbal death threats, the violent elements of this movement had clearly subsided. The State finally banished those returning Tory exiles not originally from South Carolina, as well as a number of South Carolinians who had been obviously too friendly with the British.[3] Washington, who had seen so much internecine bloodshed during the Revolutionary War in the South, was surely relieved that this particular episode proved quite brief.

William continued his public service career throughout the remainder of the 1780's by representing his district of St. Paul for three consecutive terms to the South Carolina House of Representatives, placed there by those "who well knew his firm virtue, and his correct principles, could not permit his time to pass in that smooth and uninterrupted leisure, which his unambitious modesty would have desired." One of Washington's contemporaries noted that "as a politician his principles were firm and liberal, for they were adopted from conviction—they were founded on reason." He was active in the Seventh (1787-1788), Eighth (1789-1790) and Ninth (1791) General Assemblies. During his first year he was selected by the House to serve on then Governor Thomas Pinckney's Privy Council. This small group of legislators served as advisors to the governor.[4]

During his first term in the House, he regularly attended his sessions and served on the following committees: Navigable Rivers, Regulation of Trade, Election of Public Offices, Canals and a number of single item committees. His peers frequently selected him to "carry" official messages and papers from the House to the Senate and to the Governor. He usually voted with the majority on matters decided by the House. The Seventh Assembly deliberated such matters as confiscation and amercement relating to executors of estates, debtor relief, elections, Indian affairs, paper money, public salaries, requests for incorporation, restoring citizenship, roads and taxes. The benevolent Washington donated the salary he received as a legislator to the charity fund for the poor of his parish. He voted with the minority to oppose the House vote to reduce salaries of the Governor and several other offices in 1787. He again voted with the minority when conservatives in the House tried to delay holding a state constitutional convention in early 1787 to amend and revise the state constitution. When a vote came up in 1788 to move the site of the state capital from Charleston to the more central site of Camden while the new site at Columbia was still under construction, he and a number of his colleagues unsuccessfully opposed the measure. However, Washington voted with the majority in January 1788 not to resume the "importation of Negroes" for slaves, and he also voted in November to extend the ban until 1793. The aspiring planters in the back country were opposed to the ban, since it continued to prevent their acquisition of larger numbers of slaves, and of course the ban had little effect on the large number of slaves already owned by the low country planters. As a member of the Privy Council during his first term, he participated in advisory discussions with the governor on such matters as pay for "minute Men," a new jail in

Charleston, arrangement of the state militia and the Fort Johnson garrison, border problems with the Cherokees (where General Pickens commanded the militia) and frequent attempts by ships carrying slaves to dock in Charleston (in violation of the state's importation ban). William was on the Council in September 1788 when the Congress reported that eleven states had ratified the Constitution and that it would be put into operation. He was selected to help oversee the first United State Congressional election to be held the next year in accordance with the Constitution.[5] While a member of the Eighth Assembly, he also served on numerous committees and participated in votes on such matters as debtor relief and installment laws, fees and salaries, using paper money to speed up the growth of the state's inland navigation (William opposed this practice, but was on the losing side) and censuring and reprimanding Samuel Beach for his satirical piece, "Bread of Privilege," which appeared in the *City Gazette.* Washington voted with the minority of moderates who only called for Beach to apologize. When a vote came up to finally move the capital to Columbia and to hold a state constitutional convention there as well, Washington and a minority of his fellow low country legislators symbolically voted against both acts. When the new state constitution was adopted, it provided minimum eligibility provisions to be met by prospective legislators. House members had to own at least 500 acres and either ten slaves or real estate worth at least £150 free of debt; State Senators had to meet the same criteria but at a higher level of £300 free of debt. Washington found himself again among a minority of wealthier legislators who opposed additional taxes on slaves and land for the purpose of "raising supplies" to support the state government.[6]

William served his third term in the House in 1791, as a member of the Ninth General Assembly now meeting in the new capital of Columbia. He was a member of several committees, including Privileges and Elections, Courts of Justice, Indigent Veterans, joint committees with the Senate, a Committee to Inspect the Printing of Acts and a Committee of Relief for the Chickasaw Indians. During the Revolutionary

War these Native Americans had remained neutral and lost considerable property. He voted in support of higher salaries for the governor and state judges, but then found himself among the minority who unsuccessfully tried to raise the state's tax rates.[7]

Following his career in the House, William represented the district of St. Paul in the State Senate for the Tenth (1792-1794) through the Fifteenth (1802-1804) General Assemblies. There he served on the Committee to Inspect Printing of Acts, a Committee to Consider the Governor's Message and a Committee to Examine Accounts of the City of Charleston. With the passage of the Militia Act of 1792, William became commander of the 7th Brigade, whose responsibility included the defense of Charleston and the immediate vicinity around the city. This proved more an honorary post than it was an active field command. In May 1794, he was re-appointed Brigadier General of the "Seventh Brigade of Militia," whose area of responsibility still encompassed the District of Charleston. One duty of this honorary post included inspecting the local militia when they paraded in honor of George Washington's birthday. An account on February 22, 1797 mentioned that "the two regiments of the city, together with the battalion of artillery, had been reviewed by Gen. William Washington, near the Tobacco Inspection [buildings near which a parade ground was located]."[8]

William Washington was one of fifteen members of a Charleston committee elected in July 1795 to consider the state's reaction to the controversial Jay Treaty with England. The committee unanimously urged President George Washington not to sign the treaty and not appear to side with England in its war with France. The President chose to ignore such widespread opposition, however. The debate over the treaty also divided the Federalists. William was also a John Adams presidential elector in 1796, but the state failed to support Adams and native son Thomas Pinckney for Vice President. This marked the beginning of the decline in the Federalist domination of state politics as well. Despite his being "a good deal indisposed," William successfully ran for reelection to his Senate seat in 1800 at the urging of Federalist leaders who hoped to keep control of the General Assembly. President Adams and his running mate, C.C. Pinckney, failed to carry the state in 1800, and by 1804, the Republicans went on to take control of the State government.[9]

When France and the United States eventually became embroiled in a brief undeclared war largely as a result of the Jay Treaty, newly elected President John Adams appointed William Washington in 1798 to be a brigadier general on a recalled "General" George Washington's staff. When French ships preyed on British commerce inside the Charleston bar, South Carolina Republicans stood together with the eminent Federalists C.C. Pinckney, Thomas Pinckney and William Washington. William resigned his Senate seat in the thirteenth General Assembly to accept his military post, which commission ran from July 19, 1798 through June 15, 1800. He held an independent command of what was actually a provisional paper army in South Carolina and Georgia. He and his Commanding General, Major General C.C. Pinckney, occasionally inspected the coastline of Georgia and South Carolina from March through May of 1799. Cousin George trusted William's judgment entirely and he directed him to prepare a list of officers to serve in the Carolinas and Georgia if needed. Although he had hoped to continue his peaceful life at Sandy Hill, William Washington responded to his appointment with patriotism characteristic of such a dedicated American, asserting that he "had indulged the pleasing hope that I had made a final retreat into the peaceful shades of retirement, but I shall not hesitate at this momentous crisis...to obey the summons of my country." George also was no doubt sympathetic to William's desire that they could live in peace after the War of the Revolution. With the exception a number of naval engagements, the war with France never escalated to the point of requiring either of the Washingtons' services in a real campaign. George Washington wrote to Pinckney in March 1799 that he would "be very glad to see Brigdr. General Washington on his rout to Princeton; but he will find but little to do (in the military line) in this State."

Near the close of 1799, Alexander Hamilton had procured several British and French military manuals and directed Major General Charles Cotesworth Pinckney to work with William Washington, John Watts (a former lieutenant colonel of the 1st Dragoons in the Revolutionary War) and a Lieutenant Walbach to create a similar manual for the non-existent American cavalry. Pinckney asked Hamilton in January 1800 to raise two troops of cavalry because "they will be really necessary to enable us to form a perfect system." In February and March, the officers spent time "hard at work" at the army's headquarters near Shepherdstown, Virginia and an encampment at Harper's Ferry composing a manual entitled "Instructions... for... Formation and Movement of the Cavalry." By April and May, international tensions had subsided and Pinckney noted that the army was left with "our unfinished compilation of a system for the...Cavalry." Pinckney also relied on Washington's advice regarding such matters as sending the skeleton infantry regiments to be near the states where they were recruited so as to create fewer problems when the coming reductions took place."[10]

William Washington was an active member of the South Carolina General Assembly for seventeen years, but he was not ambitious for a political career. He refused to run for governor after the Revolutionary War, primarily because he did not think it would be fair for a non-native Carolinian to run for the office and he also insisted that he could not make a speech. He preferred the more congenial life of a planter, and once reportedly remarked that "my ambition is to devote my services to my country, but there are two powerful reasons which render it impossible for me to aspire to the honor of governing the state. The first is, that till lately I was a stranger among you; and in my opinion the chief executive officer should be a native of the land over which he presides. Nor would I, on the score of qualification, put my talents in competition with those of many able men, who are ambitious of the honor. My other reason is insurmountable. If I were elected governor, I should be obliged to make a speech; and I know, that in doing so, without gaining credit in your estimation, the consciousness of inferiority would humble me in my own—I cannot make a speech."[11]

His Famous Cousin

William regularly corresponded over the post-war years with George Washington about agricultural and family matters. In November 1784 George asked William to look after his nephew, George Augustine, who was traveling abroad and probably headed for Charleston short of money. In the same letter he mentioned that "I saw your brother [Bailey, Jr.], well, the other day at Richmond. It is said he is on the point of Matrimony; but of this and other matters of family concern, I presume you receive regular and better advice than I can give. tho' unknown I beg leave to offer my best respects to your Lady." The young traveler indeed arrived in bad financial condition and spent the winter of 1784-1785 in the shelter of his cousin's generous hospitality at Sandy Hill. George was grateful to William for taking care of his stranded nephew, thanking him on June 30, 1785 "For the kind attention shown him by Mrs. Washington and yourself he entertains a grateful sense, and I offer you my sincere thanks, which I should be glad to renew to you both in person at this place [Mount Vernon]." He also thanked William for the additional favor of sending with his nephew a parcel of nuts, acorns and seeds for him to plant at Mount Vernon in Virginia. William sent another parcel the following December, and Washington responded in April that he had received the acorns and that he would "nurture the young trees, when they arrive, with great care." Evidently, he wasted little time and planted them in May. He then became adventurous enough to ask William for palmetto seeds to see if that South Carolina tree might grow in Virginia! It appears that they did grow in the experimental botanical garden and greenhouse at Mount Vernon.[12]

The two Washingtons next corresponded in 1787 regarding a Philadelphia coach-maker who had done some work for George. William was evidently doing well enough to be in the market for a carriage. The coach-maker saw an opportunity to expand his business to more than one Charleston planter if

William Washington could be encouraged by George Washington's recommendation, "if you [William], or any of your friends should have occasion for Carriages."[13]

Early in 1790, William finally received from now "President" George Washington his long overdue "Cowpens medal," originally ordered ten years prior by the Continental Congress shortly after the hard-fought American victory in 1781. Thomas Jefferson and Alexander Hamilton had personally intervened in 1789 to hasten the minting of medals for several heroes of the War of the Revolution. On one side of the medal, Washington is depicted at the head of his charging cavalry with Victory overhead holding a laurel crown in one hand and a palm branch in the other. The Latin inscription translates as: "The American Congress to William Washington, Commander of a regiment of cavalry." The other side of the medal contains a Latin inscription within a wreath of laurel, and the translation is "Through the determined pursuit of the enemy with a small group of soldiers, he gave a distinguished example of inborn valor in the battle at Cowpens, January 17, 1781." In November 1790, William wrote President Washington to express his gratitude for the medal, and invited him to stay at Sandy Hill for a few days when his travels took him into South Carolina. The President responded in January 1791 that although he planned a tour of the South in the coming spring, he could not accept his cousin's invitation. He had always been careful "not to incommode any private family by taking up my quarters with them during my journey," and because he apparently did not want to appear to show favoritism. The President accomplished this for the most part by avoiding overnight stays in private homes while he traveled.[14]

William Washington had occasion to come to the aid of his former commander, Nathanael Greene, in November 1790. He wrote to Alexander Hamilton loyally supporting Greene's claim of innocence in a resurfaced controversy over a speculation allegation originally made in 1783. It is interesting to note that although he had chosen not to return to Virginia after the war, William was also still held in high regard by such prominent men of that state as George Mason, who in early 1791 expressed his "greatest regard" for him.[15]

In the spring of 1791, President Washington arrived in South Carolina on his promised trip through the South. William Washington led an advance party up the Coastal Road toward the North Carolina border to meet his cousin and escort him into South Carolina. However, since the President had made such rapid progress, they actually met at Georgetown Ferry on April 29. The party spent the next two days at Hampton's plantation on the Santee and Joseph Manigalt's Salt Ponds Plantation. William, Charles Cotesworth Pinckney, William Moultrie, Edward Rutledge and Charleston's City Recorder John Bee Holmes personally escorted the President across the Cooper River on May 2. The crossing was quite festive, including a flotilla of barges, sailboats and rowboats. One craft carried musicians, and twelve local rowing masters rowed the President's elegant barge. The party then paraded into the city "to the accompaniment of enthusiastic cheers." That William accompanied the other two South Carolina personages spoke well of his position in his adopted state.

While in Charleston for the next seven nights, the President stayed at the Heyward House, which had been rented by the City for this occasion. The week-long celebration throughout which Charleston's "who's who" turned out included a Society of Cincinnati dinner, several other dinners, banquets and balls (including the Governor's Ball on May 6), meeting with the General Assembly and finally fireworks on Saturday, May 7. The President was up early on May 9 to continue his tour on into Georgia. William, Charles Cotesworth Pinckney, William Moultrie and Senators Ralph Izard and Pierce Butler accompanied him. The party rode northwest from the city and crossed the Ashley River after breakfasting at Frazer's tavern. Bending his rule about avoiding overnight stays in private homes, the President chose to spend the afternoon and evening of May 9 and the morning of May 10 at Sandy Hill, ascribing the visit to "motives of friendship and relationship."[16] The two men, obviously pleased with their reunion, toured the plantation, reminisced about the War of the Revolution and surely conversed at length on their favorite topic—agriculture.

When the President eventually returned to Mount Vernon, he continued a lively correspondence with William. He again recommended his Philadelphia coach-maker, David Clarke, who had made the coach he had taken on his Southern tour. William was at the time apparently considering having a coach made in Philadelphia. The President also sent his favorite jack, *Royal Gift*, to William for breeding purposes from 1792 through 1795. Mules were a superior alternative to oxen and draft horses, but to produce them a prize stud jack was required to breed with good coach mares. The Spanish jacks were reputedly the best for siring good mules, but Spain had forbidden their export. However, the king of Spain made an exception for George Washington and sent him two jacks—one Washington named appropriately *Royal Gift*. Although the President had received many generous offers for the mule's stud services, he preferred to lend it to his cousin (whom he exempted from breeding fees), writing him on January 30, 1793: "Whatever sum shall be found due to me [from other South Carolinians] on acct. of Royal Gift (after all the charges are paid, and such other deductions made as may be satisfactory for your expense and trouble in this business) I would thank you for remitting me in the manner most convenient to yourself." The "trouble in this business" proved considerable, because *Royal Gift* was unable to perform in Charleston as famously as he had in Virginia. When William observed that only one mule had been produced, the President advised his cousin in February that he had just learned of the probable cause of *Royal Gift's* problems: "he was most abominably treated on the journey by the man [a stable groom] to whom he was entrusted; for instead of moving him slowly and steadily along as he ought, he was prancing (with the jack) from one public meeting, or place to another in a gate which could not but prove injurious to an Animal who had hardly ever been out on a walk before." He asked William to keep the jack for another year in hopes that he would recover. The two men kept up a steady correspondence about the famous animal, but by July 1795 the disappointed President finally requested the return, by sea voyage, of his prize jack, "whose ruin was predicated by all those who were witnesses of the manner in wch. he was treated, before he left Virginia."[17]

George Washington was not the only former comrade in arms to pay a visit to William in the 1790s. Otho Williams, his former commander during the famous race to the Dan River and other maneuvers preceding the Battle of Guilford Courthouse, spent time with William and Jane at their Charleston home in March and April of 1793. Within the past year both men had learned of the death of Robert Kirkwood, one of their gallant fellow officers. He had moved to Ohio after the war and was commissioned a captain in the 2nd U.S. Infantry in 1791. He was killed in action when Arthur St. Clair's army suffered a disastrous defeat in November at the hands of the Miami Indians under Little Turtle.[18]

A Conspicuous Gentleman of the Turf

William Washington's fervor for horse racing was also one of the major passions of his fellow low country plantation owners. A historian of the South Carolina Jockey Club listed Washington as one of the five "most conspicuous gentlemen of the Turf" in the two decades following the American Revolution. These years were a "golden age of racing." Race week was held every February, and it was always the most anticipated social event on the Charleston calendar and the equivalent of an annual state fair. Planters and their families came to the city for parties and balls held almost every night, and the courts, stores, businesses and schools closed each day in time for the races. Always in evidence were decorated booths at the racecourse, elegant coaches, liveried servants and new fashions—especially among the planters' wives and daughters. Given William's active participation, Jane was surely present for these festivities. In the early years of these races, the owners never ran their horses for money, but "solely for the honor that a horse of their own breeding and training should distinguish himself." Washington took great pride in breeding and training his own horses. His horse, *Ranger*, won the earliest recorded race held in 1786. The horse became the "cock of the walk" of the state by winning most of the main events for the next two years.

William served as chairman of the third South Carolina Jockey Club in 1790. Washington, Charles Cotesworth Pinckney, William Moultrie, William Alston, Wade Hampton and a few other gentlemen organized the fourth South Carolina Jockey Club in 1792. The Club became one of the most prestigious organizations in the state and purchased the new Washington Race Course the same year (named in honor of President George Washington). William also became a member and supporter of the Pineville Track in St. Stephen's County in 1794. Two of his horses in particular, *Rosetta* and *Shark*, became quite famous, and there was a great rivalry between *Rosetta* and Alston's *Betsy Baker*. Each horse had its following of loyal fans among the crowd at the races, and Washington's horses were constantly in top contention throughout the following decade. At the New Market Course he raced four horses in four different heats in 1790 and two horses in two heats in 1791. His *Rosetta*, measuring "16 hands high with prodigious shoulders," won the four-mile heat in 1790 and placed second in 1791. Also in the 1791 race, his horse *Childers* placed second behind old General Sumter's *Ugly*. At the new Washington Course, *Rosetta* won her four-mile heats for the next three years in a row. By 1794, William had three more horses in contention, in addition to *Rosetta* and *Childers*: *Shark*, *Actaeon*, and *Soldier*. *Rosetta* won the three-mile heat in 1795 and *Shark* moved up to take the four-mile honors. Although Washington did not enter the 1796 events, *Shark* returned in 1797 to win a £1200 sweepstakes. This prize racer, a distinguished dark bay, continued to win or place almost every year until 1801. He was then retired and became a popular stud horse and later was buried with honors and a marble slab at the Jamesville Race Course. William's other horses entered through 1803 included *Telegraph*, *Trumpetta*, *Ariadne*, *Surry Doe* and *Achilles* (*Rosetta's* colt). It also appears that William once took *Trumpetta* to Petersburg, Virginia, where she won her heat. William really pampered his horses by not letting them loose with his cows, oxen, pigs or other livestock to inexpensively forage in the woods near his plantation. Instead, these beauties grazed in his fallow fields where there was an abundance of green, tasty crab grass.[19]

The Peaceful Planter

In contrast to his six active years as a soldier, William Washington was content to enjoy the three decades after the war in the affluent, relatively peaceful pursuit of agriculture as a South Carolina planter. The extensive real estate holdings brought to the marriage by rice heiress Jane were all near the Elliott family mansion at Sandy Hill. According to the 1789 tax returns, the four largest parcels of an estate exceeding 12,000 acres included 4,975 acres in St. Paul's Parish, 2,550 in St. Bartholomew's Parish, 1,000 in Orange Parish, 1,250 in Granville County and 1,850 in the Ninety Six District. The mansion house reportedly stood in a cluster of oak trees at the end of a private avenue, complete with an ornamental pond in the front lawn. William, ever the horseman, added a practice racecourse to the grounds for training his dear thoroughbreds. The Washingtons' first years were not easy, since the plantations had to be reinvigorated after the war and harvests for 1783-85 generally were very poor in South Carolina. Indeed, the even meager total $3,600 value for St. Paul's rice crop in 1784 had fallen to zero by 1785! William's careful management soon turned this situation around, however.

The family spent much of their time at Sandy Hill, and the somewhat isolated life apparently wore on the more sociable Jane. Most plantation mistresses also managed the daily activities of their large households, and this would have required considerable attention at one the size of Sandy Hill. Perhaps in response to Jane, and for social, health and business reasons, William purchased a fine city home in December 1785 for his family to live in when they were in Charleston. This sojourn usually included the four hot summer months and the time of the February horse races. Originally built by Thomas Savage in the 1760s, and sold to William by Mary Elliott Savage for £4,460, the handsome house still stands at the northwest corner of Church Street and South Battery. Charleston residents were all very proud of their city, and the small society of rice and cotton planters to which Jane and William belonged worked very hard at developing and showing off what were the refined and hospitable habits of the time. The primary events for William and Jane Washington that occurred during the rest of the otherwise tranquil decade of the 1780's were the births of their two children: Jane on August 1, 1783 and William, Jr. on September 17, 1785.[20]

In 1784, Bailey Washington recorded a deed of gift to William's younger brother, Bailey, Jr. for 500 of the 1,200-acre tract at Aquia that comprised his Stafford County plantation in Virginia. He no doubt took this step because he was satisfied that William had married into property and that his prospects as a planter seemed assured. At the time, there were five white persons residing at the original Virginia homestead (probably William's parents, his two younger sisters and his youngest brother). The 1787 Personal Property Tax List for Stafford County enumerated two separate households: Bailey, Sr. as owning a 4-wheel carriage, 9 horses, 30 cattle and 15 black slaves, and Bailey, Jr. as owning a 2-wheel carriage, 4 horses and 23 black slaves. Bailey, Jr. followed his father in the General Assembly, representing Stafford County in the 1784-1785 and 1787-1788 terms. By 1800, the elder Bailey retained only 412 acres, after apparently providing daughter Mary Butler with 300 acres when she married Valentine Peyton. William was also generous to the newlyweds, when in 1801 he assigned them nearly half of the 7,000 acres in the Virginia Military District of Ohio that Virginia had awarded him in 1784 for his military service in the War of the Revolution. He assigned 2,000 of the remaining acres to his brother Bailey, and by 1808 he assigned 540 acres to Charles A. Stuart. The 1810 Census lists Bailey, Jr. and his wife and eleven children less than sixteen years old, along with 45 black slaves. Bailey died in 1814, and after the property passed through several owners, a forest fire destroyed the buildings in the early 1930s. The Marine Corps base at Quantico had to be expanded during World War II, resulting in the federal government's 1943 acquisition of the property.[21]

Slave Ownership

Like his fellow plantation owners, William also owned a large number of slaves. According to the first United States Census taken in 1790, there were 380 slaves living and working on his plantations and another thirteen were at his Charleston house on South Bay and Church Street. This contrasted with the twelve white persons living at Sandy Hill (i.e., four males over sixteen years and one under sixteen and three females) and five in Charleston. William was listed as "head of household" here and Jane or another white female as "head of family" along with one male under 16 years old and two other females. He also owned a tenant farm in Pendleton County, Ninety Six District, where eight white persons lived (i.e., one male over sixteen and four under sixteen and three females; no slaves were enumerated). At the time of the 1800 Census, there were 423 slaves listed in St. Paul's Parish at Sandy Hill and another eighteen located at his Charleston home. This Census also reported seven white males (i.e., the one over 45 years old probably being William, while three were under sixteen and three were sixteen to 45 years old) and seven white females (i.e., one each over 45 and between 26 and 45 years old, two ages 16 to 26 years old and three under 16 years old) living at Sandy Hill. Although he was one of the largest slaveholders in the Charleston district, he reportedly was considered by his peers to be a benevolent master *for his time.* Yet in 1795 he was clearly opposed to including any language in new Federal Constitution regarding emancipation or ending this peculiar institution. It is not known if Washington purchased any new slaves when the foreign slave trade reopened in 1804, however. He obviously preferred his plantation life to that of starting anew on the frontier and fighting the Shawnee for ten years to secure his 7,000 acres in the Virginia Military District of Ohio (southwest of modern Columbus). William's decision to marry Jane and remain in South Carolina proved quite profitable, and he became a very successful and wealthy rice planter.[22]

During his 1796 tour of the United States, French Duc de La Rochefoucault spent some time at Sandy Hill and recorded a number of observations about Washington's life at his

plantation.   After his "genteel reception," the Frenchman
noted that Washington "is now one of the most opulent
planters, and possesses from four to five hundred slaves, by
whose number wealth is *justly* estimated in South Carolina, as it
is by their labour that riches are amassed in this country." He
saw a number of William's plantations, "all situated in the
vicinity of his mansion, without adjoining each other...the rice
fields are *inland swamps*." Washington employed one "director
with superintendance over all the plantations, and under him
special inspectors...for every plantation." About one third of
the slaves worked in the fields; the rest were too old, too young,
sick or employed around the house. He further observed that
"each black slave cultivated about four acres of rice, plus two or
three acres of provisions—chiefly Indian corn and potatoes.
An average yield was considered to be two barrels of rice per
acre. Rice then was bringing an excellent price of six to seven
dollars per barrel—three times the pre-war price." According
to the Frenchman, William had little doubt about the
profitability of the slave economy, calculating that every slave
earned annually, all expenses considered, about $250 – "the
expense for a negro, including duty, board, clothing and
medicines, he estimates from twelve to thirteen dollars."
However, the visitor described Washington as a benevolent
master, noting that "They [the slaves] are not overburdened
with labour, and they are at liberty to cultivate for themselves as
much land as they choose."

William was also planning to erect a mill for the grinding
and sifting, which was at that time done by hand, "the most
painful toil." The rice was transported to Charleston on carts,
although the planters in the area tried to raise money for a
canal across the swamps. He was also one of several planters
who directly chartered ships to transport the rice to England
themselves to avoid the heavy commissions and freight charges
of the Charleston factors (i.e., commission merchants). While
noting that the Carolina planters retired to Charleston for four
months each June, La Rochefoucault found that "They are
fond of residing on their plantations; and thus save most of
their household expenses."   The typical season included

clearing ditches or drains in late fall and early winter, harrowing and trenching in March, sowing in April, weeding and maintenance through August and harvest beginning in September. Provision crops (e.g., sweet potatoes and corn) were planted in June and harvested in October and November.

The Frenchman noted that one must get used to plantation life to like it; there was little variety, only a few neighbors and the homes were surrounded by mud and water. He particularly observed that "Mrs. Washington seems less pleased with the plantation-life than her husband, whom business frequently calls away, and whom a pipe or a good dinner often retains in the place, whither he is obliged to go." When the distinguished visitor attended a dinner given by local planters and hosted by William Washington, he left this almost humorous picture of the event: "this dinner was given, not in a good tavern, but in a miserable inn, where, from the ruinous state of the stair-case, the guests were under the necessity of working up their way to the dining-room by the aid of a ladder. It was a cold dinner, and the liquors served up were rum, brandy, and geneva, which the gentlemen of the meeting quaffed, as if they had been the most delicious champagne."[23]

In the summer of 1799, William traveled with his young son, William, Jr., to Virginia for about a month. They were delayed briefly in North Carolina, where the thirteen-year-old lad became ill. They spent August 6-8 at Mount Vernon visiting with George and Martha Washington, and left for a visit to Philadelphia "both in good health and Spirits." Father and son made a return visit to their kinsman on the weekend of September 7 and 8. George Washington recorded that the pair were anxious to get home and that they were off again after breakfast on Sunday morning, "His [William's] anxiety to get to Carolina as soon as possible (having been detained to the Eastward longer than he expected) prevented his passing more time with me."[24] Not long after returning to South Carolina, William received the sad news of George's death in December.

William and his son were "detained to the Eastward" for the purpose of enrolling William, Jr. at Princeton. Young William joined the Cliosophic Society at Nassau Hall on September 25,

1799 and he adopted his mother's maiden name "Elliott" for society use. He received his Bachelor of Arts degree in 1802, but he evidently did not take part in the commencement exercises.[25]

Later Years

William, Sr. spent his later years in active, comfortable retirement at Sandy Hill. He served on the Board of Trustees for the College of Charleston (1800-1803) and was still serving his St. Paul's Parish in 1806-1807—this time as a vestryman. When he learned that Thomas Paine, author of "American Crisis" in 1776, was in financial distress in Philadelphia, Washington immediately forwarded one hundred guineas to him, "as a tribute of gratitude and respect." He supported an 1803 pension request for Lawrence Everhart, one of his sergeants who rode with the 3rd Dragoons at Cowpens, writing, "I cannot be influenced to believe that Congress will reject the just claim of an old soldier." Daughter Jane married James Hasell Ancrum at a ceremony at Sandy Hill in 1803 as well. A proud grandfather soon doted over his first two grandchildren. Jane Washington Ancrum was born in 1804, the same year William's mother died in Stafford County. Three years later he received the sad news of his father's death (in 1807). William Washington Ancrum was born in 1808 at the Church Street house in Charleston. In the meantime, after graduating from Princeton in 1802 and spending the next three years in Europe, William, Jr. had returned home and began managing the plantation for his father. In November 1807, William, Jr. married Martha Ferguson Blake, who was the daughter of John and Margaret Mercier Blake of Charleston. The first of their ten children, William Washington, III, was born on March 24, 1810—unfortunately two weeks after his grandfather's death. Observers would later recall William in his twilight years when "His countenance was composed and rather of serious cast, but evinced the benevolence that characterized all his actions. In social life he was retiring and taciturn."

At the age of fifty-eight, William contracted an unknown illness, and after a long and painful time, he passed away on

Friday, March 6, 1810. The exact nature of his illness is not known, other than newspaper accounts of his death indicating that his health had been bad for some years and that during the last six months of his life "he sustained a complication of disorders, become too powerful for longer resistance." Moravian residents of Salem, North Carolina had noted his passing through the town in June 1805, on his way to Warm Springs, Virginia to possibly seek relief from whatever his painful conditions were. They also recalled that "He inspected our Boarding School with pleasure." He no doubt carried on the normal affairs of life as long as he was able and would have avoided imposing his problems on others. He was said to have viewed his approaching death "with a composure and equanimity truly characteristic."[26]

William Washington and his wife Jane, who outlived him by twenty years, are both buried in the old Elliott private cemetery seven miles from Sandy Hill at the "Live Oak" plantation Jane had acquired from her father. This site is near Rantowles Bridge, the scene of his first successful cavalry skirmish against the dreaded Tarleton in 1780. The grave is unmarked except for their daughter Jane's initialed inscription on the stone: "My Father and Mother Dear lie buried here." His friends remembered him as moderate, generous and benevolent. With typical modesty, William had requested on his deathbed that he not be given a military funeral. He was opposed to such trappings for himself, regardless of his military accomplishments during the War of the Revolution.[27] A roadside plaque now marks the nearby grave on U.S. Route 17 where the road now crosses Rantowles Creek.

The Sword of His Country

The death of such a local Revolutionary War hero was publicly mourned by the state Society of Cincinnati, and the American Revolution Society resolved on April 14 to "wear crepe on their left arm for thirty days, as a tribute of respect." The Society of Cincinnati also held a long memorial service at Saint Michael's Church in Charleston on June 10. In a Society resolution passed in his honor, he was fondly remembered as "one of our oldest officers - one of our brightest ornaments. His mild, yet dignified deportment - his amiable and affectionate manners, had endeared him to every individual of this society...a Modern Marcellus, the sword of his country." A similar resolution of the American Revolution Society affirmed that their comrade possessed

> *a felicitous combination of mind and heart, rearly [sic] united, which qualified him to be eminently distinguished as a soldier, and esteemed as a citizen...which rendered him modest, without timidity; generous, without extravagance; brave, without rashness; and disinterested, without austerity - which imparted firmness to his conduct, and mildness to his manners; solidity to his judgement, and boldness to his achievement...a gallant soldier, enterprising without ambition; encountering danger not for his own renown, but for his country's independence.*

His eulogist described William variously in glowing and affectionate terms: "his virtues rendered him alike conspicuous and beloved, in public and private life...dignified without austerity...affable without familiarity...of soul sincere...in action faithful, and in honor clean...broke no promise...[and] lost no friend."[28]

William Washington's memory would be publicly honored several times after his death. On April 19, 1827 Jane presented his scarlet battle flag—made by her own hands in 1780 and carried from Cowpens through Eutaw—to the Washington Light Infantry at a ceremony held in front of her house at South Bay and Church streets. She entrusted "this banner, which has been unfurled on the field on some memorable occasions, particularly at Eutaw" to this Charleston militia unit she considered to be "a band of citizen soldiers, who would on no occasion suffer its honor or lustre to tarnish." Jane died at the age of sixty-seven on December 14, 1830. The Washington Light Infantry has continued to preserve the relic. In 1857, this organization decided to erect a monument in memory of both William and Jane, but they were unable to place it at the couple's gravesite. Since the family was also unwilling to have the remains moved, a site in Magnolia Cemetery was chosen for the monument. The Washington Light Infantry sponsored an elaborate dedication ceremony on May 7, 1858. On the base of this seventeen-foot tall marble monument the names of William's Revolutionary War battles are inscribed: Trenton, Cowpens, Hobkirk's Hill and Eutaw Springs. Speakers at the ceremony recalled Washington as "a faithful friend, a devoted husband, an affectionate father, a kind master, a public spirited citizen, a Christian gentleman."[29]

William Washington, Jr. took over the management of Sandy Hill after his father's death. He followed somewhat in his namesake's footsteps in terms of living a planter's life, limited public service but active in community associations. He represented St. Paul's Parish for four terms in the General Assembly (1816-1819 and 1822-1825) and served on a number of committees, including the judiciary, ways and means, internal improvements, banks, public schools, privileges and elections. He inherited an honorary membership in the Society of Cincinnati and through his father and also became a member of the South Carolina Society, the Agricultural Society of South Carolina, Charleston Library Society, Charleston Board of Health and the College of Charleston board of trustees (1821-1830). In the 1820s he was commissioner of the Charleston Orphan House. His mother survived his father by twenty years, passing the Charleston house on to his sister Jane Washington Ancrum in 1830.

February 1830 was a tragic month for the Washington family, who was at the time staying at the Charleston home. Over the weekend of February 27 and 28 William, Jr. and his wife, Martha died. Although the causes of death are not known, Charleston experienced frequent and deadly outbreaks of yellow fever, smallpox and influenza in the nineteenth century. Jane died on December 14, closely following the untimely deaths of her beloved son and daughter-in-law. All three were buried at the family cemetery where William reposed. William III, (who had attended the College of

Charleston in 1825 and 1826), the twenty-year-old son of William, Jr. and Martha, inherited Sandy Hill and lived there until 1849. The 1830 Census and an 1831 estate inventory reveals a plantation enterprise somewhat reduced from its pinnacle at the turn of the century. For example, the number of William, Jr.'s black slaves were estimated to be 127-167 on the plantation and seven to nine in Charleston. Decades later, the colonial mansion at Sandy Hill accidentally burned down in 1864, long after it had passed out of the family's hands to J. B. Campbell, "who had preserved and restored it from decay."[30]

William Washington's military career reflected both the glorious and the desperate times of the War of the American Revolution. He was one of a vital core of young officers who risked everything and remained with their commanders throughout the war. They often proved that they could accomplish much with meager manpower and resources under dreadful conditions. Brave and often impetuous to a fault, Washington was a commander who personally led his men in battle. He was seldom discouraged by defeat and he was often magnanimous in victory. His sometimes-mercurial military exploits must on balance be judged as a successful record. His cavalry command was essential to Nathanael Greene's ultimately successful campaign to drive the British from the Carolinas and confine them to a couple of seaports by late 1781. That William Washington embodied the spirit of resistance until the end is certain. It was the very spirit that was required to defeat the British in North America.

After the War of Independence, William Washington continued to serve his new nation, although more at the local level as a man dedicated to his family, community and the success of his plantation. At the 1858 ceremony at Magnolia Cemetery one speaker offered an eloquent summary of Washington's life,

> ...the name and reputation of Col. Washington are indissolubly united with South Carolina. Upon her soil, when overrun by the enemy, in defense of her people, when almost in despair, he fought long and well. With her he

*triumphed. Within her borders, which, by choice, became his
own loved Country, he lived out his honorable and well-spent
life, in her bosom his bones repose.*[31]

His fellow officers and other contemporaries did not
question his record of courage, humility, kindness and
benevolence—and that record remains intact.

Cowpens Silver Medal awarded to William Washington.
Eastern National.

Washington's Church Street House in Charleston.
Photograph by Barbara Haller.

William and Jane Washington Memorial in Magnolia Cemetery
Washington Light Infantry

NOTES: CHAPTER VI

[1] Charles Coleman Sellers, *Portraits and Miniatures by Charles Wilson Peale.* (Philadelphia: American Philosophical Society, 1952), 17 and 243-244. Although Sellers believed that Washington's portrait was done in 1781 or 1782, this is highly unlikely. Washington was campaigning in the Carolinas throughout 1781 until his capture at Eutaw in September. He was wounded at the battle and remained a British prisoner in the Charleston area until December 1782. The staff at Mount Vernon have been unable locate the later one.

[2] Theodora J. Thompson (ed.), *Journals of the House of Representatives, 1783-1784* (Columbia: University of South Carolina Press, 1977), 229 and 263; N. Louise Bailey (ed.), *Biographical Directory of the South Carolina House of Representatives, 1775-1980* (Columbia: University of North Carolina Press, 1981), III, 751; George C. Rogers, Jr., *Evolution of a Federalist: William Loughton Smith of Charleston, 1758-1812* (Columbia: University of South Carolina Press, 1962), 253-254.

[3] William Washington to Nathanael Greene, July 8, 1784, MS, Greene Collection, Clements Library; John Alden, *The South in the Revolution* (Baton Rouge: Louisiana State University Press, 1957), 327-328; July 12 and September 8, 1784, in Adele Stanton Edwards (ed.), *Journals of the Privy Council, 1783-1789* (Columbia: University of South Carolina Press, 1971), 119-120 and 136; Walter Edgar, *South Carolina: A History* (Columbia: University of South Carolina Press, 1998), 247; Marvin R. Zahniser, *Charles Cotesworth Pinckney, Founding Father* (Chapel Hill: University of North Carolina Press, 1967), III, 75-76.

[4] Bailey (ed.), *Directory of the South Carolina House*, III, 750-751; Warley, *Oration*, 16 and 19; Michael E. Stevens (ed.), *Journals of the House of Representatives, 1787-1788* (Columbia: University of South Carolina Press, 1981), 9, 119 and 637.

[5] Stevens (ed.), *Journals of the House*, 3-615 passim, 43-89 passim, 217-218, 482 and 496, 344 and 615; Warley, *Oration*, 20; Edwards (ed.), *Journals Privy Council*, 185-221 passim; Edgar, *South Carolina*, 247-249.

[6] Michael E. Stevens (ed.), *Journals of the House of Representatives, 1789-1790* (Columbia: University of South Carolina Press, 1984), 4-323 passim; Edgar, *South Carolina,* 248-255.

[7] Michael E. Stevens (ed.), *Journals of the House of Representatives, 1791* (Columbia: University of South Carolina Press, 1985), 3-418 passim.

[8] N. Louise Bailey (ed.), *Biographical Directory of the South Carolina Senate, 1776-1985* (Columbia: University of South Carolina Press, 1986), III, 1687-1688; Michael E. Stevens (ed.), *Journals of the Senate, 1792-1794* (Columbia: University of South Carolina Press, 1988), 249-570 passim; Jean Martin Flynn, "South Carolina's Compliance with the Militia Act of 1792," *The South Carolina and Historical and Genealogical Magazine,* Vol. 69 (January 1968), 43; Charles Fraser, *Reminiscences of Charleston* (Charleston: John Russell, 1854, 24.

[9] Bailey (ed.), *South Carolina Senate,* III, 1687-1688; Stevens (ed.), *Journals of the Senate,* 249-570 passim; George C. McCowen, Jr., "Chief Justice John Rutledge and the Jay Treaty," *The South Carolina Historical and Genealogical Magazine,* Vol. LXII (January 1961), 16-17; Edgar, South Carolina, 253-254; David Duncan Wallace, *South Carolina, A Short History: 1520-1948* (Chapel Hill: University of North Carolina Press, 1951), 347; Rogers, *Evolution of a Federalist,* 348-351.

[10] Officers Appointed under the Act of July 16, 1798, in U. S. Congress, *American State Papers, Military Affairs* (Washington, D. C.: Gales and Seaton, 1832-1861), I, 147; Proposed Arrangement of General Officers and Other Officers, July 14, 1798, and George Washington to William Washington, September 27 and December 28, 1798, and to C. C. Pinckney, March 31, 1799, in Fitzpatrick (ed.), *Writings of Washington,* XXXVI, 334 and 468-469 and XXXVII, 74-75 and 166-169; William Washington to George Washington, October 19, 1798, in Washington, "William Washington," 106-107; William Washington," *William and Mary Quarterly,* 133-134; Bailey (ed.), *South Carolina Senate,* III, 1687-1688; Edgar, *South Carolina,* 261; Broadus Mitchell, *Alexander Hamilton: The National Adventure, 1788-1804* (New York: MacMillan Co., 1962), 440, 449 and 727-728; Alexander Hamilton to James McHenry, November 30, 1799 and to Charles Cotesworth Pinckney, December 2, 1799, and Charles Cotesworth Pinckney to Alexander Hamilton, December 12, 1799, January 9 and 21, March 28 and May 30, 1800, in Harold C. Syrett (ed.), *The Papers of*

Alexander Hamilton (New York: Columbia University Press, 1961-1987), XXIV, 81-83, 96, 181, 208, 379, and 542.

[11] James Barton Longacre and James Herring (comp.), *The National Portrait Gallery of Distinguished Americans* (Philadelphia: H. Perkins, 1834-1839), IV, 156; *Monument to Washington*, 35; Washington, "William Washington," 103; and "William Washington," *William and Mary Quarterly*, 133; Cowpens Committee, *Proceedings*, 118.

[12] Deas, "Genealogy of William Washington;" George Washington to William Washington, November 25, 1784, April 10, 1785 and June 30, 1785, in Fitzpatrick (ed.), *Writings of Washington*, XXVII, 405-406 and 503 and XXVIII, 101; William Washington to George Washington, December 18, 1785 and George Washington to William Washington, April 10, 1786, MS, Library of Congress; May 1 and 2, 1786 in John C. Fitzpatrick (ed.), *The Diaries of George Washington, 1748-1799* (Boston: Houghton, Mifflin Company, 1925), III, 53-54; Elizabeth Kellam de Forest, *The Gardens & Grounds at Mount Vernon* (Mount Vernon, Virginia: The Mount Vernon Ladies Association, 1982), 110.

[13] George Washington to William Washington, September 17, 1787, in Fitzpatrick (ed.), *Writings of Washington*, XXIX, 275.

[14] William Smith to Otho Williams, July 7, 1789, in *Williams Papers*, 179; Boyd (ed.), *Papers of Jefferson*, VII, 67-76 passim and 289n; William Washington to George Washington, November 7, 1790, in Washington, Cowpens Committee, *Proceedings*, 117; "William Washington," 107; George Washington to William Washington, January 8, 1791, in Fitzpatrick (ed.), *Writings of Washington*, XXXI, 192-193.

[15] William Washington to Alexander Hamilton, November 6, 1790, in Syrett (ed.), *Papers of Hamilton*, X, 467-468; Thayer, *Greene*, 417-418; George Mason to John Mason, January 10, 1791, in Robert A. Rutland (ed.), *The Papers of George Mason* (Chapel Hill: University of North Carolina Press, 1970), III, 1219.

[16] Archibald Henderson, *Washington's Southern Tour: 1791* (Boston: Houghton, Mifflin and Company, 1923), 155 and 201; Terry W. Lipscomb, *South Carolina in 1791: George Washington's Southern Tour* (Columbia: South Carolina Department of Archives and History,

1993), 10-46 passim; B. A. Salley, *President Washington's Tour Through South Carolina in 1791* (Columbia: Historical Commission of South Carolina, 1932), Bulletin No. 12, 6; April 29 and May 9 and 11, 1791 in Fitzpatrick (ed.), *Diaries of Washington,* IV, 169 and 174-175.

[17] George Washington to Joseph Williams, January 14, 1792, and William Washington, January 30, 1793, April 26, 1793, February 9, 1794, and July 14, 1795, in Fitzpatrick (ed.), *Writings of Washington,* XXXI, 457; XXXII, 319-320 and 433; XXXIII, 261-263; XXXIV, 240-241; William Washington to George Washington, October 15, 1792, April 20, 1793 and January 6, 1794, MS, Library of Congress; Lipscomb, *South Carolina in 1791,* 47-48.

[18] Memo, April 13, 1793, in *Williams Papers,* 284; Mark Mayo Boatner, *Encyclopedia of the American Revolution* (New York: D. McKay Co., 1966), 585 and 957.

[19] Bailey, (ed.), *South Carolina Senate,* III, 1688; John B. Irving, *The South Carolina Jockey Club* (Charleston: Russel & Jones, 1857), 11-22 and 163-167; Lipscomb, *South Carolina in 1791,* 47; George C. Rogers, Jr., *Charleston in the Age of the Pinckneys* (Norman: University of Oklahoma Press, 1969), 114; Wallace, *South Carolina,* 351; Duc de La Rochefoucault Liancourt, *Travels Through the United States of North America, the Country of the Iroquois, and Upper Canada, in the Years 1795, 1796, 1797* (London: R. Phillips, 1799), 598.

[20] Bailey (ed.), *South Carolina Senate,* III, 1688; Edgar, *South Carolina,* 246; Henderson, *Washington's Southern Tour,* 201-202; Lipscomb, *South Carolina in 1791,* 45-46; Salley, *Washington's Tour,* 6; Alice R. and D. E. Huger Smith, *The Dwelling Houses of Charleston, South Carolina* (Philadelphia: J. B. Lippincott Company, 1917), 187-188; Wallace, *South Carolina,* 350.

[21] Stafford County, Virginia, Will Book S, 127; Virginia State Library, *Embrey's Index,* Vol. 6, 2020-2021; U. S. Department of Commerce and Labor, Bureau of the Census, *Heads of Families at the First Census of the United States Taken in the Year 1790 and Records of the State Enumerations, 1782 to 1785: Virginia* (Baltimore: Southern Book Company, 2nd Ed., 1952), 108; Netti Schreiner-Yantis and Florence Speakman Love. (comps.), *The Personal Property Tax List for the Year 1787 for Stafford County, Virginia* (Springfield, Va.: Genealogical Books, 1987), 1003;

Gaius Marcus Brumbaugh (ed.), *Revolutionary War Records, Volume I, Virginia* (Lancaster, Pennsylvania: Lancaster Press, Inc., 1936), 85, 440 and 519; Clifford Neal Smith (comp.), *A Calendar of Archival Materials on the Land Patents Issued by the United States Government, with Subject, Tract and Name Indexes, Vol. 4, Part 1: Grants in the Virginia Military District of Ohio* (Chicago: American Library Association, 1982), 10-205 passim; U. S. Department of the Interior, Bureau of Land Management, *The Official Federal Land Patent Records Site* (Washington, D.C.: Land Patent Databases at www.glorecords.blm.gov, 2000); A. Maxim Coppage and James W. Tackett (comp.), *Stafford Co., Virginia: 1800-1850* (Concord, California: Printed for the Compilers, 1982), 4-5, 12 and 24; Eby, *Stafford Home,* 143; Swem, *General Assembly,* 442.

[22] Alden, *The South in the Revolution,* 42; Bailey (ed.), *South Carolina Senate,* III, 1688; U. S. Department of Commerce and Labor, Bureau of the Census, *Heads of Families at the First Census of the United States Taken in the Year 1790: South Carolina* (Washington, D.C.: U.S. Government Printing Office, 1900), 37-39 and 82; U. S. Department of Commerce and Labor, Bureau of the Census, *Census of the United States Taken in the Year 1800: South Carolina* (Washington, D.C.: National Archives Microfilm); J. H. Easterby (ed.), *The South Carolina Rice Plantation As Revealed in the Papers of Robert F.W. Allston* (Chicago: University of Chicago Press, 1945), 31-37; Lipscomb, *South Carolina* in 1791, 47; Rogers, *Evolution of a Federalist,* 268.

[23] Liancourt, *Travels,* 595-599; Wallace, *South Carolina,* 350.

[24] August 6 and 7, and September 7 and 8, 1799, in Fitzpatrick (ed.), *Diaries of Washington,* IV, 311-312; George Washington to Charles Cotesworth Pinckney, August 10, in Fitzpatrick (ed.), *Writings of Washington,* XXXVII, 325; George Washington to Gov. John Rutledge, September 9, 1799, in Joseph W. Barnwell (comp.), "Letters to General Greene and others," *The South Carolina Historical and Genealogical Magazine,* XVII (April 1916), 56.

[25] "William Washington, Jr.," Alumni Files, MS, Princeton University, 456; Lansing Collin Varnum (comp.), *General Catalogue of Princeton University, 1746-1906* (Princeton: Princeton University, 1908), 114.

[26] Bailey (ed.), *South Carolina Senate,* III, 1688; J. H. Easterby, *A History of the College of Charleston* (Charleston: The Scribner Press, 1935), 262,

285 and 289; Cowpens Committee, *Proceedings*, 118-119; Elizabeth Heyward Jervey (comp.), "Marriage and Death Notices in The City Gazette," *The South Carolina Historical and Genealogical Magazine*, XXXI, (October 1930), 317 and XXXIV, (July 1933), 166-169; Barnwell Rhett Heyward, "The Descendants of Col. William Rhett, of South Carolina," *The South Carolina Historical and Genealogical Magazine*, IV (January 1903), 72; William Washington to James Simons, November 13, 1803, in Balch (ed.), *Maryland Line*, 46; Henry A. M. Smith, "The Grave of Colonel William Washington," *The South Carolina Historical and Genealogical Magazine*, X (October 1909), 247; Warley, *Oration*, 20; Alumni Files, Princeton University, 456; Deas, "Genealogy of William Washington;" Adelaide L. Fries (ed.), *Records of the Moravians in North Carolina* (Raleigh: North Carolina Historical Commission, 1943), VI, 2809; King (comp.), *Overwharton Parish*, 123; Lee, *Memoirs*, I, 403; Washington, "William Washington," 104. Unfortunately, the estate records for Charleston and the church records for St. Paul's Parish were burned during the Civil War.

[27] Smith, "Grave of William Washington," 245; Ellen C. Holmes, "The Hero of Cowpens and Eutaw Springs with nothing to mark his grave," Unpublished Paper, South Carolina Historical Society, Charleston; *NCAB*, II, 492; Wilson and Fiske (eds.), *Appleton's*, VI, 384.

[28] "The City Gazette," in *The South Carolina Historical and Genealogical Magazine*, XXXIV, (July 1933), 166-167; Warley, *Oration*, 18-21 and 49.

[29] Cowpens Committee, *Proceedings*, 49 and 119-120; *Monument to Washington*, 5 and 35; "Charleston" in *The Charleston Courier*, April 20 and 21, 1827, No 8441 and 8443, 2.

[30] Smith, *Houses of Charleston*, 188; Smith, "Grave of William Washington," 246; Mabel L. Weber (ed.), Bailey (ed.), *South Carolina Senate*, III, 1689; Princeton University Alumni Files, 457-458; Easterby, *College of Charleston*, 262; "Records from the Elliott-Rowland Bible," *The South Carolina Historical and Genealogical Magazine*, XI (January 1910), 66; "Destruction of Ancient Mansion House," in *Daily South Carolinian*, Columbia, S. C., April 15, 1864, Vol. 15, No. 89, 2.

[31] *Monument to Washington*, 15.

chronology

WILLIAM A. WASHINGTON

February 28, 1752	Born in Stafford County, Virginia (Son of planter Bailey Washington and Catherine Storke Washington)
September 12, 1775	Elected captain of one of the Stafford County's companies in Colonel Hugh Mercer's regiment of "minute-men"
February 25, 1776	Commissioned captain in command of the 5th Company, 3rd Virginia Continental Infantry Regiment
September 16, 1776	Fought and possibly wounded at Battle of Harlem Heights
December 26, 1776	Fought and wounded at Battle of Trenton
January 27, 1777	Promoted to major and assigned to the 4th Continental Light Dragoons
Fall, 1777	Served with the 4th Dragoons in the Brandywine-Germantown Campaign
November 20, 1778	Promoted to Lieutenant Colonel and given command of the 3rd Continental Light Dragoons

March, 1780	Led the 3rd Dragoons to Charleston, South Carolina
March 27, 1780	Fought at Skirmish near Rantowle's Bridge
April 6, 1780	Fought at Skirmish near Middleton's Plantation
April 14, 1780	Fought at Battle of Monck's Corner
May 6, 1780	Fought at Battle of Lenud's Ferry
Summer, 1780	Rebuilt a combined unit of the 3rd and 1st Dragoons in North Carolina
December 4, 1780	Used "Quaker Gun" strategy to capture Rugeley's Farm
December 28, 1780	Fought at Battle of Hammond's Stores
January 17, 1781	Fought and possibly wounded at Battle of Cowpens
March 2, 1781	Fought at Skirmish near Alamance Creek
March 6, 1781	Fought at Battle of Wetzell's Mills
March 15, 1781	Fought at Battle of Guilford Court House
April 20, 1781	Led Cavalry Raid on Camden outposts
April 25, 1781	Fought at Battle of Hobkirk's Hill
May 21, 1781	Fought at Skirmish near Fort Ninety Six

May & June, 1781	Present for Siege of Fort Ninety-Six
July & August	Led Cavalry in "Dog Days" campaign
September 8, 1781	Fought at Battle of Eutaw Springs — wounded and captured by the British
September, 1781 – December, 1782	Held as prisoner of war in Charleston by the British
April 21, 1782	Married Jane R. Elliott in Charleston
December 12, 1782	"Released" when the British evacuated Charleston
1783	Became member of Society of Cincinnati
August 1, 1783	Daughter Jane Washington born
September 17, 1785	Son William A. Washington, Jr. born
1787 – 1791	Elected and served as Representative from St. Paul's Parish in the South Carolina General Assembly (also named to Governor's Privy Council)
May, 1791	Escorted George Washington in South Carolina while on his "Southern Tour"
1792 - 1798	Named and served as a Brigadier General of the 7th Militia Brigade under the United States Militia Act
1792 - 1804	Elected and served as Senator from St. Paul's Parish senate district in the South Carolina General Assembly

1798 - 1800	Named and served as a Brigadier General of the U.S. Army during the "Quasi War" with France (vacated his Senate seat)
1800 - 1803	Served on Board of Trustees, College of Charleston
March 6, 1810	Died at Sandy Hill Plantation
December 14, 1830	Wife Jane Washington died in Charleston

bibliography

PRIMARY SOURCES

MANUSCRIPTS:

Baylor Family Papers. Charlottesville: University of Virginia
  Library. Military Papers.

The Charleston Courier. "Charleston," April 20 and 21, 1827, No.
  8441 and 8443.

The (Charleston) Royal Gazette. Return of Losses at Guilford, May
  23, 1781; Accounts of the Battle of Eutaw Springs,
  September 8-12, 1781, 15-19, and 26-29; Marriage Notice,
  April 27-May 1, 1782.

"Destruction of Ancient Mansion House." *Daily South
  Carolinian.* Columbia, April 15, 1864, Vol. 15, No. 89, 2.

The Emmett Collection. New York: The New York Public
  Library.

Greene, Nathanael. Ann Arbor, Michigan: William L.
  Clements Library. Nathanael Greene Collection.

Greene, Nathanael. Washington, D. C.: Library of Congress.
  Papers.

National Archives and Records Administration. Revolutionary
  War Rolls. Washington, D. C. Record Group 97. Microfilm
  Publication M246.

Stafford County, Virginia. Will Book Volume S. Richmond: Virginia State Library. Microfilm.

U. S. Department of Commerce and Labor, Bureau of the Census. *Census of the United States Taken in the Year 1800: South Carolina.* Washington, D.C.: National Archives and Records Administration Microfilms.

The Virginia Gazette. Williamsburg: Alexander Purdie, September 22, 1775, August 9, 1776, October 4, 1776, and November 15, 1776; Dixon & Hunter, January 1, 1776 and July 20, 1776.

Warley, Felix B. *An Oration, Delivered in Saint Michael's Church, in the City of Charleston, the 19th June, 1810, on the Death of the Late Gen. William Washington.* Charleston: W. P. Young, 1810.

"Washington, William, Jr." Alumni Files. Princeton University. Item 456.

PUBLICATIONS:

Anderson, Thomas. "Journal of Lieutenant Thomas Anderson of the Delaware Regiment, 1780-1782." *The Historical Magazine,* I (April 1867).

Balch, Thomas (ed.). *Papers Relating Chiefly to the Maryland Line During the Revolution.* Philadelphia: The Seventy-Six Society, 1857.

Barnwell (comp.) Joseph W. "Letters to General Greene and Others." *South Carolina Historical and Genealogical Magazine,* XVI, No. 3 (July 1915) and XVII, No. 2 (April 1916).

Boyd, Julian P. (ed.). *Papers of Jefferson.* 18 vols. Princeton: Princeton University Press, 1950-1971.

Brumbaugh, Gaius Marcus (ed.). *Revolutionary War Records, Volume I, Virginia.* Lancaster, Pennsylvania: Lancaster Press, Inc., 1936.

Burnett, Edmund C. (ed.). *Letters of Members of the Continental Congress.* 8 vols. Washington, D. C.: Carnegie Institute, 1921-1936.

Campbell, Charles (ed.). *The Bland Papers: Being a Selection of from the Manuscripts of Colonel Theodoric Bland, Jr.* 2 vols. Petersburg: Edmund and Julian C. Ruffian, 1840.

Clark, Walter (ed.). *The State Records of North Carolina.* 15 Vols. Raleigh: P. M. Hale, 1886-1907.

Committee of Safety of Virginia, Journal of the. *Calendar of Virginia State Papers and Other Manuscripts.* Richmond: Secretary of the Commonwealth, 1890. Vol. VIII.

Conrad, Dennis M. (ed.). *The Papers of Nathanael Greene, Vol. VIII: 30 March 1781 - 10 July 1781.* Chapel Hill: University of North Carolina Press, 1995.

Conrad, Dennis M. (ed.). *The Papers of Nathanael Greene, Vol. IX: 11 July 1781 - 2 December 1781.* Chapel Hill: University of North Carolina Press, 1997.

Conrad, Dennis M. (ed.). *The Papers of Nathanael Greene, Vol. X: 3 December 1781 - 6 April 1782.* Chapel Hill: University of North Carolina Press, 1998.

Conrad, Dennis M. (ed.). *The Papers of Nathanael Greene, Vol. XI: 7 April 1782 - 30 September 1782.* Chapel Hill: University of North Carolina Press, 2000.

Dann, John C. (ed.). *The Revolution Remembered: Eyewitness Accounts of the War for Independence.* Chicago: University of Chicago Press, 1977.

Duc de La Rochefoucault Liancourt. *Travels Through the United States of North America, the Country of the Iroquois, and Upper Canada, in the Years 1795, 1796, 1797.* London: R. Phillips, 1799.

Edwards, Adele Stanton (ed.). *Journals of the Privy Council, 1783-1789.* Columbia: University of South Carolina Press, 1971.

Fitzpatrick, John C. (ed.). *The Diaries of George Washington, 1748-1799.* 4 vols. Boston: Houghton, Mifflin and Company, 1925.

Fitzpatrick, John C. (ed.). *The Writings of George Washington from the Original Manuscript Sources, 1745-1799.* 39 vols. Washington, D. C.: U. S. Government Printing Office, 1932.

Force, Peter (ed.). *American Archives.* 5th Series. 3 vols. Washington, D. C.: U. S. Congress, 1837-1846.

Ford, Worthington Chauncey (ed.). *Journals of the Continental Congress.* 34 vols. Washington, D. C.: Library of Congress, 1904-1937.

Ford, Worthington Chauncey (ed.). *The Writings of George Washington.* 14 vols. New York: G. P. Putnam's Sons, 1893.

Fraser, Charles. *Reminiscences of Charleston.* Charleston: John Russell, 1854.

Fries, Adelaide L. (ed.). *Records of the Moravians in North Carolina.* Raleigh: North Carolina Historical Commission, 1943. Vol. VI.

Gibbs, R. W. (ed.). *Documentary History of the American Revolution, Chiefly in South Carolina.* 3 vols. New York: D. Appleton and Company, 1853-1857.

Gordon, William. *The History of the Rise, Progress, and Establishment of the Independence of the United States of America.* 4 vols. London: Printed for the author, 1788.

Graham, William A. (ed.). *General Joseph Graham and his Papers on North Carolina Revolutionary History.* Raleigh: Edwards & Broughton, 1904.

Hammond, Otis G. (ed.). *Sullivan Papers.* 3 vols. Concord: New Hampshire Historical Society, 1930.

Hayes, John T. (ed.). *A Gentleman of Fortune: The Diary of Baylor Hill, First Continental Light Dragoons, 1777-1781.* 3 vols. Fort Lauderdale, Florida: The Saddlebag Press, 1995.

"Heads of Families–Virginia, 1785." U.S. Bureau of the Census. *Heads of Families at the First Census of the United States Taken in the Year 1790 and Records of State Enumerations: 1782 to 1785.* Baltimore: Southern Book Company, 1952.

Hemphill, William Edwin (ed.). *Journals of the General Assembly and House of Representatives, 1776-1780.* Columbia: University of South Carolina Press, 1970.

Higginbotham, Don (ed.). *The Papers of James Iredell; Vol. II: 1778 - 1783.* 2 Vols. Raleigh: Department of Cultural Resources, 1976.

Hillman, Benjamin J. (ed.). *Executive Journals of the Council of Colonial Virginia, Vol. VI: June 20, 1754 - May 3, 1775.* Richmond: Virginia State Library, 1966.

Howland, H. R. "The Second Battle of Camden, S. C. – Account of it, Written at the Time, by Gen. Otho H. Williams," *Potters American Monthly,* IV (1875).

Hunt, Gaillard (ed.). *Fragments of Revolutionary History.* Brooklyn: The Historical Printing Club, 1892.

Jervey, Elizabeth Heyward (comp.). "Marriage and Death Notices in The City Gazette," *The South Carolina Historical and Genealogical Magazine*, XXXI (October 1930) and XXXIV (July 1933).

Johnson, Joseph (ed.). *Traditions and Reminiscences Chiefly of the American Revolution in the South.* Charleston: Walker & James, 1851.

Kennedy, John Pendleton (ed.). *Journals of the House of Burgesses of Virginia, 1766-1769.* Richmond: MCMVI, Vol. 11.

Kennedy, John Pendleton (ed.). *Journals of the House of Burgesses of Virginia, 1770-1772.* Richmond: MCMVI, Vol. 12.

King, George Harrison Sanford (comp.). *The Register of Overwharton Parish, Stafford County, Virginia, 1723-1758.* Fredericksburg: Published for the Compiler, 1961.

King, George Harrison Sanford (comp.). *The Register of St. Paul's Parish, 1715-1798 – Stafford County, Virginia, 1715-1776.* Fredericksburg: Published for the Compiler, 1960.

Lee, Henry. *Memoirs of the War in the Southern Department of the United States.* 2 vols. Philadelphia: Bradford and Inskeep, 1812.

Lee, Henry. *The Campaign of 1781 in the Carolinas.* Philadelphia: Bradford and Inskeep, 1824.

"Letters to General Greene and Others," *South Carolina and Genealogical Magazine*, Vol. XVI (July 1915), No. 3.

MacKenzie, Roderick. *Strictures on Lieutenant Colonel Tarleton's History* Cornhill: Printed for the Author, 1787.

McCall, Hugh. *The History of Georgia.* Atlanta: A. B. Caldwell, 1909 reprint of original 1811 edition.

McIlwaine, H. R. (ed.). *Official Letters of the Governors of the State of Virginia, Vol. I: The Letters of Patrick Henry.* Richmond: The Virginia State Library, 1926.

McIlwaine, H. R. (ed.). *Official Letters of the Governors of Virginia, Vol. II: The Letters of Thomas Jefferson.* Richmond: Virginia State Library, 1928.

Marshall, John. *The Life of George Washington.* 5 Vols. Fredericksburg: Citizens Guild, 1926 reprint of the original 1805 edition.

Moore, Frank (ed.). *Diary of the American Revolution.* 2 vols. New York: Washington Square Press, 1858.

Morris, Richard B. and Commager, Henry S. (eds.). *The Spirit of Seventy-Six.* New York: Harper and Row, 1958.

Moultrie, William. *Memoirs of the American Revolution.* 2 vols. New York: David Longworth, 1802.

Moylan, Stephen. "Correspondence of Moylan, Stephen." *Pennsylvania Magazine of History and Biography,* XXXVII (1913).

Myers, Theodorus Bailey (comp.). "Cowpens Papers, being correspondence of General Morgan and the prominent actors," Charleston *News and Courier* (Tuesday, May 10, 1881), 1.

O'Neal, J. B. (ed.). "Memoir of Major Joseph McJunkin." *The Magnolia,* II (1843).

Roberts, James M. (ed.). *Autobiography of a Revolutionary Soldier.* New York: Arno Press, Inc., 1979.

Rutland, Robert A. (ed.). *The Papers of George Mason.* Three volumes. Chapel Hill: University of North Carolina Press, 1970.

Ryden, George Herbert (ed.). *Letters to and from Caesar Rodney, 1756-1784.* Philadelphia: University of Pennsylvania Press, 1933.

Salley, Alexander S. (comp.). *South Carolina Provincial Troops Named in Papers of the First Council of Safety of the Revolutionary Party in South Carolina, June-November, 1775* (Baltimore: Genealogical Publishing Co., Inc., 1977.

Schreiner-Yantis, Netti and Love, Florence Speakman (comps.). *The Personal Property Tax List for the Year 1787 for Stafford County, Virginia* Springfield, Va.: Genealogical Books, 1987.

Scribner, Robert L. and Tarter, Brent (comps.). *Revolutionary Virginia: The Road to Independence, Volume IV: The Committee of Safety and the Balance of Forces, 1775.* Charlottesville: University Press of Virginia, 1978.

Scribner, Robert L. and Tarter, Brent (comps.). *Revolutionary Virginia: The Road to Independence, Volume VI: The Time of Decision, 1776.* Charlottesville: University Press of Virginia, 1981.

Scribner, Robert L. and Tarter, Brent (comps.). *Revolutionary Virginia: The Road to Independence, Volume VIII: Independence and the Fifth Convention, 1776.* Charlottesville: University Press of Virginia, 1983.

Seymour, William. "A Journal of the Southern Expedition, 1780-1783." *The Papers of the Historical Society of Delaware.* Vol. XV. Wilmington: 1883.

Showman, Richard K. (ed.). *The Papers of Nathanael Greene*, Vol. II: 1 January 1777 - 16 October 1778. Chapel Hill: University of North Carolina Press, 1980.

Showman, Richard K. (ed.). *The Papers of Nathanael Greene, Vol. V: 1 November, 1779 - 31 May, 1780.* Chapel Hill: University of North Carolina Press, 1989.

Showman, Richard K. (ed.). *The Papers of Nathanael Greene, Vol. VI: 1 June 1780 - 25 December 1780.* Chapel Hill: University of North Carolina Press, 1991.

Showman, Richard K. (ed.). *The Papers of Nathanael Greene, Vol. VII: 26 December 1780 - 29 March 1781.* Chapel Hill: University of North Carolina Press, 1994.

Sparks, Jared (ed.). *Correspondence of the American Revolution: Being Letters of Eminent Men to George Washington.* 4 vols. Boston: Little, Brown and Company, 1853.

Smith, Clifford Neal (comp.). *A Calendar of Archival Materials on the Land Patents Issued by the United States Government, with Subject, Tract and Name Indexes*, Vol. 4, Part 1: Grants in the Virginia Military District of Ohio. Chicago: American Library Association, 1982.

Sparks, Jared (ed.). *The Writings of Washington.* 12 vols. Boston: Hillard, Gray and Company, 1834-1837.

Stedman, C. *The History of the Origin, Progress, and Termination of the American War.* 2 vols. London: Printed for the Author, 1794.

Stevens, Michael E. (ed.). *Journals of the House of Representatives, 1787-1788.* Columbia: University of South Carolina Press, 1981.

Stevens, Michael E. (ed.). *Journals of the House of Representatives, 1789-1790.* Columbia: University of South Carolina Press, 1984.

Stevens, Michael E. (ed.). *Journals of the House of Representatives, 1791.* Columbia: University of South Carolina Press, 1985.

Stevens, Michael E. (ed.). *Journals of the Senate, 1792-1794.* Columbia: University of South Carolina Press, 1988.

Stryker, William S. (ed.). *Archives of the State of New Jersey. Second Series: Extracts from American Newspapers, 1776-1782.* 5 vols. Trenton: John L. Murphy Publishing Co., 1901-1917.

Syrett, Harold C. (ed.). *The Papers of Alexander Hamilton.* 27 vols. New York: Columbia University Press, 1961-1987.

Tallmadge, Benjamin. *Memoir of Col. Benjamin Tallmadge.* New York: Thomas Holman, 1858.

Tarleton, Banastre. *A History of the Campaigns of 1780 and 1781 in the Southern Provinces of North America.* London: T. Cadwell, 1787.

Thompson, Theodora J. (ed.). *Journals of the House of Representatives, 1783-1784.* Columbia: University of South Carolina Press, 1977.

Turner, Joseph Brown (ed.). *The Journal and Order Book of Captain Robert Kirkwood.* Wilmington: The Historical Society of Delaware, 1910.

Uhlendorf, Bernard A. (ed.). *Revolution in America: Confidential Letters and Journals, 1776-1784, of Adjutant General Major Baurmeister of the Hessian Forces.* New Brunswick: Rutgers University Press, 1957.

Uhlendorf, Bernard A. (ed.). *The Siege of Charleston.* Ann Arbor: University of Michigan Press, 1938.

U. S. Congress. *American State Papers: Military Affairs.* 7 vols. Washington, D. C.: Gales and Seaton, 1832-1861.

U. S. Department of Commerce and Labor, Bureau of the Census. *Heads of Families at the First Census of the United States Taken in the Year 1790: South Carolina.* Washington, D.C.: U.S. Government Printing Office, 1900.

U. S. Department of Commerce and Labor, Bureau of the Census. *Heads of Families at the First Census of the United States Taken in the Year 1790 and Records of the State Enumerations, 1782 to 1785: Virginia.* Baltimore: Southern Book Company, 2nd Ed., 1952.

U. S. Department of the Interior, Bureau of Land Management. *The Official Federal Land Patent Records Site.* Washington, D.C.: Land Patent Databases at www.glorecords.blm.gov, 2000.

Van Schreeven, William J. (comp.) and Scribner, Robert L. (ed.). *Revolutionary Virginia: The Road to Independence. Volume I: Forming Thunderclouds and the First Convention, 1763-1774.* Charlotte: University Press of Virginia, 1973.

The Virginia State Library. *Embrey's Index of Records: Stafford County Virginia Index of Grantees, 1664-1914.* Richmond: Virginia State Library Microfilm Roll No. 13. Vol. 6.

Webber, Mabel L. (comp.). "Death Notices from the South Carolina and American General Gazette, and its Continuation, The Royal Gazette." *The South Carolina Historical and Genealogical Magazine,* XVII, No. 4 (October 1916).

Webber, Mabel L. (ed.). "Records from the Elliott-Rowland Bible." *The South Carolina Historical and Genealogical Magazine*, XI, No. 1 (January, 1910).

Wilcox, William B. (ed.). *The American Rebellion: Sir Henry Clinton's Narrative of his Campaigns, 1775-1782.* New Haven: Yale University Press, 1954.

Wilkenson, James. *Memoirs of My Own Times.* 3 vols. Philadelphia: Abraham Small, 1816.

Works Progress Administration (comp.). *Calendar of the General Otho HollandWilliams Papers in the Maryland Historical Society.* Baltimore: Maryland Historical Records Survey Project, 1940.

Young, Thomas. "Memoir of Thomas Young, A Revolutionary Patriot of South Carolina," *The Orion*, III, Nos. 2 and 3 (October and November 1843).

SECONDARY SOURCES

Adams, Charles Francis. *Studies Military and Diplomatic, 1775-1865.* New York: The MacMillan Company, 1911.

Alden, John. *The South in the Revolution.* Baton Rouge: Louisiana State University Press, 1957.

Babits, Lawrence E. *A Devil of a Whipping: The Battle of Cowpens.* Chapel Hill: University of North Carolina Press, 1998.

Bailey, N. Louise (ed.). *Biographical Directory of the South Carolina House of Representatives, 1775-1980.* Vol. III. Columbia: University of South Carolina Press, 1981.

Bailey, N. Louise (ed.). *Biographical Directory of the South Carolina Senate,* Vol. III. Columbia: University of South Carolina Press, 1986.

Baker, Thomas E. *The Monuments at Guilford Courthouse National Military Park.* Greensboro, North Carolina: National Park Service, 1991.

Baker, Thomas E. *Another Such Victory: The Story of the American defeat at Guilford Courthouse that helped win the War for Independence.* New York: Eastern Acorn Press, 1981.

Bass, Robert Duncan. *The Green Dragoon; the Lives of Banastre Tarleton and Mary Robinson.* New York: Henry Holt, 1957.

Bass, Robert Duncan. *Ninety Six: The Struggle for the South Carolina Back Country.* Lexington, South Carolina: The Sandlapper Store, Inc., 1978.

Bass, Robert D. *Swamp Fox: The Life and Campaigns of General Francis Marion.* Orangeburg, South Carolina: Sandlapper Publishing Company, Inc., 1974.

Bauer, Frederick. "Notes on the Use of Cavalry in the American Revolution," *Cavalry Journal,* XLVII (1938).

Bearss, Edwin C. *Battle of Cowpens: A Documented Narrative and Troop Movement Maps.* Johnson City, Tenn.: The Overmountain Press, 1996 reprint of the original 1957 National Park Service edition.

Berg, Fred Anderson. *Encyclopedia of Continental Army Units.* Harrisburg: Stackpole Books, 1972.

Boatner, Mark Mayo. *Encyclopedia of the American Revolution.* New York: D. McKay Co., 1966.

Boatner, Mark Mayo. *Landmarks of the American Revolution.* Harrisburg: Stackpole Books, 1973.

Brown, Stuart Gerry (ed.). *The Autobiography of James Monroe.* Syracuse: Syracuse University Press, 1959.

Buchanan, John. *The Road to Guilford Courthouse: The American Revolution in the Carolinas.* New York: John Wiley and Sons, Inc., 1997.

Byrd, Francis J. *William Washinton: Continental Cavalryman.* Chapel Hill: University of North Carolina M.A. Thesis, 1971.

Callahan, North. *Daniel Morgan: Ranger of the Revolution.* New York: Holt, Rinehart and Winston, 1961.

Cann, Marvin. *Old Ninety Six in the South Carolina Backcountry, 1700-1781.* Troy, South Carolina: Sleepy Creek Publications, 1996.

Clark, Jewell T. and Long, Elizabeth Terry (comp.). "A Guide to Church Records in the Archives Branch of the Virginia State Library." Richmond: Virginia State Library, n.d.

Coleman, Charles Washington, Jr. (ed.). "The Southern Campaigns, 1781 From Guilford Court House to the Siege of York." *The Magazine of American History,* VII (1881).

Cook, Fred J. "Francisco the Incredible." *American Heritage,* X (October 1959).

Coppage, A. Maxim and Tackett, James W. (comp.). *Stafford Co., Virginia: 1800-1850.* Concord, California: Printed for the Compilers, 1982.

Cowpens Centennial Committee, *Proceedings at the Unveiling of the Battle Monument in Spartanburg, S.C., in Commemoration of the Centennial of the Battle of Cowpens.* Charleston, 1896.

Cresson, W. P. *James Monroe*. Chapel Hill: University of North Carolina Press, 1946.

Cureton, Charles H. and Zlatich, Marko. "4th Regiment of Continental Light Dragoons, 1777-1778." *Military Collector & Historian*, XXXVII, No. 3 (1985).

Davis, Gherardi. *Regimental Colors in the War of the Revolution*. New York: Gilliss Press, 1907.

Davis, W. W. H. "Washington on the West Bank of the Delaware, 1776." *Pennsylvania Magazine of History and Biography*, IV (1880).

Deas, Alston. "Genealogy of Lt. Col. William Washington." Unpublished Paper. South Carolina Historical Society, Charleston.

De Forest, Elizabeth Kellam. *The Gardens & Grounds at Mount Vernon*. Mount Vernon, Virginia: The Mount Vernon Ladies Association, 1982.

"Descendants of Two John Washingtons." *Virginia Historical Magazine*, XXII (1914).

Douwes, William. "Logistical Support of the Continental Light Dragoons." *Military Collector & Historian*, XXIV, No. 4 (1972).

Dupuy, R. Ernest and Trevor N. *The Compact History of the Revolutionary War*. New York: Hawthorn Books, Inc., 1968.

Easterby, J. H. *A History of the College of Charleston*. Charleston: The Scribner Press, 1935.

Easterby, J. H. (ed.). *The South Carolina Rice Plantation As Revealed in the Papers of Robert F. W. Allston*. Chicago: University of Chicago Press, 1945.

Eben, Jay. *Dragoon Sketchbook: 1776-1798.* Springfield, Ohio: Published by the Author, 1990.

Eby, Jerrilynn. *They Called Stafford Home: The Development of Stafford County, Virginia, from 1600 until 1865.* Bowie, Maryland: Heritage Books, Inc., 1997.

Edgar, Walter B. (ed.). *Biographical Directory of the South Carolina House of Representatives.* 3 Vols. Columbia: University of South Carolina Press, 1974.

Edgar, Walter B. *South Carolina: A History.* Columbia: University of South Carolina Press, 1998.

Ellet, Elizabeth F. *The Women of the American Revolution.* 3 Vols. Williamstown, Mass.: Corner House Publishers, 1980 reprint of the original 1848 edition.

Emmett, Thomas Addis (ed.). "The Southern Campaign, 1780; Gates at Camden." *The Magazine of American History,* V (1880).

Fast, Howard. *The Crossing.* New York: William Morris and Company, Inc., 1971.

Fisher, Therese A. (comp.). *Marriage Records of the City of Fredericksburg, and of Orange, Spotsylvania, and Stafford Counties, Virginia: 1722*-Bowie, Md.: Heritage Books, Inc., 2nd Ed., 1990.

Fleming, Thomas S. *Cowpens: "Downright Fighting".* Washington, D.C.: National Park Service, 1988.

Flynn, Jean Martin. "South Carolina's Compliance with the Militia Act of 1792," *The South Carolina and Historical and Genealogical Magazine.* Vol. 69 (January 1968).

Foote, William Henry (ed.). *Sketches of North Carolina, Historical and Biographical.* New York: Robert Carter, 1846.

Fortesque, John W. *A History of the British Army.* Vol. III: 1763-1793. London: MacMillan and Co., 1911.

Freeman, Douglas Southall. *George Washington: A Biography, Vol. I: Young Washington.* New York: Charles Scribner's Sons, 1948.

Freeman, Douglas Southall. *George Washington: A Biography, Vol. IV: Leader of the Revolution.* New York: Charles Scribner's Sons, 1951.

Goolrick, John T. *The Life of General Hugh Mercer.* New York: The Neale Publishing Company, 1906.

Graham, James. *The Life of Daniel Morgan.* New York: Derby and Jackson, 1856.

Greene, George Washington. *The Life of Nathanael Greene, Major General in the Revolution.* 3 vols. Boston: Houghton, Mifflin and Company, 1884.

Gregorie, Ann King. *Thomas Sumter.* Columbia: R. L. Bryan, 1931.

Griffin, Martin J. *Stephen Moylan.* Philadelphia: Printed for the author, 1909.

Gunby, A. A. *Colonel John Gunby of the Maryland Line.* Cincinnati: Robert Clarke Company, 1902.

Haller, Stephen E. *William Washington: Cavalryman of the Revolution.* Oxford, Ohio: Miami University M.A. Thesis, 1975.

Hanser, Richard. *The Glorious Hour of Lt. Monroe.* Battleboro, Vermont: The Book Press, 1975.

Harrison, Peleg D. *The Stars and Stripes and Other American Flags.* Boston: Little, Brown, and Company, 1914.

Heitman, Francis B. *Historical Register of Officers of the Continental Army during the War of the Revolution, April, 1775 to December, 1783.* Washington, D. C.: The Rare Book Shop Publishing Company, Inc., 1914.

Henderson, Archibald. *Washington's Southern Tour: 1791.* Boston: Houghton, Mifflin and Company, 1923.

Heyward, Barnwell Rhett. "The Descendants of Col. William Rhett, of South Carolina." *The South Carolina Historical and Genealogical Magazine,* IV (January 1903).

Higgenbotham, Don. *Daniel Morgan: Revolutionary Rifleman.* Chapel Hill: University of North Carolina Press, 1961.

Hilborn, Nat and Sam. *Battleground of Freedom: South Carolina in the Revolution.* Columbia: Sandlapper Press, Inc., 1970.

Holmes, Ellen C. "The Hero of Cowpens and Eutaw Springs with nothing to mark his grave." Unpublished Paper. South Carolina Historical Society, Charleston.

Huger Smith, Alice R. and D.E. *The Dwelling Houses of Charleston, South Carolina.* Philadelphia: J.B. Lippincott Company, 1917.

Irving, John B. *A Day on the Cooper River.* Columbia: R. L. Bryan Co., original 1842 monograph enlarged and edited by Louisa Cheves Storey, 1932.

Irving, John B. *The South Carolina Jockey Club.* Charleston: Russel & Jones, 1857.

Johnson, William. *Sketches of the Life and Correspondence of Nathanael Greene.* 2 vols. Charleston: A. F. Miller, 1822.

Johnston, Henry P. *The Battle of Harlem Heights.* New York: The MacMillan Company, 1897.

Jones, Newton B. "The Washington Light Infantry Company at the Bunker Hill Centennial." *The South Carolina Historical and Genealogical Magazine,* LXV (October 1964).

Katcher, Philip. *Uniforms of the Continental Army.* York, Pennsylvania: George Shumway, 1981.

Ketchum, Richard M. *The Winter Soldiers.* Garden City, N. J.: Doubleday & Company, Inc., 1973.

Lefferts, Charles M. *Uniforms of the American, British, French and German Armies in the War of the American Revolution, 1775-1783.* New York: The New York Historical Society, 1926.

Leonard, Cynthia Miller (comp.). *The General Assembly of Virginia, July 30, 1619 - January 11, 1978: A Bicentennial Register of Members.* Richmond: Virginia State Library, 1978.

Lipscomb, Terry W. *South Carolina in 1791: George Washington's Southern Tour.* Columbia: South Carolina Department of Archives and History, 1993.

Loescher, Burt G. *Washington's Eyes: The Continental Light Dragoons.* New York: The Old Army Press, 1977.

Longacre, James Barton and Herring, James (comp.). 4 vols. *The National Portrait Gallery of Distinguished Americans.* Philadelphia: H. Perkins, 1834-1839.

Lossing, Benson J. *Pictorial Fieldbook of the Revolution.* 2 vols. New York: Harper and Brothers, 1851.

Lumpkin, Henry. *From Savannah to Yorktown: The American Revolution in the South.* Columbia: University of South Carolina Press, 1981.

McCowen, George C., Jr. "Chief Justice John Rutledge and the Jay Treaty." *The South Carolina and Historical and Genealogical Magazine,* Vol. LXII (January 1961).

McCrady, Edward. *The History of South Carolina in the American Revolution, 1780-1783.* New York: The MacMillan Company, 1902.

Manning, Clarance A. *Soldier of Liberty, Casimir Pulaski.* New York: Philosophical Library, 1945.

Mitchell, Broadus. *Alexander Hamilton: The National Adventure, 1788-1804.* New York: MacMillan Co., 1962.

Morrill, Dan L. *Southern Campaigns of the American Revolution.* Baltimore: Nautical & Aviation Publishing Company of America, 1993.

Moss, Bobby Gilmer. *The Patriots at the Cowpens.* Greenville: A Press, 1985.

The National Cyclopaedia of American Biography; Being the History of the United States. 47 vols. New York: James T. White & Company, 1898-1965.

Pancake, John S. *This Destructive War: The British Campaign in the Carolinas, 1780-1782.* University, Alabama: University of Alabama Press, 1985.

Proceedings at the Inauguration of the Monument Erected by the Washington Light Infantry to the Memory of Col. William Washington at Magnolia Cemetery, May 5, 1858. Charleston: Steam Power Press, 1858.

Ramsay, David. *Ramsay's History of South Carolina.* 2 vols. Newberry, South Carolina: W. J. Duffle, 1858.

Ranke, Vinnetta W. (comp.). *Justices of the Peace of Colonial Virginia* Washington, D.C.: Private Printing, 1945.

Rankin, Hugh F. *Francis Marion.* New York: Thomas Y. Crowell Company, 1973.

Rankin, Hugh F. *Greene and Cornwallis: The Campaign in the Carolinas.* Raleigh: North Carolina Department of Cultural Resources, 1976.

Reed, William Bradford (ed.). *The Life of Joseph Reed.* 2 vols. Philadelphia: Lindsay and Blakiston, 1847.

Reid, Courtland T. *Guilford Courthouse National Military Park, North Carolina.* Washington, D. C.: National Park Service, 1959.

Richardson, Edward W. *Standards and Colors of the American Revolution.* Philadelphia: University of Pennsylvania Press, 1982.

Ripley, Warren. *Battleground – South Carolina in the Revolution.* Charleston: Evening Post Publishing Co., 1983.

Risley, Clyde A. and Zlatich, Marko. "3rd Regiment of Continental Light Dragoons, 1778-1783," *Military Collector & Historian,* XLIV (1992), No. 3, Plate No. 689.

Robinson, Blacknell P. *William R. Davie.* Chapel Hill: University of North Carolina Press, 1957.

Rogers, George C. Jr. *Charleston in the Age of the Pinckneys* (Norman: University of Oklahoma Press, 1969.

Rogers, George C. Jr. *Evolution of a Federalist: William Loughton Smith of Charleston, 1758-1812.* Columbia: University of South Carolina Press, 1962.

Salley, B. A. *President Washington's Tour Through South Carolina in 1791.* Columbia: Historical Commission of South Carolina, 1932. Bulletin No. 12.

Scheer, George P. and Rankin, Hugh F. *Rebels and Redcoats.* Cleveland: World Publishing Co., 1957.

Schenck, David. *North Carolina 1780-81: Being a History of the Invasion of the Carolinas by the British Army under Lord Cornwallis* (Raleigh: Edwards & Broughton, Publishers, 1889. Reprinted, Bowie, Md.: Heritage Books, Inc., 2000.)

Schermerhorn, Frank Earle. *American and French Flags of the Revolution, 1775-1783.* Philadelphia: Pennsylvania Society of the Sons of the Revolution, 1948.

Sellers, Charles Coleman. *Portraits and Miniatures by Charles Wilson Peale.* Philadelphia: American Philosophical Society, 1952.

Sellers, John R. *The Virginia Continental Line.* Williamsburg: The Virginia Independence Bicentennial Commission, 1978.

Simms, William Gilbert. *South Carolina in the Revolutionary War.* Charleston: Walker and James, 1853.

Smith, Henry A. M. "The Grave of Colonel William Washington." *The South Carolina Historical and Genealogical Magazine,* X (October 1909).

Smith, Samuel Steele. *The Battle of Brandywine.* Monmouth Beach, N. J.: Philip Freneau Press, 1976.

Smith, Samuel Steele. *The Battle of Monmouth.* Monmouth Beach, N. J.: Philip Freneau Press, 1964.

Smith, Samuel Steele. *The Battle of Trenton.* Monmouth Beach, N. J.: Philip Freneau Press, 1965.

Steffen, Randy. *The Horse Soldiers, 1776-1943, Vol. I: The Revolutionary War, The War of 1812 and The Early Frontier: 1776-1850.* Norman, Oklahoma: University of Oklahoma Press, 1977.

Stryker, William S. *The Battles of Trenton and Princeton.* Boston: Houghton, Mifflin and Company, 1898.

Swem, Earl G. and Williams, John W. *A Register of the General Assembly of Virginia.* Richmond: Superintendent of Public Printing, 1918.

Thayer, Theodore George. *Nathanael Greene: Strategist of the American Revolution.* New York: Twayne, 1960.

Treacy, Mildred P. *Prelude to Yorktown: The Southern Campaigns of Nathanael Greene.* Chapel Hill: University of North Carolina Press, 1963.

Urwin, Gregory J.W. *The United States Cavalry: An Illustrated History.* Poole, U.K.: Blandford Press, 1983).

Varnum, Lansing Collin (comp.). *General Catalogue of Princeton University, 1746-1906.* Princeton: Princeton University, 1908.

Wallace, David Duncan. *South Carolina, A Short History: 1520-1948.* Chapel Hill: University of North Carolina Press, 1951.

Ward, Christopher L. *The Delaware Continentals: 1776-1783.* Wilmington: Historical Society of Delaware, 1941.

Ward, Christopher L. *The War of the Revolution*. 2 vols. New York: The MacMillan Company, 1952.

Ward, Harry M. *Duty, Honor or Country: General George Weedon and the American Revolution*. Philadelphia: American Philosophical Society, 1979.

Waring, Alice Noble. *The Fighting Elder: Andrew Pickens, 1739-1817*. Columbia: University of South Carolina Press, 1962.

Washington, Ella Basset. "William Washington, Lieut.-Colonel Third Light Dragoons, Continental Army." *The Magazine of American History*, IX (February 1883).

Weigley, Russell F. *The Partisan War: The South Carolina Campaign of 1780-1782*. Columbia: University of South Carolina Press, 1970.

Wells, Guy Fred. *Parish Education in Colonial Virginia*. New York: Columbia University, 1923.

"William Washington of Stafford County, Virginia." *The William and Mary Quarterly*, 1st Ser., XV (October 1906).

Wilson, James Grant and Fiske, John (eds.). *Appleton's Cyclopaedia of American Biography*. 8 vols. New York: D. Appleton and Company, 1898-1918.

Wood, W. J. *Battles of the Revolutionary War, 1775-1781*. Chapel Hill: Algonquin Books, 1990.

Woodson (comp.), Robert F. and Isobel B. *Virginia Tithables From Burned Record Counties*. Richmond: Published for the Compilers, 1970.

Zahniser, Marvin R. *Charles Cotesworth Pinckney, Founding Father*. 3 vols. Chapel Hill: University of North Carolina Press, 1967.

illustrations

Virginia Continentals capturing the Hessian cannon at the
Battle of Trenton in 1776 painted by Charles McBarron
(courtesy of Army Art Collection, U.S. Army Center of
Military History)

CHAPTER II
4th Regiment of Continental Light Dragoons, 1777-1778
drawn by Charles Cureton (Plate #577 in *Military Collector
and Historian*, XXXVII, No. 3, 1985 courtesy of the
Company of Military Historians)

CHAPTER III
3rd Regiment of Continental Light Dragoons, 1778-1783
drawn by C.A. Risley (Plate #689 in *Military Collector and
Historian*, XLIV, No. 3, 1992 courtesy of the Company of
Military Historians)

"Eutaw Flag" of Colonel Washington's Cavalry preserved by
Mrs. Jane Washington until 1827 (a 1883 photograph of
the original battle flag in the custody of the Washington
Light Infantry since 1827, courtesy of the Washington
Light Infantry, Charleston)

CHAPTER IV
"Battle of Cowpens" painted by William Ranney in ca. 1845
(Permission courtesy of Eastern National Park &
Monument Association)

"Col. William Augustine [sic] Washington at the Battle of
Cowpens" painted by S.H. Gunbar in 1849 for Graham's
Magazine, (#148-GW-390 courtesy of the National Archives
and Records Administration)

"Battle of Cowpens, South Carolina: Conflict between Cols. Washington and Tarleton" by Alonzo Chappel in 1858 (from Negative #41454 courtesy of the New-York Historical Society)

"The Combat between Colonels Washington and Tarleton at the Battle of the Cowpens" by T. de Thulstrup in 1898 for Henry Cabot Lodge's *The Story of the Revolution*, Vol. II (out of copyright; Scribner's, now owned by Simon & Schuster, New York)

CHAPTER IV

William Washington's Light Dragoons and the First Maryland Continentals preparing to charge the British Guards at the Battle of Guilford Courthouse on 15 March 1781 painted by Charles McBarron (courtesy of Army Art Collection, U.S. Army Center of Military History)

Guilford Courthouse National Military Park: Third Line Field and Cavalry Monument (Permission courtesy of Eastern National Park & Monument Association)

CHAPTER V

"The Battle of Hobkirk's Hill: Charge of Colonel Washington's Cavalry" by F.C. Yohn in 1898 for Henry Cabot Lodge's *The Story of the Revolution*, Vol. II (out of copyright; Scribner's, now owned by Simon & Schuster, New York)

Memorial erected in Charleston's Magnolia Cemetery in honor of William and Jane Washington by the Washington Light Infantry in 1858 (a 1998 photograph, courtesy of the Washington Light Infantry, Charleston)

"Battle of Eutaw Springs" after Alonzo Chappel's c. 1850s painting showing Washington's cavalry preparing to charge the British right (courtesy of South Caroliniana Library, University of South Carolina, Columbia)

CHAPTER VI

Cowpens silver medal awarded to Lieutenant Colonel William Washington by Congress on March 9, 1781 and delivered in 1790 with a letter from President George Washington (Permission courtesy of Eastern National Park & Monument Association)

William and Jane Washington's Church Street House in Charleston, built in 1768 and purchased by Washington in 1785 (2001 photograph by Barbara Haller of the house still standing near The Battery)

Memorial erected in Charleston's Magnolia Cemetery in honor of William and Jane Washington by the Washington Light Infantry in 1858 (a 1998 photograph, courtesy of the Washington Light Infantry, Charleston)

MAPS:

CHAPTER I

MAP 1. THE WAR IN THE MIDDLE STATES: 1776-79, (Map by Steve Haller and Nick Ackermann)

CHAPTER III

MAP 2. THE WAR IN THE SOUTH: 1779-81, (Map by Steve Haller and Nick Ackermann)

CHAPTER IV

MAP 3. THE BATTLE OF COWPENS (2 phases) (Map by Steve Haller)

index

about the author

Stephen E. Haller brings his 25 years as a professional archivist together with a life-long interest in the Revolutionary War in the Carolinas to tell the exciting story of William Washington, the Patriot cavalry commander brave enough to cross sabers with Tarleton's dreaded "green dragoons." Steve is currently the Manager of Archives and Records for the Colonial Williamsburg Foundation in Virginia. After serving in military intelligence with the U.S. Army in the Vietnam War, Steve received his BA (Phi Beta Kappa) and MA degrees in American History from Miami University in Oxford, Ohio. He is the author of *The Management of Local Government Records on Limited Resources* (1991) and "An Officer's Button of an Unidentified 7th Regiment," in *The Web of Time: Pages from America's Past* (Internet magazine, May 2000). Steve also collects and paints military miniatures representing historical regiments of the Revolutionary War, contributes to historical gaming magazines and is the author of a set of war game rules for fighting Revolutionary War battles in miniature—*The Whites of Their Eyes*. He lives with his wife and son in Williamsburg, Virginia, and his daughter is an architect in Columbia, South Carolina.